POLITICS
FOR
THE LOVE
OF
FANDOM

POLITICS FOR THE LOVE OF FANDOM

Fan-Based Citizenship in a Digital World

ASHLEY HINCK

LOUISIANA STATE UNIVERSITY PRESS

BATON ROUGE

Published by Louisiana State University Press
Copyright © 2019 by Louisiana State University Press
All rights reserved
Manufactured in the United States of America
First printing

DESIGNER: Michelle A. Neustrom
TYPEFACE: Whitman
PRINTER AND BINDER: Sheridan Books, Inc.

Portions of this book appeared previously as "Ethical Frameworks and Ethical
Modalities: Theorizing Communication and Citizenship in a Fluid World."
Communication Theory 26, no. 1 (2016): 1–20. It is reprinted here
courtesy John Wiley and Sons Ltd. Copyright © 2015.

LIBRARY OF CONGRESS CATALOGING-IN-PUBLICATION DATA

Names: Hinck, Ashley, author.
Title: Politics for the love of fandom : fan-based citizenship in a digital world /
Ashley Hinck.
Description: Baton Rouge : Louisiana State University Press, 2019. | Includes
bibliographical references and index.
Identifiers: LCCN 2018037602 | ISBN 978-0-8071-7034-2 (cloth : alk. paper) |
ISBN 978-0-8071-7125-7 (pdf) | ISBN 978-0-8071-7126-4 (epub)
Subjects: LCSH: Public interest groups. | Fans (Persons)—Political activity. |
Political participation—Social aspects. | Popular culture—Political aspects.
Classification: LCC JF529 .H56 2019 | DDC 324/.4—dc23
LC record available at https://lccn.loc.gov/2018037602

CONTENTS

ACKNOWLEDGMENTS

This book had its beginnings more than a decade ago. While I had read the Harry Potter novels as a child, I didn't discover fandom until I was in high school. My friends Anne Szczubelek and Monica Muzzin introduced me to the Harry Potter fandom and guided me through it, recommending Harry Potter news websites to visit and wizard rock bands to listen to. Anne and Monica took me to two Harry Potter conventions, and Anne helped me host the Whomping Willows band for two unforgettable concerts during college in my little rental house in Omaha, Nebraska. That was all I needed to fall down the rabbit hole of fandom. And I've loved every minute of it. In many ways, I owe my love of fandom to Anne and Monica.

But most importantly, Anne introduced me to the Harry Potter Alliance (HPA), my first encounter with fan activism and fan-based citizenship performances. I volunteered with the Harry Potter Alliance as a staff member briefly in 2009 before starting graduate school that fall. The HPA staff members were extraordinary, and looking back now, I realize just how little I contributed. I was eclipsed by remarkably smart, dedicated, and experienced staff members. I am sure the staff members of the HPA hardly remember me, but I certainly remember them. Their innovative vision, relentless dedication, and remarkable organization and experience make fan activism like the HPA's possible, inspiring millions of Harry Potter fans just like me. I hope this book can be more helpful to them than I was as a staff member. I hope this helps them form new coalitions, develop new strategies, and see their activist work in new ways.

While I owe much to Anne and the Harry Potter Alliance for taking me into the world of fandom and fan-based citizenship, this project also owes its existence to my academic colleagues and mentors. I owe much to Marty Birkholt, Sue Zaeske, Rob Asen, Steve Lucas, Mike Xenos, Jonathan Gray, Jim Brown, and Karma Chávez, who read many of those early ideas and more polished papers, and ultimately took me, my fandom, and the Harry Potter Alliance seriously. I owe the most to Rob Howard. Rob immediately saw the value in my research, despite having no experience with fandom.

I also owe thanks to the Wisconsin Rhetoric Writing group members, Andrew Peck, Jennie Keohane, Kelly Jakes, and Casey Schmitt. Thank you to members of my 2015 Rhetoric Society of America (RSA) working group, who workshopped the introductory book chapter with me: Damien Pfister, Kate Zittlow Rogness, Matthew Houdek, and Nikki Weickum. Thank you to Kyra Hunting, who generously read my manuscript and offered brilliant insights. And thank you to Nicky Kurtzweil, who helped me copyedit in the last throes of this work. Thank you to cheerleading colleagues like Amber Davisson and Leslie Rasmussen, who kept reminding me that I had something important to say in this book. The creation of this book was also supported by a University of Wisconsin Vilas Travel grant and the Xavier University Garry Fund.

While my academic colleagues and mentors taught me what it meant to be a member of a community of scholars, fans were the ones who taught me what it meant to be a fan in their fandoms. I owe an enormous debt to all the fans who agreed to do interviews with me and answered my surveys. They taught me what it means to be a Husker fan, a nerdfighter, a LEGO fan, and a Star Wars fan. I appreciate all the time they gave and their willingness to give me a glimpse into their beloved fan communities. Without the generosity of these fans, this work would not have been possible.

Lastly, I want to thank my family and friends for helping me logistically and supporting me emotionally throughout my work on this book. Thank you to Alise Hernandez and Nikki Elsasser, who gave me couches to sleep on so that I could visit Nebraska and conduct participant observation during my research. Thank you to everyone who accompanied me to Husker football games, including my friends Alise Hernandez and Nikki Elsasser; my father, Ed Hinck; and my partner, Eric Miller. All of those football games were either remarkably hot and humid or cold and snowing.

Thank you for braving the elements with me. Thank you to my parents, Ed and Shelly Hinck, who, despite having little experience with fandom, believed in my work and listened to me ramble on about the importance of both fandom and the internet to the field of communication. After six years, I think I have them convinced. Lastly, I want to thank Eric Miller, my partner, who suffered through many work-filled weekends and evenings and who embarked on many of these fandom adventures with me. Thank you, Eric, for your unwavering support.

POLITICS
FOR
THE LOVE
OF
FANDOM

INTRODUCTION

FAN-BASED CITIZENSHIP
Public Engagement for the Love of Harry Potter

On October 10, 2005, a unique Amnesty International fund-raiser took
place in a basement theater in Somerville, Massachusetts. The event included performances of Harry Potter comedy skits, storyteller Brother
Blue's exploration of the importance of stories and storytelling, and a musi-
cal performance by the band Harry and the Potters. At the end of the night,
Andrew Slack, comedian, teacher, and Harry Potter fan, asked the crowd
to help him form "Dumbledore's Army for the real world."[1] And the Harry
Potter Alliance (HPA) was officially launched.

Since that night, the Harry Potter Alliance has used parallels between
the Harry Potter story and our world to engage in social justice activism
focusing on equality, human rights, and literacy. Harry Potter Alliance cofounder Andrew Slack explained the motivation for the Harry Potter Alliance: "If Harry Potter was in our world, wouldn't he do more than celebrate
the fact he is Harry Potter? Wouldn't he fight for justice in our world the
way he did in his?"[2] Inspired by the kind of social change Harry brought
about in the fictional universe of J. K. Rowling's Harry Potter books, Slack
envisioned the Harry Potter Alliance as Dumbledore's Army for the real
world. Since Harry and his friends can't be here with us to take action on
genocide, climate change, and fair trade, Harry Potter fans have taken it
upon themselves to fill that gap. And fans have answered Slack's call to
action enthusiastically. Since 2005, the HPA has launched more than forty
campaigns, mobilized millions of Harry Potter fans, and organized more
than 275 chapters in twenty-five countries around the world.[3] Their activist
work has taken many forms, including petitions, book drives, donations,

flash mobs, boycotts, new voter registration, and letters to government officials.

Now more than ten years old and an officially registered nonprofit organization, the Harry Potter Alliance has demonstrated that its brand of activism is more than a fleeting fad or a silly game. Indeed, the Harry Potter Alliance has become a mainstay in online geek culture with an important presence at fan conventions like GeekyCon and VidCon, earning coverage from major news outlets like the Daily Dot, The Mary Sue, Alternet, and Wired, and periodically finding itself receiving prominent coverage on sites like Reddit, Mashable, and BuzzFeed.[4] But the Harry Potter Alliance has also gained significant attention beyond online geek culture. The HPA has been covered by mainstream news publications like the New York Times, the Washington Post, the New Yorker, Time magazine, Guardian, Forbes, MTV, and People magazine.[5] Furthermore, Slack's work building the HPA has been recognized by major foundations like the Nathan Cummings Foundation and the Ashoka Foundation, both of which award fellowships to "leading social entrepreneurs."[6]

The Harry Potter Alliance certainly doesn't look like other political organizations. Yet it has succeeded in recruiting millions of Harry Potter fans for political campaigns that have had major impacts on circulating discourses, statewide issues, and media company policies through protests, letter writing, voter registration, phone banking, and more. This book takes these actions and the fans who participate in them seriously, asking what has enabled the emergence of these actions, how these actions work, what possibilities they open up, and what limitations they bring. The Harry Potter Alliance is not alone in this kind of work. Many fan groups are enacting these kinds of citizenship performances. This book examines the many groups of fans who have used fandom to develop new public values, envision a different status quo, and find passion, enthusiasm, and commitment for public issues. Ultimately, I argue that these citizenship performances are powerful, productive, and more widespread than we may expect.

Conceptualizing Citizenship in Rhetoric and Media Studies

Framing actions like the Harry Potter Alliance's as citizenship may seem surprising at first. Citizenship in the US is often framed as serious business, performed by adults within traditional institutions like political parties. The HPA's actions are couched in a fantastical story and often performed by teenagers in online spaces, movie theaters, and fan conventions. But popular conceptions of citizenship emphasizing seriousness and traditional institutions show only a sliver of possibilities for what citizenship can be and what it can show us about politics, rhetoric, and public life.[7]

The *Oxford English Dictionary* defines citizenship in two ways: first, as the "position or status of being a citizen," and second, as "engagement in the duties and responsibilities of a member of society."[8] Scholars have come to refer to the first definition as legal-judicial citizenship, in which citizenship is based on legal residence.[9] Legal-judicial citizenship requires that citizens fulfill certain obligations, like paying taxes. These are legal requirements—not optional. The second definition from the *Oxford English Dictionary* has come to be encapsulated in what scholars call political citizenship.[10] Unlike legal-judicial citizenship, political citizenship is about more than what you are legally required to do—political citizenship is about being an active participant within your civic community and the nation's body politic. When we talk about being a "good citizen," this is the type of citizenship we are referring to. Practices like information gathering, deliberation, and active participation have come to function as important civic norms that define being a good citizen today.[11] In addition to the two definitions of citizenship offered by the *Oxford English Dictionary,* scholars have articulated a third type of citizenship: affective citizenship.[12] Affective citizenship is defined as feelings of belonging and togetherness. Invoked through national anthems and flags, affective citizenship is about the feeling of loyalty to one's government. These three types of citizenship are not mutually exclusive. Rather, they often occur together in the same actions.[13] For example, one can vote if one is a legal-judicial citizen, voting is a way to be an active citizen in the body politic, and wearing an "I Voted" sticker can induce a feeling of belonging within the nation-state.

These categories of citizenship help us understand the "what" of citizenship. They help us understand what citizenship is and allow us to identify what citizenship is being enacted where, when, and by whom. We can track how many people have voted, what factors lead to voting, and what the long-term shifts are in voting patterns. Social scientists in political science, journalism, and mass communication have done much to help answer this "what" question of citizenship.[14] But for scholars, activists, and citizens interested in communication, we must also ask *how* citizenship is performed, or, as Rob Asen puts it, "how citizenship proceeds."[15] Rather than counting and tracking citizenship across time, as a scholar of rhetoric and media using critical and ethnographic methods, I attend to the ways in which a citizenship performance emerges from a particular context and the meanings it activates and connects to in the process. This type of investigation requires a theorization of citizenship suited to the intricacies of performance, discourse, and media.

Following Rob Asen, I understand citizenship to be a mode of public engagement—that is, a process of engaging others.[16] Theorizing citizenship as a mode, or "a manner of doing something,"[17] draws our attention to how citizenship is performed. In performances, the audience, the performer, the context, and available resources all contribute to the emergent meaning of the performance.[18] Thus, viewing citizenship as a performance allows us to attend to varied and particular meanings that might emerge from the same act. For example, in a study of disenfranchised women attempting to register to vote from 1868 to 1875, rhetorical critic Angela Ray draws attention to the ways in which voting was performed as part of personal networks. Women came to register or vote with other family members, including sisters, sisters-in-law, mothers, husbands, and fathers, "performatively rebutting the common claim that women's voting would destroy the family."[19] Ray identifies the arguments that voting made by pointing to the manner in which the act of voting was done.

Viewing citizenship as a performance also means that we can attend to the ways in which power and identity matter in citizenship. In the same article, Ray describes the ways in which women faced the impossible task of making the body appear "as a representative of a gender-neutral, race-neutral, class-neutral abstraction."[20] When Carrie S. Burnham voted at the polls in Philadelphia in 1871, Ray explains, the *Inquirer* described her as wearing "a black silk dress, lace collar and white gloves."[21] This description, Ray asserts, demonstrates that "conventions of femininity, wedded to expectations of class and race, thus threatened to transmute the universalist argument [for voting rights] into one emphasizing attributes that might *earn* a person the right to civic involvement."[22] Ray's analysis points to the ways in which power and identity emerge in the manner of citizenship performances. As Asen puts it, "examining modes of engagement undoes the status bracketing sustained by viewing citizenship through constitutive acts."[23] Angela Ray's research demonstrates that analyzing how citizenship is performed allows us to pay attention to power and identity. In the case of fan-based citizenship performances, we can attend not only to the number of votes that former US president Barack Obama received or the money raised by Harry Potter fans but also to how those civic actions were performed in order to understand how identity and power are implicated.

Viewing citizenship as a performance also means that we can examine the ways in which citizenship emerges out of particular contexts. Citizenship practices do not exist in a vacuum; rather, the relationship between the citizen and the state is made and remade through public culture. Rhetorical scholars Robert Hariman and John Lucaites define public culture as the "oratory, posters, print journalism, literary and other artistic works, documentary films, and other media" that function to "define audiences as citizens, uphold norms of political representation and institutional transparency, and promote the general welfare."[24] The texts, images, and media of public culture function to provide "vehicles for thought and feeling, for imagination and disputatious argument."[25] What rhetorical scholars call public culture, political communication scholar Peter Dahlgren calls civic culture.[26] Dahlgren asserts that civic cultures are the "cultural patterns in which identities of citizenship, and the foundations for civic agency, are embedded."[27] This is where civic values, civic affinity and trust, civic knowledge, civic practices, civic identities, and civic spaces are articulated and thus also where definitions of the "good citizen" emerge and shift.[28] Public culture and civic values are anything but static. Indeed, we are not born knowing that voting is an important duty—we learn this through public culture. Conceptualizing citizenship as rising out of public culture calls us to see citizenship as culturally, socially, and historically situated.[29] Historically situated at a moment when networked and digital media have proliferated, when fan affiliations and communities have grown in importance, and when citizenship practices seem to be in flux, the civic actions of the Harry Potter Alliance and the many other similar groups have emerged as a powerful form of citizenship. This book argues that these groups and organizations are enacting a new mode of citizenship—one that engages the public and other citizens in very specific and powerful ways.

Fan-Based Citizenship as a New Mode of Citizenship

I call this new mode of citizenship, enacted by organizations like the Harry Potter Alliance, "fan-based citizenship": public engagement that emerges from a commitment to a fan-object. I call it fan-based citizenship and not fan activism, as other scholars and some fans do, because citizenship describes a wider variety of civic and political actions.[30] While most of the Harry Potter Alliance's actions can be described as activism, not all of their actions can be. Karma Chávez defines activism as "a particular form of politics that is explicitly designed to effect social change with a specific agenda, usually enacted outside traditional, deliberative modes of decision-making conducted within established institutions."[31] Thus, we can understand the Harry Potter Alliance's actions that convinced Warner Brothers to use fair-trade chocolate in its Harry Potter–brand candy as activism. But many of the Harry Potter Alliance's other actions, like Wizard Rock the Vote, the Accio Books campaign, a fund-raiser for Partners in Health, and the Grainger Leadership Academy, fall outside of the definition of activism. Actions like registering new voters, donating money to nonprofits, and phone banking for state referenda all take place within established institutions. Thus, the Harry Potter Alliance utilizes its unique fan-based strategies not only in activism but also in other types of civic action. In this sense, the term "fan activism" fails to capture the full range of the HPA's activities. I use "fan-based citizenship" to encompass a wider range of performances of political participation and civic engagement that draw on one's commitment to a fan-object.

In calling the actions of the Harry Potter Alliance fan-based citizenship, I set aside questions of media engagement or cultural engagement in which fans deploy activist tactics like petitions, boycotts, and letter-writing campaigns aimed at media companies and cultural representations, often called fan activism or media activism.[32] In these campaigns, fans may try to save a show from cancellation, like in the cases of *Star Trek* (1966–69), *Once & Again* (1999–2002), and *Another World* (1964–99).[33] Or, they may seek to influence story lines or production decisions, like in the case of the casting of white actors in *The Last Airbender* (2010) and the death of Tara in *Buffy the Vampire Slayer* (1997–2003).[34] Or, they may seek changes in policies regarding professional athletes, like in the case of the Australian football group Footy Fans Against Sexual Assault.[35] This type of fan activism, enacted as media or cultural engagement, has significant implications for fan communities and politics embedded within media systems. Media studies scholar Henry Jenkins argues that this kind of media engagement functions to "cement social ties between fans, define their shared interests, and shape their public status."[36] Additionally, some media activism tries to impact media representations and policies that have important political implications for the way belonging is constructed for fans. But issues taken up in media and cultural engagement are sources of concern for particular groups of fans, not the general public. Indeed, it seems natural that fans would act on issues in which they have a stake—*media* issues that affect their experiences as *fans*. However, in cases of fan-based citizenship, fans take action on *public* issues that affect their experiences as *citizens*. In this book I analyze how fan experiences come to be made relevant to public issues (e.g., climate change, fair trade, access to clean water, and local mentoring), resulting in civic action that is grounded in one's experience and identity as a fan.

While I use the term "fan-based citizenship" to make a theoretical argument about the serious and significant public engagement of fans, the fans I met while researching this book conceptualized their civic actions in a variety of ways. Many Harry Potter fans were quick to call their actions activism and embrace the political connotations of that term. Other fan communities saw their actions as community engagement, while still others saw their actions as participation in the fandom.[37] Fans have not developed an agreed-upon emic term for their unique brand of citizenship, at least in part because their actions blend fandom and citizenship in new and unique ways and have emerged at a time when citizenship is undergoing significant change.

Fan-based citizenship has emerged as a new mode of citizenship at a time when the whole of citizenship seems to be in flux. Ethan Zuckerman, an internet studies scholar and director of MIT's Center for Civic Media, points to instances like the Harry Potter Alliance's Hunger Games campaign, Kiva.org, Indiegogo, and Kony 2012 as proof that "civics is changing."[38] Media and cultural studies scholars Henry Jenkins and Sangita Shresthova call actions like the Harry Potter Alliance's "a new mode of civic engagement" and call scholars to turn their attention to this new mode:[39]

"All of this suggests the urgent need for scholars to explore more fully the many different potential relationships between fandom and political life."[40] Like media and cultural studies scholars, political communication scholars including Lance Bennett, Peter Dahlgren, Bruce Williams, and Michael X. Delli Carpini have recognized that major shifts in political communication and civic practices are occurring.[41]

Today, the texts, artifacts, and media that make up the center of public culture and discourses of citizenship are increasingly blurring the boundary between entertainment and politics. Media scholar Sonia Livingstone argues that increasingly publics are mediated and media audiences are diffused.[42] These changes function to "blur traditional boundaries between work and leisure, education and entertainment, domestic and civic, local and global."[43] This shift is especially visible in satirical television news shows like *The Daily Show* (1996–present) and *The Colbert Report* (2005–15). Scholars like Jeffrey Jones, Michael Xenos, and Geoffrey Baym have found that young people are increasingly getting their political information from these humorous and entertaining news programs.[44] *The Daily Show* and *The Colbert Report* demonstrate that entertainment with a political bent can have productive impacts on citizens. But fan-based citizenship performances like those of the Harry Potter Alliance take this merger between entertainment and politics one step further.

As Andrew Slack explains: "The truly radical thing we've done is show that fantasy is not an escape from our world, but an invitation to go deeper into it. By encouraging young people to be like the heroes they read about, this enthusiastic generation really can change the world."[45] The Harry Potter Alliance does more than present a political argument couched in play or humor. It is a political argument authorized and justified by a fictional story and a commitment to that fan identity. Slack says in a separate interview, "If Harry were in our world . . . he would fight injustice in our world the way he fought injustice in his."[46] Members of the Harry Potter Alliance choose to support fair trade because Harry and Hermione worked to protect and free Dobby, a house-elf who served as a kind of indentured servant, valuing workers' rights in the process. In other words, for Harry Potter Alliance members, popular culture serves as a guiding framework for civic action. This is what makes civic appeals for citizenship performances like the Harry Potter Alliance's so different from most other civic appeals.

By blending popular culture and civic action, the Harry Potter Alliance represents an important new mode of citizenship. The Harry Potter Alliance's political actions question the assumed relationship between citizenship performances, civic groups, and ethics. Communication scholars have traditionally understood civic actions as deeply connected to social institutions, like family and church, and civic groups like the Democratic Party, Greenpeace, or the Southern Christian Leadership Conference. In this book, I argue that in fan-based citizenship, citizens choose popular culture over civic institutions to guide their civic action—Harry Potter fans choose Harry Potter over the Republican Party to guide their action on same-sex marriage.

Understanding Fandom

Fan-based citizenship like the Harry Potter Alliance's is grounded in one's experience as a fan. Therefore, in order to understand fan-based citizenship, we must also understand what it means to be a fan. One's fandom or fannishness can be best understood as an intense engagement with a fan-object. Fan-objects are the popular culture objects fans love, including books, television shows, comics, video games, sports teams, celebrities, etc. Fan studies scholars Jonathan Gray and Kristina Busse and sociologists Nick Abercrombie and Brian Longhurst have articulated defining characteristics of the fan experience.[47] Here, I organize those characteristics into four continua that define one's experience as a fan and thus undergird fan-based citizenship performances.

First, fans experience an emotional/affective tie to their object of fandom.[48] This is the close connection fans often feel toward their object of fandom. When fans express how much they love a television show or how committed they are to attending every home football game, they are expressing their emotional and affective tie to their fan-object. Second, fans cultivate a specialization of knowledge regarding their object of fandom.[49] For example, baseball fans memorize RBIs (runs brought in) of their favorite players, while fans of *Friends* (1994–2004) memorize their favorite lines from the show. Third, fans participate in a community of fans.[50] For example, fans may post on online discussion boards or attend tailgating events. An organized, online community of fans is often referred to as a fandom.

Fourth, fans engage in a range of activities that result in material productivity.[51] This includes fanfiction, which is fiction written by fans based in the universe of their fan-object.[52] Through fanfiction, fans continue the story with their favorite characters and reimagine new situations and plotlines. Material productivity includes making crafts, like *Doctor Who* (1963–89; 2005–present) scarves, and making music, what is often known in fan circles as filk.[53] Scholars and fans frame the practices in this category as either affirmational or transformative in their purpose.[54] Affirmational engagement "analyzes and interprets the source text, creating shared meaning and characterizations," while transformational engagement "aggressively alters and transforms the source text, changing and manipulating it to the fans' own desires."[55] One fan may create a cosplay costume that is affirmational—a costume re-created from their fan-object that is true to the source text's every detail, while another fan may create a cosplay costume that changes a character's gender—thus transforming the source text in significant ways. Paul Booth adds, "Fan practices hover between these categories, enacting them not as absolute polarities but as shifting interpretations and identities."[56]

The behaviors or fan practices described in these continua (affective ties, specialization of knowledge, community, and material productivity) are performed in fluid ways depending upon fan, community, context, and audience. For example, each continuum may take on a different level of importance for individual fans or collective fan communities. In communities like comics fandom, acquiring a specialization of knowledge might be more important than building community. Or a particular *Doctor Who* fan may value material productivity over the other continua, focusing most of her time on creating *Doctor Who* cosplay costumes rather than acquiring extensive knowledge of every episode of *Doctor Who*.

I hope that viewing these practices as fluid continua helps us conceptualize fan experiences without creating a set of minimum criteria that fans must meet in order to count as "real fans." Indeed, gendered, racialized, and class-based logics are present across each continuum. For example, material productivity that is gendered feminine, like cosplay, in comic book fandom is sometimes undervalued, while memorizing quotes, issues, and facts—gendered masculine—is praised as the demonstration of a "true fan."

Fans of color are routinely rendered invisible within geek fan communities to such a degree that Jamie Broadnax founded a blog and podcast to offer her own answer to the far too prevalent question, "Do black girl nerds exist?"[57] These continua not only help us understand the axes of fan experiences but also invite us to examine how fan practices, communities, and identities maintain exclusions. At stake is who gets to be a fan.

Even defining fans through the most common fan practices can maintain problematic exclusions. In a study of football fans, sports studies scholars Anne Osborne and Danielle Sarver Coombs found that by defining football fandom through common fan practices like boisterous expressions of emotion at sports bars during football games, some fans get excluded by definition.[58] For example, Natalie, an Asian American woman football fan, enacts her fandom by wearing a jersey and watching the game at a sports bar, but she refrains from loud, boisterous cheering because that practice comes into conflict with her identity as an Asian American woman. As an Asian American woman, she is expected to be quiet and reserved—at odds with white men football fans' loud cheering.[59] Osborne and Coombs demonstrate that fans negotiate their fan identity alongside their many other identities (gender, race, sexuality, etc.) and many other roles (wife, mother, etc.). Fans often find innovative ways to perform their fan identity even alongside these other constraints. But both fans and scholars need to recognize such varying performances.

Fans themselves play a key role in pushing back against exclusionary discourses and making room for themselves and others in fan communities. News sites like *The Mary Sue* pay particular attention to issues related to gender and social justice, and sites like *Blerds Online* and *BlerdNation*™ give voice and visibility to fans of color.[60] This also extends to critiques of fan-objects. For example, *Doctor Who* fans on Tumblr have pointed to the problematic ways in which *Doctor Who* writer and showrunner Steven Moffat writes women characters. In other examples, fans organize themselves into organizations and movements. Fans of Nickelodeon's animated show *The Last Airbender* (2003–8) protested the casting of white actors for the starring roles in the live-action movie version, also titled *The Last Airbender* (2010).[61] The Harry Potter Alliance criticized Warner Brothers' choice to use non-fair-trade chocolate in Harry Potter candy. Fans are not universally blind to the shortcomings of their fan-objects and fan communities. Indeed, it is often precisely because of their deep love for their fan-object and community that fans push their fan-objects and fan cultures to be better.

Understanding fan practices, identities, and communities is becoming increasingly important as fandom has become more popular, visible, and accessible than ever before.[62] Scholars like Kristina Busse, Paul Booth, and Henry Jenkins argue that "fandom has entered the mainstream."[63] At the local level, newspapers regularly cover fan conventions that come to town. Even media giants like MTV have tried to tap into the cultural cachet of fandom by hosting events like the Fandom Awards, which were filmed live at San Diego Comic-Con in 2014.[64]

Fandom's mainstreaming and the increased visibility that comes with it have occurred in part as a result of the development and growing power of neoliberalism in our contemporary world. Media industries have come to see fans as enthusiastic consumers who can be courted with minimal effort, but who routinely donate innumerable amounts of free labor for the fan-object they love.[65] Media companies are cultivating and supporting their fan followings, though for their own profit.[66] Put simply, fans have become a powerful and valuable audience.

Digital Technologies Enable Community

The growth in visibility, accessibility, and size of fandoms in recent years is also due to technological developments. The development of networked computing (the precursor to the contemporary World Wide Web) in the 1980s and 1990s enabled communities to emerge across great geographic distances.[67] Online communities developed and continue to develop around shared interests like fandom as well as parenting, technology, religion, and the news.[68] Writing about the Whole Earth 'Lectronic Link (WELL) founded in 1985, Howard Rheingold describes online communities as "social aggregations that emerge from the Net when enough people carry on those public discussions long enough, with sufficient human feeling, to form webs of personal relationships in cyberspace."[69] Feelings of connection, belonging, and identity are just as much at the center of online communities as offline communities.

But Rheingold cautions that "you have to be careful to not mistake the tool for the task and think that just writing words on a screen is the same thing as real community."[70] We make this error when we assume that the existence of a website or platform like Twitter or Facebook automatically signals the existence of online communities.[71] Indeed, creating and sustaining online community takes work. It is not automatic or self-sustaining. Rhetoric and folklore scholar Rob Howard explains how online communities sustain themselves without geographic boundaries or anchors: "Unlike geographical communities, online communities are often based solely on the discursive behaviors that express these social relationships. Because they have no physical or geographic markers, online communities are radically dependent on the ongoing enactment of the shared expectations that are both witnessed and enacted by participants in discourse."[72] Community emerges when members continually enact their community membership through discursive practices.

Before the internet, fan communities like those that emerged around *Star Trek* were built using fan zines (homemade magazines) that circulated through the postal service and face-to-face meetings at local clubs or fan conventions.[73] However, participation in the community often depended on word of mouth, and fans were restricted by geographic location. The development of the internet made community building across geographic distance significantly easier for fans.[74] And many fans enthusiastically adopted these new media technologies. Henry Jenkins points out that fans "were often early adopters of new media platforms and practices. . . . They were historically among the first to interact within geographically dispersed communities of interest."[75] For example, Usenet listservs in the 1990s enabled soap opera fans to construct an online community for themselves, as Nancy Baym demonstrates.[76] Live Journal in the 2000s allowed fanfiction writers to easily share their stories and find other fanfiction to read, as Karen Hellekson and Kristina Busse detail.[77] Networked technologies have been essential to the robust development of fan communities in recent decades. And networked technologies continue to develop in new ways that allow fans to easily create media, share media, and construct and maintain community even across great geographic distances.

These shifts, which have made fandom an increasingly important identity in our contemporary world while also making fan activities easier to organize, host, and participate in, have laid the foundation for actions like the Harry Potter Alliance's. Thanks in part to networked technologies, the Harry Potter Alliance has a large audience for its Harry Potter–themed civic agenda. Fan-based citizenship has emerged as a new mode of public engagement in large part because of the development of networked technologies.

Locating Fan-Based Citizenship Scholarship

Consideration of fan-based citizenship like the Harry Potter Alliance's has primarily been located in fan studies and audience studies.[78] This means that scholars have paid close attention to the ways in which the particularities of fandom enable productive political participation, while setting aside questions of persuasive appeals in communication. Fan studies scholar Liesbet van Zoonen argues that fan activities help fans cultivate skills that are important for democratic participation.[79] For example, when Harry Potter fans discuss who the half-blood prince might be before the sixth Harry Potter book is released, fans practice deliberation, information filtering, and even consensus seeking. Van Zoonen argues that these are important skills for political action and democratic participation, positioning fans who have mastered these skills as potentially efficacious citizens.[80] Media studies scholar Jonathan Gray finds evidence of this kind of action in the case of the 2011 Wisconsin protests over anti-union legislation.[81] Fans used their specialized knowledge of fan-objects to create protest signs that critiqued Governor Scott Walker through references to Star Wars, Lord of the Rings, and Harry Potter.[82] When fans practice deliberation, careful research, writing, and art within fan communities, they are preparing themselves to participate in politics.

In addition to helping fans cultivate skills necessary for participating in democracies, fandom also provides key structures important in political mobilization. Tight-knit and well-developed fan communities serve as foundations for public formation. Alex Leavitt and Andrea Horbinski demonstrate how this occurred in the case of Japan's 2010 Nonexistent Crimes Bill (Bill 156), which threatened heavy censorship of manga, anime, and other visual arts.[83] Fans argued against the draconian bill by drawing on the fan community structures already in place. They composed their critique in the form of popular fan-made comics known as dôjin, and fans circulated their critique of the bill at dôjin conventions.[84] In this way, fan communities can serve as ready-made audiences for political arguments, providing important structures and norms of circulation. Henry Jenkins argues that fan communities have envisioned and developed unique and innovative social structures that enable them to take political action. Jenkins explains that "the political effects of these fan communities come not simply through the production and circulation of new ideas (the critical readings of favorite texts) but also through access to new social structures (collective intelligence) and new models of cultural production (participatory culture)."[85] For example, in the case of the Harry Potter Alliance, Jenkins argues that the organization utilizes structures like strong leadership, dispersed membership, social networks, and flexibility.[86] When these types of structures are absent from fan communities, they can discourage and even prevent the development of fan-based citizenship. Cheuk Yin Li argues that this occurred in the Canto-Pop singer Ho Denise CC's (HOCC) fandom.[87] While queer readings, images, and invitations existed within the HOCC fan community, hierarchical structures in the fan community limited queer activities to creative fan endeavors rather than queer activism engaging China on a national level. Fan community structures play a key role in fostering fan-based citizenship performances.

Fan-based citizenship is enabled not only by the structures of fan communities but also by fan-objects. Scholars like Matt Yockey and Stephen Duncombe argue that fan-based citizenship emerges around fan-objects that offer depictions of social change through utopian explorations.[88] In television shows like *Star Trek* (1966–69) and comics like *Wonder Woman*, fans are invited to imagine a better world. Fan-based citizenship performances become concrete actions fans can take to bring the status quo closer to ideal futures. While utopian fan-objects may at times seem abstract, television characters, actors, and creators model what social change may look like.[89] Fans of Joss Whedon's work, including *Firefly* (2002–3) and *Buffy the Vampire Slayer* (1997–2003), took inspiration from him and his strong female characters when they answered his call in 2006 and 2007 to support Equality Now, a nonprofit organization that supports women and girls. Tanya Cochran argues that by donating to Equality Now, fans took on the role of Joss Whedon, who writes strong women characters, and took on the role of strong women characters like Buffy and Zoe, who consistently defeat evil.[90] Across these cases of utopian visions and role models, a vision of a different status quo is strengthened by the affective bond fans feel toward their fan-objects.[91] In a study of *X-Files* (1993–2002) fandom, Bethan Jones argues: "Honesty, dedication, strength, and loyalty are attributes given to Scully, and Anderson, by fans. These characteristics are important to fans, and as a result, they model themselves on or undertake work for Scully and Andersen."[92]

But how are fans invited to undertake such work? Fan structure and fan skills provide the means for civic action, while fan-objects provide the inspiration, but what remains unclear is how fans are invited to take such action. Scholars have carefully documented cases of fan-based citizenship performances, but little is known about the persuasive communication strategies used to invite fans to take action. That is—scholars know much about the fandom aspects of fan-based citizenship but little about the rhetorical aspects of fan-based citizenship. If fan structures are used to enact civic action, as Henry Jenkins argues, then how are fans invited to take such action? If an affective bond is present, as Matt Yockey argues, how is it invoked? If role modeling occurs, as Bethan Jones and Lucy Bennett argue, then how does a character become a call to action for fans? This book seeks to fill this gap by examining the rhetorical strategies deployed by fans in fan-based citizenship performances. I ask, how are fans invited, encouraged, and persuaded to take civic action on behalf of their fan-object?

To analyze rhetorical strategies that rhetors (or speakers and writers) use to invite fans to participate in civic engagement, I focus my attention on how rhetors pair ethical frameworks from popular culture fan-objects with civic actions, and how these pairings might be productive for public culture and under what conditions these pairings are empowering and for whom.[93] An increasingly fluid world offers new possibilities for identity formation, community membership, and institutional participation. Answering these research questions will enable a better understanding of a new type of civic action emerging in our fluid world: fan-based citizenship performances. Thus, this book argues that fan groups, not just civic institutions/ groups, can guide citizenship practices.

To do this, I examine four case studies: (1) Husker football and the TeamMates' Coaches Challenge campaign, (2) the VlogBrothers and Nerd-fighteria's Project for Awesome, (3) Greenpeace's LEGO and Shell Oil campaign, and (4) the Star Wars Force for Change campaign. These case studies capture variation across two vectors: fan-object and fan membership. First, my case studies explore a variety of fan-objects by examining fandom around sports, vlogs (video blogs), toys, and movies. Second, these fandoms vary in terms of demographic membership. The University of Nebraska Husker football fandom is comprised predominantly of adult white men who perform a hegemonic form of masculinity reinforced by football's valued place in mainstream culture. Nebraska football fans are geographically located in Nebraska primarily, though fans often retain their fan identity even after moving great distances.[94] The nerdfighter fandom is predominantly comprised of white women who are in high school or college, but who are diverse sexually. Nerdfighteria is a global fandom with about 40 percent of fans living outside of the United States. LEGO fandom is primarily comprised of adult fans of LEGO in their thirties and forties, mostly white men, who collect, build, and discuss LEGO. LEGO has unique cultural standing because of its framing as an educational toy, both in engineering and art. Star Wars fandom skews heavily toward white men and is characterized by generational membership as the movies have been released in three waves: 1977–83, 1999–2005, and 2015–19, with fans ranging from teenagers to people in their sixties. While *Star Wars'* futuristic view of a universe with space travel places it firmly within the science fiction genre, its widespread success and popularity has lent it cultural cachet not available to other science fiction fandoms. By studying cases of fan performances of citizenship that fall across a spectrum of fan-objects and fan membership, we can begin to understand how widespread fan-based citizenship performances can be, as well as the variety of opportunities that exist for fan-based citizenship performances.[95] These cases demonstrate that fan-based citizenship performances are not simply "flukes" but rather occur across varying fan-objects and fan membership.

Preview of Chapters

I begin the book by articulating a theoretical context that has enabled fan-based citizenship performances to emerge. Following theorists like Anthony Giddens and Zygmut Bauman, I argue that our contemporary world is characterized by a fluidity of institutional membership, in which individuals have increased choice between institutional and group membership. This means that worldviews that lead to political actions are no longer limited to political institutions. Rather, citizens can take political actions on behalf of Harry Potter.[96] This fluidity provides us with a context for understanding the emergence of fan-based citizenship performances like the Harry Potter Alliance. Because of the way in which fluidity unsettles traditional understandings of civic action as tied to institutional and group membership, fluidity requires new theoretical terms. I offer *ethical framework* as a worldview or a frame of understanding based on an ethic that is theoretical and all-encompassing and *ethical modality* as a particular mode of action that falls under an ethical framework. Turning to an example from the Harry Potter Alliance, I illustrate the use of these key terms briefly. Then I identify the methodological assumptions that must undergird a study of fan-based citizenship performances in a fluid world using these terms, before detailing my own methodological process.

Chapters 2–4 consider three different strategies for pairing ethical frameworks with ethical modalities. In chapter 2, I examine the strategy of *connecting*, in which citizens draw parallels between the popular culture fan-object and a real-world public issue. To illustrate this, I analyze the case of the University of Nebraska Husker football team and the mentoring nonprofit TeamMates. Founded by former football head coach Tom Osborne, TeamMates connects Husker football to mentoring and, in the process, pairs a Husker ethical framework with a mentoring ethical modality. TeamMates draws on a Husker ethical framework that calls Huskers to be neighborly, to work hard, and to stay down-to-earth. TeamMates invokes these ethical obligations as it draws connections between joining the football team and volunteering to mentor. In the process, TeamMates transfers the importance of Husker football to mentoring, a public issue often ignored and underdiscussed. By pairing Husker football with volunteering, TeamMates provides an additional entry to public culture, while also recasting public priorities around mentoring, youth, and poverty in Nebraska.

While chapter 2 analyzes *connecting* as a strategy for pairing, chapter 3 considers *expanding* as a strategy for pairing noncivic popular culture ethical frameworks with civic ethical modalities. This strategy involves expanding or pushing ethical frameworks beyond fan activities to also include civic actions. To examine this strategy, I turn to the case of the Nerdfighteria fandom surrounding John and Hank Green's YouTube channel called The VlogBrothers. The Nerdfighteria ethical framework consists of five values that all aim to increase "awesome" in the world. Typically, these values are deployed in fan activities, like attending fan conventions, participating in collaborative projects, and posting comments in the online forums. But John and Hank extend the Nerdfighteria ethical framework beyond these fan activities to also include charitable donations and deliberation about those donations during their annual Project for Awesome. By pairing a Nerdfighteria ethical framework with charitable giving, the Project for Awesome makes participation in digital culture an entry to public culture, while also creating a new kind of civic space online, departing from problematic sexist norms and practices of internet culture.

Chapter 4 analyzes how *retelling* reenvisions the story told by a fan-object and thus pairs a popular culture ethical framework with a civic modality. In this chapter, I consider how Greenpeace utilized this strategy in its 2014 YouTube video *LEGO: Everything is NOT Awesome*. Receiving more than eight million views, the video was the most visible part of a campaign to convince LEGO to end its contract with Shell, which included advertising on the children's toy. The video draws upon a LEGO ethical framework that places creativity, imagination, and originality at the center. Greenpeace's video shows a fictional LEGO world built in creative, original, and imaginative ways, threatened by an oil spill. By retelling LEGO's story, Greenpeace casts Shell as a threat to LEGO, the fan-object. Thus, fans are called to take civic action to protect the LEGO ethical framework and their beloved fan-object. The campaign had different implications for two different audiences: parents of kids who play with LEGO who were more willing to boycott LEGO and LEGO fans who loved LEGO and thus were unwilling to boycott. The LEGO case demonstrates that even a successful pairing must be consistent with fan priorities: love of the fan-object.

In chapter 5, I analyze *absent pairings* by turning to the case of the Star Wars Force for Change. In 2014, Disney launched the Force for Change campaign ahead of the release of *Episode VII: The Force Awakens* as a way to raise money for UNICEF. If we define success as the amount of money raised, focusing on the "what" of citizenship, we ought to consider the campaign a wild success because it raised more than $4 million. But if we define success not by the "what" of citizenship but by the "how" of citizenship, we might begin to tease out success and failure in terms of a campaign's relationship to public culture. Did the campaign engage and enrich public culture in powerful ways? In this chapter, I argue that the Star Wars Force for Change campaign did little to engage or enrich public culture, with little relationship to public culture and public issues at all, making the campaign a civic failure. Across the campaign's website and videos, the Force for Change called upon fans to take a civic action, but it failed to pair a Star Wars ethical framework with a civic ethical modality. Instead, the Force for Change relied on noncivic appeals for their donations, inviting fans to participate in the campaign not out of a commitment to a public issue or civic action but only to be a good fan. Without the pairing of a popular culture ethical framework with a civic ethical modality, there is no connection between fandom and public culture. The Star Wars campaign enriches fan culture through its exclusive merchandise and grand prizes but doesn't significantly engage public culture.

In the conclusion, I argue that this book not only helps us understand fans as citizens but also helps us understand public culture in our contemporary world. I explore how fan-based citizenship shapes our contemporary public culture and how online communities ground citizenship performances. I also consider the predominantly white demographics of this book's case studies, exploring the problematic implications those demographics have for civic action. Last, I explore some of the possible futures for fan-based citizenship performances.

In the coda, I turn my attention to practitioners like activists, politicians, and media industry representatives. Here I identify the takeaways or lessons the research in this book offers for engaging fans and for inventing and developing fan activist campaigns.

Ultimately, this book demonstrates that even as the Harry Potter Alliance may be the most well-known case of fan-based citizenship performance, it is hardly the only one.[97] Across football, YouTube, movies, and toys, fandom can function as an important grounding for citizenship. Emerging from a fluid and digital world, fan-based citizenship performances blend fandom and civic action in a variety of ways. By doing so, they open up new entries to public culture and new possibilities for civic space.

THEORIZING CITIZENSHIP
IN A DIGITAL, FLUID WORLD

During the 2008 US presidential election, Paul DeGeorge, cofounder of the Harry Potter Alliance and cofounder, with his brother Joe DeGeorge, of the popular "wizard wrock" band Harry and the Potters, made "Wizards for Obama" T-shirts.[1] In an interview, Paul explains, "I knew a lot about fandom, and I know that people like to flash their nerdy pride around. So I figured . . . why not use that as a way to help people express their support for Obama's candidacy?"[2] On these T-shirts, Paul creatively riffed on the typical campaign slogans like "Women for Obama," "African Americans for Obama," and "Union Workers for Obama," with new slogans like "Wizards for Obama." Harry Potter fans reacted enthusiastically to the shirts. By the end of the 2008 election cycle, Paul knew he had to expand the operation for the 2012 election. In 2012, Paul created a website and online store called Nerds for Obama.[3] Paul continued to sell Harry Potter–themed merchandise that proclaimed, "Wizards for Obama," "Hufflepuffs for Obama," and "Voldemort Can't Stop Barack" (fig. 1). But this time, Paul sold bumper stickers and buttons in addition to T-shirts, offered free digital image files for users to download and use on their social media pages, and offered merchandise for fandoms other than Harry Potter. The Nerds for Obama store connected Obama support to *Firefly,* Settlers of Catan, *Game of Thrones,* Star Wars, *Sherlock,* the VlogBrothers, Mario Brothers, *Doctor Who,* and Pokémon. While not formally endorsed by the Obama campaign, Obama lent his support to the project by retweeting and reblogging images from the Nerds for Obama site. Paul explains that the Nerds for Obama store wasn't about satire: "I was trying to link up a member group, like

Teachers for Obama. . . . [I]t was much more in line with the existing infra-structure of ways people would support candidates rather than satire."[4] For Harry Potter fans like Paul, their fandom is a key aspect of their identity—one that guides their political actions just as much as identities like union member or teacher.

By replacing traditional political institutions and identities (like union membership) with a fan identity (wizards and Hufflepuffs), Paul's "Huf-flepuffs for Obama" T-shirts question the assumed relationship between citizenship performances, civic groups, and ethics. Communication schol-ars have traditionally understood civic actions as deeply connected to social institutions like family, church, and civic groups. In this chapter, I argue that economic, social, and political shifts since the late 1970s have made the membership in those social institutions and civic groups more fluid than ever before. In a fluid world, citizens may easily choose Harry Potter over the Democratic Party to guide their civic action on voting in presiden-tial elections. It is this fluidity that provides us with a context for under-standing the emergence of fan-based citizenship performances like Paul DeGeorge's "Wizards for Obama" T-shirts and the Harry Potter Alliance's fair-trade campaigns.

A fluid world that enables citizens to choose popular culture media texts to authorize civic actions demands new theoretical terms, theoretical assumptions, and methodological approaches. First, I offer *ethical frame-work* and *ethical modality* as terms to enable researchers to investigate this shift and the civic actions it enables.[5] Through processes of pairing and unpairing, fan-based citizenship performances combine noncivic ethical frameworks from popular culture with civic ethical modalities, civic ac-tions like voting, petitioning, etc. These terms allow researchers to fully examine a wide range of fan-based citizenship performances, including performances that are emancipatory and problematic, effective and inef-fective, and grassroots and industry organized. In this chapter, I use the example of the Harry Potter Alliance's "Not in Harry's Name" campaign to illustrate how these terms can be used to investigate fan-based citizenship performances.

Second, a fluid world also demands a new set of theoretical assump-tions for rhetoricians and political communication scholars. A fluid world means that political groups are no longer limited to social institutions like

Figure 1. Images from the Nerds for Obama online store (www.nerdsforobama.org).

political parties, unions, and churches. Popular culture fan communities can guide civic action as well. Thus, rhetoricians studying public culture and political scientists studying civic action must now come to terms with questions about popular culture, meaning, and action. In this section, I offer three theoretical assumptions that must undergird research into fan-based citizenship performances.

Third, a fluid world that enables citizens to choose popular texts to authorize civic actions pushes the methods rhetoricians and political communication scholars are accustomed to using. While rhetoricians could faithfully assume that significant political texts would find their way into mainstream discussion determined both by national political actors and journalistic coverage, the texts that emerge in fan-based citizenship achieve neither. Instead, the significant political texts involved in fan-based citizenship emerge from specific online communities of thousands or millions of fans. Understanding these rhetorical texts and political actions requires understanding these fan communities. In this section, I argue that internet-based methods and fieldwork can meet that need. Thus, in a fluid world where civic belonging is found in any number of noncivic communities, fieldwork becomes not just peripheral to the discipline but central.

The theoretical framework and methodology outlined here will be used to analyze the rest of the case studies in this book. A theoretical framework that examines the complexity and depth of these fan-based citizenship performances must integrate research not only from fan studies but also from political communication, internet studies, and social movement studies. While I argue that fluidity makes fan-based citizenship performances easier than ever for citizens to enact, this does not necessarily mean that fan-based citizenship performances have not existed historically—only that they were more difficult and likely existed in smaller numbers.[6] As political communication researcher Michael Delli Carpini points out, being confronted with new civic actions in a changing political landscape can call us to develop new theories or modify old ones, helping us to look back historically to see things we, as researchers, might have missed before.[7]

Overall, this chapter articulates a context, theoretical terms, and a set of methods for research into fan-based citizenship performances. By doing so, I hope to provide a theoretical and methodological foundation for scholars across the communication and media disciplines to consider the myriad ways (positive or negative) in which fan-based citizenship performances impact our public culture, deliberation, and civic identities. To begin, I turn to the context from which these citizenship performances have emerged.

A Fluid World: Choice among Institutions

Scholars have generally recognized that civic actions are deeply connected to social institutions, civic groups, and religious organizations.[8] In social institutions and groups like families, churches, schools, unions, and community groups, we learn how to participate in public culture. For example, during the civil rights movement, black churches served as locations where citizens could be mobilized and learn civic skills.[9] These social institutions and civic groups are locations for invitations for public participation, discussion of public issues, and guidelines for right action in the world, and as such function as entries to public culture.

However, the relationship between institutions, politics, and social organizations began to change in the 1970s as major social, political, and economic shifts occurred.[10] Globalization, neoliberal policies, the privatization of public goods, services, and safety nets, and the diffusion of personal technologies like computers and smartphones contributed to restructuring within government institutions and social organizations.[11] These economic, technological, and social changes have had a profound impact on social institutions. Participation in groups and associations like unions, civic clubs, churches, and political parties has taken a significant downward turn.[12] Now membership in institutions that had traditionally provided economic security, social orientation, and ethical guidance is anything but guaranteed or automatic.

Zygmunt Bauman, Anthony Giddens, and Ulrich Beck describe this shift in modern life as characterized by a sense of fluidity in which individuals easily choose between multiple institutions, organizations, and groups and fluidly move between those institutional and group frameworks, resources, and requirements.[13] Both institutions and individuals are liquid, changing quickly and easily moving into new configurations.[14] Whereas in the past, individuals inherited membership within institutions through generations or by way of geographic limits, they now face choices among many institutions and groups.[15]

A fluid society requires individuals to choose their own worldviews, activities, and ethical systems. The guidance that tradition, family structures, and other institutions or social organizations used to provide for individuals has been weakened.[16] Giddens puts it this way: "In a post-traditional social universe, an indefinite range of potential courses of action (with their attendant risks) is at any given moment open to individuals and collectivities. Choosing among such alternatives is always an 'as if' matter, a question of selecting between possible worlds."[17] Citing the decreasing influence of social groups, Lance Bennett says, "Contemporary young people enjoy unprecedented levels of freedom to define and manage their self-identities in contrast with earlier generations' experiences with stronger groups (denominational church, labor, class, party) that essentially assigned broad social identities to their members."[18]

One's choices among institutions, organizations, and groups are not inconsequential or random; rather, they comprise the building blocks of one's social identity and public subjectivity in a liquid world. Beck explains that "socially prescribed biography is transformed into biography that is self-produced and continues to be produced."[19] By choosing membership in a Methodist church, a volunteer firefighter association, a local gun club, or the Democratic Party, an individual builds her public subjectivity. We pick and choose from many available social organizations and civic groups, living our identities across many "institutional settings of modernity."[20] Thus, in our fluid world, the agent chooses and constructs their own lifeworld from the vast array of options available in an increasingly globalized information society.

Increasing choice among social organizations and civic groups has implications for collective action and public formation. Fluidity among organizations and groups enhances choice but increases individual responsibility.[21] The implication for civic action is that this new individualism cuts away at solidarity in community formation and collective political action.[22] This produces a world "where few if any people continue to believe that changing the life of others is of any relevance to their own life."[23] Indeed, neoliberal policies reinforce this individualism; individuals are called to assume responsibility for responding to risks and fears themselves.[24]

Civic Actions in a Fluid World

So if our world is characterized by a fluidity that enables some degree of choice among political, religious, and social institutions and groups, how has this affected the ways in which citizens engage in politics? In this section, I argue that communication scholars from across a variety of subdisciplines have begun to answer this question. By putting them into conversation with one another, we can build a more complete picture of the characteristics of shifting citizenship practices and their relationship to a fluid world.

First, the fluidity among institutions, organizations, and groups and its resulting individualism enables individuals to adopt a politics that is more personalized and privatized than ever before. Bauman argues that individuals experience a lack of connection and apathy toward collective social change.[25] Similarly, internet studies scholar Zizi Papacharissi argues that individuals are increasingly frustrated with their inability to affect political institutions within representative democracies.[26] Papacharissi finds that citizens are rejecting traditional institutional political acts, turning instead to privatized and personalized civic actions. Signing a petition online or watching a subversive YouTube video occurs in a private online media landscape, based on personal concerns about civic issues. Lance Bennett and Alexandra Segerberg found evidence of this kind of personalized politics during the 2009 G20 summit in London.[27] A group called Put People First used broad action frames that allowed citizens to insert themselves into the protest in a variety of ways and offered protesters many ways to enact the protest and share information digitally, including a #G20 hashtag on Twitter, Facebook groups, email lists, signing petitions, and more.

One form of personalized politics is what Giddens calls "life-politics" and most others call "lifestyle politics."[28] In lifestyle politics, citizens take political action out of a personal sense of self, living their civic ideals through everyday choices. For example, a citizen might make global warming a personal lifestyle issue by choosing to buy a Prius. Indeed, such consumer or commodity activism is often at the center of lifestyle politics.[29] But such lifestyle politics are not restricted to conservative or neoliberal causes or logics. In her ethnographic study of anarchism, Laura Portwood-Stacer found that by dressing, eating, and consuming in a particular way, anarchists work to dismantle hierarchies, including capitalism, racism, and the state.[30] Even as personalized politics and lifestyle politics have opened up possibilities for civic action, they have also "further eroded group memberships and loyalties to parties and political institutions," contributing to the further privileging of personalized politics.[31]

Second, a fluid society encourages fluid organizational patterns within institutions and groups. These loosely organized civic groups allow individuals to easily join, move, pause, and exit the group: membership is fluid. Bennett and Segerberg identify two types of loosely organized groups.[32] One type provides citizens with many different ways to take action on a set of issues, allowing citizens to personalize their civic actions. Citizens might tweet support and make a donation but choose not to contact their representatives. Here digital media is used to notify citizens of possible actions to take and is used to enable those personal actions. In the second type of loosely organized groups, digital media play a more central role as "organizational hubs," organizing and integrating the communication from many contributors all at once.[33] Bennett and Segerberg found that this loosely organized crowd enabled connective action in tweets utilizing the #COP15 protesting the 15th Conference of the Parties to the United Nations Framework Convention on Climate Change in 2009. Even without central actors or organizations leading the #COP15 Twitter stream, tweets protesting the Copenhagen conference maintained organization and coherence.

Preferences for fluid organizational styles are a central difference between the baby boomer generation (people born between approximately 1946 and 1964) and the millennials (people born between approximately 1981 and 1997).[34] Stephen Coleman and Lance Bennett argue that citizenship performed by young people is less institutionally based and more individually focused.[35] Youth seek out unestablished spaces like the internet to practice citizenship, forming grassroots civic groups of their own. Youth adopting this style of politics reject the obligations of government institutions in favor of finding a sense of individual purpose in loose and fluid social networks. Indeed, it makes sense that Baby Boomers accustomed to doing politics in a less fluid world would favor clear institutional boundaries, organization, and direction, while millennials, confronted with learning to do politics in a fluid world, would adopt fluid organizational styles.

Fluid organizational patterns and personalized politics are the resulting characteristics of a fluid world that offers radical choice between institutions, groups, and organizations. Of course, not all institutional membership, for all individuals, is fluid all the time. Indeed, I may still inherit membership in a local, family church even as I also choose to enact personalized politics by buying a Prius and participate in a fluidly organized social movement campaign by tweeting #COP15. The point here isn't that institutional choice is newly *universal*; rather, institutional choice is newly *possible*.

A Fluid World Necessitates New Terms

Fan-based citizenship performances represent a radical expansion of institutional choice enabled by a fluid society. Citizens not only freely choose from among civic worldviews like the Democratic or Republican Parties but can also now choose between civic and *noncivic* worldviews and apply them equally easily to civic action.[36] Both fan and industry discourses articulate the preferred uses of popular culture media objects, like Harry Potter, as noncivic. Growing out of fan experiences with popular culture, fan-based citizenship performances are connected to noncivic worldviews.[37] By creating websites centered on sharing the latest news about the Harry Potter media object and writing fan fiction that extends and rewrites the lives of their favorite characters, fans invite audiences to use Harry Potter for entertainment purposes. Similarly, industry actors like J. K. Rowling, Scholastic, and Warner Brothers frame the preferred uses of Harry Potter as leisure and entertainment.[38] Rowling, Scholastic, and Warner Brothers together invite fans to engage Harry Potter as entertainment by encouraging fans to buy movie tickets, preorder books, attend book release parties at book stores, rewatch the movies aired on television, buy merchandise, visit the Wizarding World of Harry Potter at Universal Studios, and join the official Harry Potter website and social network site, Pottermore. Fans and industry actors position the noncivic uses of Harry Potter as the preferred uses. Applying a noncivic framework like Harry Potter to civic action like phone banking in support of same-sex marriage (rather than traditionally civic frameworks like the Democratic Party's platform) represents a significant expansion of choice among institutions. Such a radical departure from our traditional notions of ethics and civic action requires new theoretical concepts: ethical framework and ethical modality.

ETHICAL FRAMEWORK AND ETHICAL MODALITY

An *ethical framework* is a worldview or frame of understanding based on an ethic that is theoretical and all-encompassing. An ethical framework could potentially be applied to any action, while an ethical modality is more specific. An *ethical modality* is a way of meeting an ethical obligation. It is a particular mode of action that falls under an ethical framework. Based on an ethic that is practical, an ethical modality is specific to particular actions, topics, or themes. Ultimately, ethical frameworks and ethical modalities are defined by their relationship to each other: an ethical modality is used to satisfy one's obligation to an ethical framework.

Imagine, for example, an ethic of "sharing with others." If I believe in an ethical framework of sharing with others, I may use an ethical modality of contributing my tools as part of a neighborhood tool-sharing program. Sharing with others is a broad theoretical framework, an ethic that can guide many types of actions. Sharing my tools with my neighbors is a more specific ethic. The ethical modality is a way of satisfying the obligations of the ethical framework. Clearly there are many ethical frameworks that could be used for many ethical modalities. I might enact the ethical modality of sharing tools using a different ethical framework, like neighborly generosity. I might also enact my ethical framework of sharing with others through other ethical modalities, like donating old clothes to Goodwill.

Philosophers like Aristotle, Mill, and Kant give us ethical systems that incorporate both ethical frameworks and ethical modalities into one, producing an all-encompassing system establishing right ways of acting.[39] Francisco Varela draws attention to this in his book *Ethical Know-How: Action, Wisdom, and Cognition.*[40] Varela seeks to tease out what he sees as the implied and understudied aspect of ethics: "know-how." Varela defines "know-how" as ethical action taken on a daily basis in situations that are infinitely unique and defines "know-what" as ethical obligations based on prescriptive principles (where Western philosophers have directed much of their attention). While Varela's terms capture a dynamic I seek to draw attention to with ethical framework and ethical modality, Varela's terms are overburdened with the critical aim of his project. Varela seeks to reverse the privileging of "know-what" against "know-how" and thus to place "know-how" at the center of any program of ethics. Unlike Varela, I seek to draw attention to both aspects of ethical action: the framework (prescriptive principles) and the modality (everyday actions).

I draw my inspiration for ethical modality from Daniel C. Brouwer and Robert Asen's deployment of modality to understand publics and their rhetorical actions.[41] Beginning from the *Oxford English Dictionary*'s definition of mode as "a way or manner in which something is done or takes place; a method of proceeding in any activity," Brouwer and Asen use modality to draw attention to public engagement as a process and argue that the choices made during that process matter.[42] In my own use of "modality" as part of "ethical modality," I want to emphasize that the manner in which an obligation to an ethical framework is met matters. Ultimately, I argue that both the broad ethical framework (moral principles) and the ethical modality (everyday action taken to enact that ethical framework) are important.

In my use of ethical framework and ethical modality, I seek to identify the ethics invoked by particular rhetors, social groups, or social movements, not to endorse their chosen and performed ethics as good or desirable. Brouwer and Asen make a similar argument in regard to public modalities: "The critical character of this project does not arise from an inherent quality of a modality per se, since processes of public engagement may advance praiseworthy or censurable ends. Rather, the critical character of public modalities arises from the intervention and judgment of the scholar, who discerns the values implicated in particular engagements and judges their progressive or regressive qualities."[43]

I understand an ethic as a particular right way of acting, a particular understanding of morality, right and wrong, or the good. Communication scholars can identify various ethics deployed in communication, but identifying ethics does not endorse such ethics as correct or good.[44] Scholars need theoretical terms to talk about civic action emanating from ethics that are both praiseworthy and problematic. I believe ethical framework and ethical modality serve that function.

PAIRING AND UNPAIRING

While the multiple ethical frameworks and ethical modalities referenced in my earlier examples about sharing with others, neighborhood tool-sharing programs, and donating clothes to Goodwill may make their connection to one another seem random, institutions influence which ethical modalities we use to enact which ethical frameworks. This is a process I call *pairing*. Pairing occurs when ethical frameworks are matched to ethical modalities in institutionally preferred ways. For example, Republicans express an ethical framework of operating small government with few social programs. One ethical modality a Republican could employ to act according to this framework would be donating money to the local food bank, thus enabling local charities rather than government programs to help struggling individuals. The ethical modality is a specific ethic that allows one to meet one's obligations to a broader ethic. Through a process of pairing conducted by institutions and community groups, ethical modalities and ethical frameworks are linked and mutually reinforce each other. This pairing of an ethical framework with an ethical modality is based on one's participation in these institutions and communities. The ethical framework is an ethic which matches the institution or group's ideology, and the ethical modality is an institutionally enabled, recommended, and preferred way of enacting the institution or group's ethical framework.

Because individuals belong to overlapping communities and institutions, they also have overlapping ethical frameworks. Citizens choose which ethical framework and modality pairing to enact based on context, cues, and other factors. For example, a member of a Catholic church community might enact an ethical framework of a church member who helps the downtrodden paired with an ethical modality of a volunteer at the church's soup kitchen. The ethical framework of a church member helping the downtrodden could be potentially applied to wide-ranging situations, offering a number of potential ethical modalities, including supporting universal healthcare, donating money to United Way, or volunteering for a charity drive at work. Yet, membership in a political community may call up a different pairing of an ethical framework and modality and thus may require different action than supporting universal health care. Membership in a local Republican Party may supersede membership in a Catholic church community as the ethical framework most applicable to the ethical modality of universal healthcare. Ultimately, different communities operate with different pairings of ethical frameworks and ethical modalities. Citizens move easily between their multiple pairings, relying on context, cues, and other factors to decide which pairing to enact.

What I have sought to do with the examples above is demonstrate how ethical frameworks and ethical modalities work in our everyday lives. I sought to demonstrate how, even though we are not accustomed to distinguishing between ethical frameworks and ethical modalities, both are always at play. In a civic world more clearly dominated by institutions, there would be little need for understanding ethical frameworks and modalities as separate entities because they would almost always be clearly paired, occurring together. Some political worldview (Democrat, Republican, independent, nonprofit, etc.) would lead to political actions. But radical choice between institutions disrupts such automatic and guaranteed pairing between ethical modalities and ethical frameworks, making these terms essential to understanding new forms of citizenship in a fluid world.

Today worldviews that lead to political actions are no longer limited to political institutions. Harry Potter, Husker football, and the Justice League are all easier than ever to use as worldviews that could lead to political actions. It is this shift that has necessitated new terms: a fluid world has made it increasingly possible and easy to choose among civic institutions and noncivic institutions when engaging in civic actions. More than ever before, scholars must consider civic and noncivic ethical frameworks applied to civic modalities. Ethical framework and ethical modality help scholars do just that. In the next section, I offer a brief example of how these terms can be used in scholarship to investigate fan-based citizenship performances.

A Brief Example: "Not in Harry's Name"

Founded in 2005 and growing out of the Harry Potter fandom, the Harry Potter Alliance (HPA) is a nonprofit organization that uses parallels from the Harry Potter story to do social justice activism. The HPA has conducted campaigns on issues like same-sex marriage, independent media, literacy, economic justice, bullying, hurricane relief, mental health, climate change, healthy body images, and fair trade.[45] The HPA takes on a liberal political agenda focused on social justice, though it refrains from endorsing political candidates in elections. The HPA is one of the most established and well-developed fan activist organizations, making it a particularly clear illustration of how ethical framework and ethical modalities can be used as theoretical terms to investigate fan-based citizenship performances.

The Harry Potter Alliance's 2013 campaign Not in Harry's Name called for Warner Brothers to use fair-trade chocolate in their Harry Potter candy. In 2010, the HPA asked Free2Work to conduct a study of Warner Brothers' chocolate, and Warner Brothers received a grade of F in the human rights category. After the HPA asked Warner Brothers about its human rights guidelines, Warner Brothers asserted that it had its own report stating that it did not violate human rights with its chocolate. But Warner Brothers refused to make the report public. The HPA's Not in Harry's Name campaign worked to get Warner Brothers to make their report public and to show proof that they use ethical sourcing practices in the making of their Harry Potter chocolate. The Not in Harry's Name campaign consisted of a website, a petition, a *Huffington Post* article by HPA cofounder Andrew Slack, and a series of YouTube videos made by Harry Potter fan community members as well as well-known vloggers. Ultimately, the campaign succeeded. On December 22, 2014, Warner Brothers sent a letter to the Harry Potter Alliance announcing that all Harry Potter chocolate "will be 100-percent Utz or Fairtrade certified" by the end of 2015.[46]

In the "Not in Harry's Name" campaign, a Harry Potter ethical framework is paired with a fair-trade ethical modality. The HPA draws two main parallels between the Harry Potter books and fair trade. First, they draw a parallel between workers' rights in the real world and the rights of house-elves in the books. In one video, Dan Brown, a well-known vlogger, asks, "What would Dobby think?"[47] In the Harry Potter story, Dobby is a house-elf who was forced to work as a kind of indentured servant. When Hermione finds out about the condition of house-elves, she forms an activist group to earn house-elves basic workers' rights like breaks and holidays. Harry, frustrated with Dobby's particularly abusive (and evil) owner, tricks the owner into freeing Dobby from service. When Dan asks, "What would Dobby think?" he invites Harry Potter fans to be like Hermione and Harry and work toward guaranteeing that all people have fair workers' rights.

The HPA also draws a parallel between Harry's activism when Voldemort returns and fans' own fair-trade activism. Addressing Warner Brothers, the HPA says: "As reasonable people who love the Harry Potter movies and want to work with Warner Bros as partners, we want to believe them! *We really do.* But Harry Potter would not simply take the Ministry on their word, and neither will we."[48] The HPA points to a part of the Harry Potter books in which the governing body of the wizarding world in Great Britain, the Ministry of Magic, was lying about Lord Voldemort's return. Choosing to deny the signs of his return to power and the threat it posed, Minister of Magic Cornelius Fudge worked with the newspaper the *Daily Prophet* to restrict citizens' information and failed to take any substantive action. Harry had seen proof that Voldemort was returning to power and tried to wake the rest of the wizarding world up to Voldemort's return, despite the misinformation spewed by the Ministry and the *Daily Prophet.* The HPA calls fans to be vigilant citizens, just like Harry. This comparison asks fans to recognize that sometimes companies and governments like the Ministry and the *Daily Prophet* cover up mistakes. But good citizens, like Harry, seek proof, agitate other citizens, and don't give up.

The HPA combines this Harry Potter ethical framework (workers' rights and skeptical activism) with signing petitions and buying alternative products as ethical modalities. The HPA invites fans to sign a petition to get Warner Brothers to show the report and to buy an alternative—Harry Potter chocolate frogs made from fair-trade chocolate. Buying alternative candy and pledging one's support with a petition signature tells Warner Brothers where fans and citizens stand on the issue. While the ethical modality that matches the Harry Potter ethical framework in the books relies on wands, house-elves, and an evil wizard, in the Not in Harry's Name campaign the HPA unpairs the Harry Potter ethical framework from its corresponding Harry Potter modality. Instead the HPA pairs the noncivic Harry Potter ethical framework (workers rights' and skeptical activism) with a fair trade ethical modality (petitions and alternative products).

While the HPA's Not in Harry's Name campaign offers only a short illustration of the ways in which ethical framework and ethical modality can be used to understand fan-based citizenship performances, I hope it makes clear how ethical framework and ethical modality can enable us to investigate these fan-based citizenship performances. Indeed, without ethical framework and ethical modality, it would be difficult to articulate the dynamics of the HPA's Not in Harry's Name campaign. Of course, not all fan-based performances of citizenship look exactly like the HPA's—indeed, not all fan-based citizenship performances oppose media industries. Some fan-based citizenship performances occur in cooperation with media industry actors and some fan activism campaigns are organized and led by media companies. The usefulness of ethical framework and modalities as terms is the ability of these terms to allow researchers to analyze any of these types of fan-based citizenship performances.

Theoretical Assumptions

Analyzing fan-based citizenship like the HPA's requires new theoretical assumptions. Because a fluid society enables noncivic groups and communities, like fan communities, to guide civic action, rhetoricians and political communication scholars are confronted with identifying new theoretical assumptions for their analysis—assumptions that previously lay outside the realm of citizenship, civic engagement, or politics. Scholars of rhetoric, civic engagement, social movements, and fandom must now ask questions like, What is the meaning of a popular culture artifact? How can we know? How are ethical frameworks extracted from popular culture objects? What is the relationship between popular culture and political action? Can one cause the other? In this section, I draw on media studies, cultural studies, and fan studies research to identify the theoretical assumptions necessary to analyze discourses that unpair and re-pair varying ethical frameworks and ethical modalities. I argue that we need to approach fan-based citizenship performances by recognizing that popular culture media objects function as resources for citizens using three central theoretical assumptions.

First, scholars ought to recognize that popular culture texts have multiple meanings but that interpretive communities and rhetors influence which interpretation of the text fans choose to adopt.[49] For example, the Harry Potter story points toward tolerance. Harry defends his friend Hermione against prejudice and ridicule because she is not a pure-blood witch and thus, according to some, not a witch worthy of attending Hogwarts School of Witchcraft and Wizardry. But the story also points toward intolerance. The goblins that run the wizarding bank are problematically imbued with characteristics reminiscent of Jewish ethnic stereotypes. These contradictory meanings aren't just theoretical. Audience and reception studies research has found empirical support for varied interpretations of media texts. For example, media studies scholars Kyra Hunting and Rebecca Hains found differing interpretations of the feminist messages in the *My Little Pony: Friendship Is Magic* (2010–present) television show.[50] While the show presented feminist messages that emphasized the value of women and girl friendships and praised values that are traditionally gendered feminine, the adult male fans of the show, who call themselves bronies, resisted some of those interpretations. When defending *My Little Pony: Friendship Is Magic* as a high-quality television show, bronies utilized justifications that relied on gendered taste discourses and hierarchies. In doing so, bronies praised the feminist messages in their fan-object while also participating in the problematic hierarchies that devalue girls' media in the first place. Multiple and contradictory meanings exist within media objects themselves, discourse about media objects, and consumption of media objects.[51] Fans emphasize and deemphasize these meanings in varying ways.

At stake here is how an ethical framework is developed from a popular culture artifact. If popular culture artifacts have multiple and even contradictory meanings, how do fans agree on an ethical framework? Fan scholars Kristina Busse and Jonathan Gray argue that fan communities are not just imagined communities but also literal instantiations of Stanley Fish's interpretive communities.[52] Interpretations and strategies for interpretations get worked out and reinforced through community discourse, social norms, and creative acts like writing, art, and music.[53] Thus, fan communities develop a set of dominant interpretations for their text, which serve as the foundations for ethical frameworks. Fan community leaders or celebrities may also play a role in supporting particular interpretations of popular culture artifacts over others.[54] For example, in the case of the Harry Potter fandom, the dominant interpretation is that the Harry Potter story supports equality. This interpretation gains traction when Harry Potter fandom celebrities like Paul DeGeorge, who formed the first band to perform songs about Harry Potter, subscribe to that interpretation and argue that others should too. Such a position makes DeGeorge remarkably influential and makes his interpretations attractive to other fans. Of course, fan communities, like any community, are not monolithic. Even while the community develops dominant interpretations of the Harry Potter story, not all Harry Potter fans will subscribe to those dominant interpretations.

Fan studies and media studies scholarship often examines the ways in which the text or the fan community's interpretation of the text is emancipatory or not. This is a significant point, but it answers a question about the media text, not about the use of that media text for civic purposes. In this book, I focus my attention on the latter. In investigating fan-based citizenship performances, we ought to be concerned with how those popular media objects are deployed in communication toward civic ends. That is, scholars ought to note which textual interpretations are invoked when, how, by whom, and with what implications. Thus, I ask, How do rhetors/creators/communicators encourage fans to adopt a particular interpretation of a media object, and how is that interpretation deployed in civic contexts?

Second, even as we direct scholarly attention to civic uses of popular culture, we must also recognize that the political use of popular culture artifacts in civic actions is not automatic. Even with dominant interpretations of popular culture artifacts emerging from communities, there is still nothing guaranteeing that fans will apply a Harry Potter framework to a particular ethical modality. Popular culture does not directly lead to political activism or citizenship performances.[55] It provides the resources. Thus, it is important to recognize that popular culture's use as a political and rhetorical resource is not automatic or guaranteed. Citizens must *choose* Harry Potter from the many other choices available in a fluid world.

For example, just because one of Harry Potter's central themes is tolerance for others does not mean that every Harry Potter fan will see that as a reason to enact tolerance in their everyday lives. Simply being a fan of Harry Potter is not enough to guarantee that I, as a fan, will apply Harry Potter to the real world. Nor is it enough to guarantee that I, as a fan, will apply Harry Potter to a particular civic issue like public health care. Citizens must choose which ethical framework to pair with which ethical modality, sometimes choosing between contradictory ethical frameworks like the Catholic Church, the Republican Party, and the Harry Potter Alliance on issues like fair trade. We must view fans and media audiences as agents who use popular culture resources toward civic ends.

Rhetors can assist in this choosing by persuading fans that their ethical framework is applicable and desirable. This may mean persuading fans to not only choose Harry Potter as an ethical framework but also to choose a *particular* Harry Potter ethical framework. Recognizing that Harry Potter supports equality, we might utilize an ethical framework focused on same-sex marriage because Dumbledore, Harry's headmaster and mentor, was gay. Or we might utilize an ethical framework focused on eliminating racial microaggressions because Harry's best friend, Hermione, was Muggle-born and thus faced considerable bullying from other students. When applying an ethical framework to an ethical modality, rhetors must first invite fans to adopt a particular interpretation of a popular culture object, and then, second, invite fans to apply that interpretation to the real world in a particular way. This perspective allows us to emphasize the role that communication plays in citizenship performances utilizing popular culture. The question for communication scholars is, How do fans invite others to adopt a particular ethical framework and apply it to an ethical modality? What strategies do rhetors/communicators use?

Last, access to popular culture artifacts varies with one's social location and power. Rhetorical and critical/cultural communication scholars have long recognized that power and social location affect our ability to access particular civic identities or institutional membership.[56] This is certainly true of popular culture media objects and fan communities. Indeed, as with any resource, access to and belonging in fan communities varies with an individual's social location and power.[57] Being a fan often requires some minimal degree of leisure time and money to access popular culture artifacts and participate in fan communities. A Harry Potter fan could check the books out from the library, download free podcasts, and follow the Leaky Cauldron website online. But a Harry Potter fan could also spend more than three thousand dollars on a weekend trip to LeakyCon, a well-known Harry Potter fan convention. Additionally, access to some popular culture artifacts varies with fans' social status and identity. For example, female comic book fans often face barriers to access and community participation, including hostile environments in comic book shops and gatekeeping discourses like the "fake geek girl."[58] Ultimately, we must understand that popular culture functions as a resource that is not universally available and requires power to exercise. Communication scholars must ask, Who has access to popular culture media objects and communities? Who is permitted to use particular popular culture media objects? Whose access is policed? Who is permitted to use popular culture as an ethical framework, and who is not? Ultimately, who gets to be a fan? Who gets to be a citizen? These three theoretical assumptions—that texts have multiple meanings, that the political use of popular culture is not automatic, and that access to popular culture texts varies with social location and power—function to guide my analysis of fan-based citizenship. These assumptions provide the grounding from which the rest of this book's case studies proceed.

Fandom and Rhetoric: Methodological Underpinnings

As I've argued so far in this chapter, a fluid world means that fan communities function as locations in which public values, rhetorical action, and civic engagement emerge. In these cases, rhetoric and fan studies are deeply intertwined. Thus, analyzing persuasive and civic appeals in fan communities requires an integration of methods from both fan studies and rhetoric. Rhetorical studies offers methods that can be used to understand public communication and persuasive appeals in civic contexts, while fan studies offers methods that can be used to understand fan culture, community, and identities in media contexts. In this section, I explain how I combined the methodological approaches for rhetorical studies and fan studies into a single research project. Ultimately, I argue that understanding citizenship performances in a fluid world requires internet-based methods and fieldwork.

While the field of rhetoric emerged around the study of speeches or oratory, contemporary rhetorical scholars define rhetorical artifacts far beyond speeches like those given by presidents or social movement leaders.[59] These artifacts are defined in part by their function. That is, how does public communication function, and with what implications? While rhetorical artifacts can be speeches, paintings, videos, or infographics, in each case, the artifact functions rhetorically. Traditionally, rhetoricians have found rhetorical artifacts in library archives, like pamphlets from the 1800s, or in public transcripts, like presidential inauguration speeches. But because much of fan-based citizenship in a fluid world emerges from online communities, their rhetorical artifacts exist primarily on the internet. These artifacts include videos, blog posts, images, websites, press releases, and more.

Accessing and saving online rhetorical artifacts requires internet-specific approaches with unique challenges. One challenge is that the internet feels like it is "always accessible"—a network connection and a computer is all one needs. This is particularly true for professors with an income that allows us to pay for internet access at home while also having access to high-speed internet on university campuses. Furthermore, popular discourses frame the internet as permanent: the popular adage reminds users, young people especially, that whatever you post online will be impossible to ever fully delete.[60] While the internet may feel permanent and always accessible, it is anything but.[61] Websites actually change quite quickly, making the archiving of digital content on the internet particularly important for rhetoricians. While the Internet Archive's Wayback Machine can sometimes be helpful in providing snapshots of past websites, the frequency with which its web crawlers archive any particular website is hard to predict. Thus, rhetoricians like myself doing internet research must create their own archives of rhetorical texts and artifacts.

I archived the rhetorical artifacts for each of the case studies in this book by downloading the artifacts from the internet onto my laptop's hard drive. I downloaded PDFs of press releases and organization reports. I downloaded YouTube videos using KeepVid.com. I made PDFs of websites and took screenshots of websites as well. I organized these files in folders, preserving as much metadata (URLs, date posted, etc.) as possible.

These archiving methods work well for rhetorical analysis because they preserve most of the details of the artifact, enabling a close reading rather than any kind of big data analysis. I also backed up my digital archive on an external hard drive and in the cloud. By doing this, I was following the advice of digital archivists who recommend following the 3–2–1 rule, which includes three copies of digital files, including the original file, a second copy on a different device, and a third copy somewhere offsite.[62] If my office on campus is broken into and I lose both my laptop and my external hard drive, I still have the third off-site copy in the cloud. If my cloud service is hacked, I still have my copies on my external hard drive. When rhetoricians create their own digital archives, computer crashes don't just threaten the research manuscript; they threaten the texts and artifacts themselves. Archiving and backing up data become necessary components of internet-based research methods.

FIELDWORK: FANS AS RHETORICAL AUDIENCES AND FAN COMMUNITIES AS CONTEXT

Part of the work of rhetorical analysis involves contextualization—that is, analyzing how a rhetorical artifact emerges from a particular rhetorical situation for a particular audience. Context, for rhetoricians, means identifying particular power relationships between people and institutions, social and cultural symbols and meanings, and prominent values and discourses circulating at the time. For rhetoricians doing historical work, this often means drawing on secondary and primary sources to articulate a historical context that includes political and social factors. For rhetoricians studying contemporary rhetoric, this often means using news articles to describe the specific situation at hand. In the case of fan-based citizenship in a fluid world, all of this unfolds within very specific fan communities, with limited secondary research and even more limited news articles (fan communities are rarely covered in national or regional news outlets). Field methods can help fill that gap.

The rhetorical field is "the nexus where rhetoric is produced, where it is enacted, where it circulates, and consequently, where it is audienced."[63] Thus, field methods are the data-gathering practices that allow the critic to enter the field: interviews, participant observation, ethnography, autoethnography, focus groups, etc. These methods help rhetoricians attend to texts, contexts, and audiences that are "live" or "in situ."[64] Fieldwork has increasingly been theorized and taken up by rhetoricians studying a wide variety of texts ranging from vernacular communities to live protests to spaces and places.[65] Lisa Silvestri argues that rhetorical field methods are particularly important to understanding the context of online rhetorical artifacts: "The proliferation of global communication technologies and the consequent digital diffusion of discourse demands that rhetoricians pay careful attention to the contexts that generate online exchanges. Internet texts are both digitally diffuse *and* culturally specific, prompting critics to immerse themselves in the emergent habits and practices of online populations."[66]

Because the audiences and the context for fan-based citizenship are fans and fan communities, rhetorical fieldwork in this case means fieldwork in and with fan communities. Fan studies researchers have long used fieldwork and autoethnography to investigate fandom, attending to the particular methodological concerns fieldwork with fans involves, including trust and privacy.[67] The goal of fieldwork is not to "uncover some 'authentic'" fan identity or culture or to "define absolutely" that identity or culture.[68] Rather, as Stefan Lawrence explains in his study of English football fandom, the goal of fieldwork is to "explore the signs, symbols, motifs and socio-cultural codes" of fan identities and cultures and how fans' "myths of belonging, are inscribed, performed, contested and imagined."[69] For this book, fieldwork in online fan communities demanded gathering two types of data. First, it required watching, reading, and otherwise engaging the fan-object. For example, for the Star Wars fan community, I watched all the Star Wars films, read Star Wars novels, and watched the *Star Wars: Rebels* and *Star Wars: The Clone Wars* animated television shows. For the Nebraska Huskers, I attended home and away football games, tailgated before games, attended local watch parties, and read head coach Tom Osborne's books about life and football. Understanding fans and their rhetoric requires understanding the fan-object, which in turn helps build trust with fans. Second, fieldwork in fan communities demanded gathering data about each fan community's history, practices, and values. To do this, I used interviews, surveys, and participant observation. The fan communities examined in this book exist both online and offline, thus requiring a blend of face-to-face and internet-based approaches. For example, I participated in the local Ohio-Kentucky-Indiana LEGO users group (OKI-LUG) and attended BrickCon, an Adult Fans of LEGO (AFOL) convention in Seattle, Washington. On the other hand, I also conducted an online, open-ended survey of AFOLs, to understand the far-reaching online AFOL community. In total, I interviewed 33 fans, and another 189 fans participated in the open-ended online surveys, resulting in a total of 222 participants.

I spent approximately four years doing fieldwork for this book, spending one year with each fan community, which included tracking the news for each, participating in fan events, and interviewing and surveying fans in the community. I spent from April 2012 to February 2013 doing fieldwork with Nerdfighteria. From April 2013 to October 2014, I did fieldwork with the Nebraska Huskers. I did fieldwork from October 2015 to February 2017 doing fieldwork with AFOLs. And from August 2016 to May 2017 I did the same with the Star Wars fan community. The research in this book offers a snapshot, at one particular time, of each fan community discussed. For example, the VlogBrothers fan community in 2012 is different from the Vlog-Brothers fan community in 2017. Since 2012, John Green's books have been made into movies, more of their original fans have grown older, John and Hank have a podcast, and Hank founded PodCon. All of these developments change the shape and nature of the fan community. Thus, I hope readers remember that fan communities have continued to grow and change since the research for this book was done. No fan community is static.

While four years of fieldwork represent a significant amount of data collection, there are still limitations to my fieldwork. I relied heavily on snowball sampling. I would meet a few fans who would later introduce me to others and help me circulate calls for interview and survey participants. Further, my location in the United States, and even more particularly in the Midwest, leant a bias toward fans in these areas. My local face-to-face research took place in Midwest locations: Husker watch parties with the MadCity Huskers while I lived in Madison, Wisconsin, and meetings of the Ohio-Kentucky-Indiana LEGO User Group (OKI-LUG) while I lived in Cincinnati, Ohio. While online interviews and online surveys enabled me to hear from fans all over the world, it is likely that I heard from a higher percentage of fans in the US and in the Midwest because of my own networks and snowball sampling.

Last, there are inevitable limits to fieldwork of a fan community completed in only one year. Indeed, I felt this keenly as a researcher, noting how often one year felt like too short a time to learn about and see every interesting corner of each fan community. Of course, longer times spent in the field would have made a book like this nearly impossible to complete. Spending even just one year on each of the four case studies has meant that this book represents nearly four years' worth of fieldwork and data collection. While each chapter in this book may not present a comprehensive picture of each fan community, I routinely found that one year of fieldwork was long enough to enable me to contextualize the fan-based citizenship performances coming out of each particular fandom. Each chapter presents the reader with what they need to know about the fan community in order to fully contextualize and understand the fan-based citizenship performances discussed. Ultimately, rhetorical field methods enabled me to parse out the specific social meanings that emerged from fan communities and were invoked through fan-based civic appeals.

ACA-FAN: THE ROLE OF THE RESEARCHER

Doing fieldwork in fan communities of which the researcher may already be a member (to varying degrees) brings up questions of objectivity and insider status. The term "aca-fan" has emerged to describe this very tension. Famously used by Henry Jenkins as the title for his well-known blog *Confessions of an Aca-Fan*,[70] "aca-fan" describes the specific subject position of folks who are both academics and fans. The term "aca-fan" asserts that the two identities need not be separate—that one need not deny one's fannish investment in one's scholarly work.[71] Indeed, this has become an important move for fan studies scholars, many of whom publish research about fan communities of which they are members. For example, Katherine Larsen and Lynn Zubernis are fans of the television show *Supernatural* (2005–17) and have published books and articles about the show.[72] For many fan studies researchers, their own fan sensibilities and experiences are deeply integrated into their research.

Scholars can navigate this tension by attending to their own affect and methodological processes openly in their research. As Louisa Stein notes, aca-fandom is "a state of engagement with media and media studies, one that's necessarily unstable and messy and that requires that we engage in a constant self-reflexive conversation with our object of study."[73] Rhetoricians George McHendry, Michael Middleton, Danielle Endres, Samantha Senda-Cook, and Megan O'Byrne make a similar call for researchers to attend to the affective and political relationships that emerge from the field.[74] In this section, I examine the ways in which my own fan sensibilities appear throughout the research discussed in this book. My aim here is transparency and reflection—to be open about the ways my own fan investment emerged and to be reflective about the ways in which that aca-fan identity steered my research.

The case studies in this book range widely, and my positionality in each fandom varied as well. Harry Potter was my gateway into fandom. Harry Potter was the fan community in which I spent countless hours well before I started this project. Thus, my discussions of Harry Potter in this book reflect that aca-fan identity. On the other hand, I didn't begin research into Nerdfighteria as a fan, but my experience lies closer to being an aca-fan than anything else. Nerdfighteria was the kind of fandom that I would have joined and loved had I found it apart from my research. Thus, my research is tinged with a realization that these folks and their community were right up my alley. Thus, I approached the Harry Potter and nerdfighter case studies with fannish investments.

In working with the Harry Potter and nerdfighter case studies as a fan myself, I found myself combining the methodological models of both Jenkins's aca-fandom and Black's openness to a text. Like aca-fans, rhetorician Edwin Black famously rejected the need for all rhetorical criticism to be objective.[75] In fact, Black argues that part of the critical process demands subjectivity: Black asserts that to fully understand the text before forming a judgment, the critic must "see the object on its own terms" with the "utmost sympathy and compassionate understanding."[76] Black asserts that objectivity and its corresponding absence of investment and affect in humanities-grounded work like rhetorical criticism is a fool's errand.[77] While we cannot exorcise individuality, bias, and investment, we can make sure that our bias doesn't blind us to parts of the text. Black's solution is a call for openness—an openness to the text and all it has to offer. The critic, he says, cannot be "closed to discovery."[78] Ultimately, our goal ought not be objectivity but openness. I followed this methodological call in my work with the Harry Potter and Nerdfighter fan communities, recognizing my own investment in the texts as aca-fans would call me to do, while also cultivating an openness to the text that extended beyond my own investments, biases, and personal experiences.

While I may have occupied an aca-fan position in the Harry Potter and VlogBrothers case studies, in the Husker football fandom, the LEGO fandom, and the Star Wars fandom, I was much further from the aca-fan position.[79] Before beginning work with the Star Wars fandom, I was mostly ambivalent. I had seen the movies and enjoyed them but had never dived deeply into the stories. My experience with LEGO was very limited as well. While my brother grew up playing with LEGO, I did not. Thus, my LEGO building skills were well below those of a six-year-old, much less those of a thirty-five-year-old fan who regularly discusses the latest building techniques. My experiences with football in general and Husker football in particular were significantly limited, in part because I spent much of my life actively avoiding football. I had lived in Omaha, Nebraska, for four years as an undergraduate but missed catching the Husker bug (I defined myself as a nerd, college debater, and book lover, and football hadn't really been part of my family culture). Before that, I had attended only one college football game in my life and didn't necessarily enjoy it. I began the Husker research project knowing very little about football at all. While I was very nearly a football antifan, I had at least spent a summer working as an intern for TeamMates as an undergraduate student at Creighton University, giving me some sense of what that organization was all about.

Part of what's at risk when we aren't aca-fans is an obligation to fans and a sense of trust between fans and scholars. We feel some safety in knowing that if a researcher is a fan as well, they are less likely to mock fans and more likely to capture the beautiful complexity of fan communities. As a member of the fan community already, the scholar can engage in a kind of autoethnography, removing the threat of the top-down analytic approach that has often unfairly framed fans as irrational, crazed, and emotional.[80] But of course, having shared identities with our participants as fans does not necessarily resolve all of the ethical dilemmas involved. For example, in her book *Out in the Country: Youth, Media, and Queer Visibility in Rural America*, Mary Gray writes both as an aged-out queer youth activist and as an anthropologist. Gray explains that these positionalities come with "divided interests": she is no longer just an activist but also a "researcher trained to build a career of investigating questions of youth, identities, and queer experience."[81] Gray asserts, "I have a growing responsibility to a community of scholars working on similar topics and to research institutions funding these investigations."[82] Even with an aca-fan positionality that aligns us with our participants, we still may face ethical obligations that pull us in different directions and position us in different ways in our research. Ultimately, in each case, in each research project, scholars will have to navigate the tension between competing interests, obligations, and accounts.

Doing research with a fan community of which one isn't necessarily a member—without that aca-fan positionality—can offer its own challenges and benefits, in particular because fan studies research and methodologies so often assume aca-fan positionalities. My approach to doing fieldwork without an aca-fan positionality was a kind of openness to becoming a fan—an openness to experiencing that passion, investment, and affect. I binge-watched all the Star Wars movies. I cheered along with Husker fans. I oohed and aahed over the most impressive LEGO creations. I opened myself to an affective experience, and eventually I found myself to be a fan. Of course, I can't claim the same level of commitment, knowledge, or excitement that my fan-participants could, but in each case, I came to love the fan-object to some degree. Now, I may never love Husker football as much as I love Harry Potter, but I believe that an openness to fandom, affect, and investment, cultivated while doing fieldwork, was productive for my research.

I came to have some degree of fannish investment in all the fan-objects and communities I studied. So much so that when it came time to transition to a new case study after having spent one year doing fieldwork in a fan community, I often found it difficult to say goodbye and disengage from all the fan practices I had come to enjoy. Of course, it would have been impossible to maintain a full, active role in all five fan communities at once. Indeed, both fandom and fieldwork are time-consuming. But that didn't make disengaging from a fan-object and exiting a fan community any easier. Even with these well-justified reasons, there was always a kind of heartbreak in disengaging. After learning to love a fan-object, it was often hard to let go.

Although they are not always a part of academic books in the humanities, I believe discussions of methods are critical as rhetoric scholars increasingly make the turn to fieldwork and as fan studies gains a wider audience within the academy. In this section, I reflect on my own methodological choices specially designed for a fluid world and the ways in which my methods and my positionality steered my research and ultimately this book. Indeed, I spent a lot of time thinking about the methods that would help me answer my questions about fan-based citizenship. What kind of data would I need to study civic appeals in fan communities? How could I apply the lessons of rhetorical criticism to online texts? How could I go about learning the histories, practices, and values of online fan communities? In answering these questions, I ultimately combined methods from both rhetoric and fan studies, bringing together rhetorical field methods with discussions of aca-fandom, and bringing together rhetorical criticism with textual methods from fan studies, all embedded in online contexts. I hope that the methods I developed here will enable other scholars to study fan-based citizenship. Reflexivity and transparency not only make scholarship better but also improve the field, making it easier for future scholars to critique our work and build new methods suited to new questions. Ultimately, both rhetoric scholars and fan studies scholars must continue to think, read, and write about methods.

Explaining my methods offers a secondary advantage as well: it offers a useful outline for how I approach each case study in the rest of this book—an outline that I follow in each chapter. The first two sections of each chapter draw on evidence from my fieldwork to undergird my argument. The first section examines the social, cultural, and political context for the fan-based citizenship performances under analysis, and the second section articulates the ethical framework that emerged from the audience of fans. With this groundwork in place, I turn my attention in the third section to the communication at play. Here I use rhetorical analysis to unpack how appeals are constructed for audiences of fans, analyzing how the ethical framework from the second section was invoked through persuasive appeals. Put another way, the third section seeks to identify the rhetorical strategy that paired the fan ethical framework to a civic ethical modality. Ultimately, across each chapter I use sections on context, ethical frameworks, and pairing strategies to answer the question, How are fans invited to participate in fan-based citizenship performances?

Conclusion: Theoretical Frameworks, Asummptions, and Methods

In this chapter, I have argued that a fluid world serves as the context for fan-based citizenship performances. A fluid world enables individuals to easily choose from among institutions, enacting personalized politics as well as fluid organization patterns. This fluid world affects the theoretical terms, theoretical assumptions, and methods scholars need in order to investigate new modes of citizenship like fan-based citizenship. First, I advanced two new theoretical terms: ethical framework and ethical modality. I defined *ethical framework* as a worldview or a frame of understanding based on an ethic that is theoretical and all-encompassing. I defined an *ethical modality* as a way of meeting an ethical obligation to the ethical framework. Institutions typically *pair* preferred ethical modalities with ethical frameworks. But with a fluid world's increased choice among institutions, such pairings can become unpaired. In cases of fan-based citizenship performances, fans unpair typical civic ethical frameworks from modalities (like Democratic Party ideology from same-sex marriage) and re-pair non-civic ethical frameworks (like Harry Potter) with civic ethical modalities (like same-sex marriage). Second, I offered new theoretical assumptions suited to investigating new citizenship performances that draw on communities of belonging that lie outside of the traditionally political. I argued that we must assume that popular culture contains many meanings, political action based on popular culture is not automatic, and engagement with popular culture varies with social status and power. Ultimately, that means seeing popular culture as a resource for citizenship. Third, this chapter outlined the methods needed to investigate the pairing of civic ethical modalities with fan-based ethical frameworks. I blended methods from rhetoric and fan studies to archive rhetorical artifacts, conduct fieldwork with fan communities, and analyze rhetoric emerging from fan cultures. These methods allow me to examine the rhetorical process of pairing civic ethical modalities with fan-based ethical frameworks across case studies as different as Nebraska Husker football and LEGO, as we will see in chapters 2, 3, and 4.

CONNECTING

The Husker Football Coaches Challenge

On November 8, 2014, the *New York Times* set out to identify the "places in America where college football means the most."[1] Correlating data from Facebook about users who "liked" college football teams and where those users lived, the *New York Times* identified the places that had the highest concentration of football fans. The *New York Times* map revealed that Nebraska had the second-highest concentration of fans, behind only Alabama, demonstrating that in Nebraska, football fandom is a common and united experience.

The *New York Times* map shows clearly that college football matters in Nebraska. And with only one college team to root for, the state forms a united front as they cheer on their University of Nebraska Huskers. But for a state with a small base population from which to fund a championship-level football team and cold winters that can make it difficult to compete with the University of Florida or the University of Southern California in recruiting, the strength of Nebraska's football fandom is somewhat surprising. Yet, Nebraskans across the state are deeply dedicated to their football team. That might be because, as communication scholar Roger Aden argues, "football is not just football" for Nebraskans.[2] "It's also about a way of being in the world," Aden says.[3] For Husker fans, being a Husker is about being Nebraskan. Fan culture and civic community merge in important ways in Nebraska.

This is what undergirds former football head coach Tom Osborne's mentoring nonprofit, TeamMates. Founded in 1991 with just a handful of volunteers from the Husker football team working in the local Lincoln, Nebraska, public schools, Tom Osborne's mentoring nonprofit now works in schools across the state. TeamMates recruits local adults to mentor youth once each week at school, often meeting with them during lunch or after school. As the nonprofit expanded beyond the original Husker football team, it never lost its Husker focus. While Osborne may have started off recruiting Husker players, now he recruits Huskers fans. Across its publicity materials and events, TeamMates draws on Husker fandom.

In this chapter, I examine how an ethical framework can emerge from a sports fandom. In fandoms like Harry Potter, rhetors constructed ethical frameworks from the narrative of Harry Potter. Harry's position as good hero and Voldemort's position as evil villain provide clear-cut lessons about who is good and which actions are desirable. Football does not offer a fictional story from which to draw an ethical framework. Instead, fans use the drama of the football field to construct an ethical framework. By identifying what causes wins, what causes losses, what characteristics or actions are required to win, and which characteristics are most important to the Husker community, Huskers construct an ethical framework. They do this through social practices, traditions, discourse, and media—articulating what values define Huskers and thus what ethics define a Husker ethical framework. Following Aden's work on Husker fan values, I explore how the values of working hard, showing respect, and helping your neighbor are maintained and enacted throughout the fan community.[4]

TeamMates draws on these values in their volunteer recruitment campaigns. I focus here on TeamMates' 2013 Coaches Challenge recruitment campaign, its largest and most well-known recruitment campaign. The Coaches Challenge campaign pits states against each other in an effort to recruit new mentors, and the state that recruits the most mentors during the campaign wins the game. The Coaches Challenge campaign doesn't invite Nebraskans to engage in civic action (mentoring) because of their political party ideology or a religious value. Rather, the campaign invites citizens to engage in civic action because of their fan identity as Huskers: TeamMates pairs a Husker ethical framework with a civic ethical modality of volunteering to mentor. TeamMates achieves this through a rhetorical strategy of *connecting*—deploying parallels, links, or metaphors that connect the fan-object to the civic action. In this case, TeamMates draws on two central *connecting* metaphors: "joining the team" and "beating Kansas."

Through this pairing, TeamMates presents citizens with a powerful call to action and helps transfer importance and visibility from Husker football to mentoring needs across the state. At the core, this chapter is about civic actions like volunteerism that are grounded in fan identities and values.

I begin this chapter by examining research on the relationship between sports fans and citizenship before contextualizing the Husker football fandom and contextualizing TeamMates. With that contextualization in place, I turn my attention to the Husker ethical framework, comprised from the characteristics fans attribute to winning on the field. Next, I argue that TeamMates utilized a *connecting* strategy to pair the Husker ethical framework to a volunteering civic modality. I define the *connecting* rhetorical strategy anchored in theories of metaphor and allegory before turning to analysis of the Coaches Challenge campaign materials. Ultimately, I argue that TeamMates draws on a strategy of *connecting*, enacted through two parallels: join the team/volunteer and beat rivals/beat the mentoring gap.

Sport Fans and Citizenship

Noreen Wales Kruse, drawing on the work of Sir Alfred Lunn, asserts, "the influence and prestige of sport in the modern world is comparable only to that of the church in medieval Europe."[5] Indeed, today sports play a central role in the lives of almost 50 percent of Americans. According to a Pew Research Center study, nearly half of all Americans report that they follow sports "somewhat closely," paying attention to scores, replays, and news on TV, in the newspaper, and on the radio.[6] In 2008, sports fans spent more than $25 million directly on spectator sports.[7] Today, the US sports industry is estimated to be worth $414 billion,[8] while globally, the sports industry is worth somewhere between $480 and $620 billion.[9] In the US, football remains the most popular sport: 34 percent of Americans list football as their favorite sport, followed by basketball and baseball.[10] More than fifty million tickets were sold to college football games in 2013, while an additional thirty-four million tickets were sold to professional football games in 2013.[11]

By connecting Nebraska football to civic engagement, TeamMates' approach to mentoring is slightly unusual. Sports culture in the US is generally considered to have little connection to politics. Michael Butterworth explains, "The prevailing wisdom in the USA is that sport and politics should not mix."[12] Fans expect their favorite athletes to avoid politics off the field: athletes ought to play the sport and collect their check.[13] Sport is seen to reward those who have talent and work hard by offering a level playing field—something that is unavailable anywhere else in society. Sport is often understood by fans and athletes as separate from or above politics.[14] Events like the 2016–17 "Take a Knee" movement in the US demonstrate just how deep-seated this discourse of "apolitical sport" can be. After San Francisco 49ers quarterback Colin Kaepernick knelt during the national anthem to protest racist treatment of black folks in America, fans boycotted, owners worried about TV ratings, and ultimately Kaepernick lost his contract.[15] While football fans may have attempted to excise the political from football, they only succeeded in "deny[ing] that the terrain of sport is already politicized"—whether Kaepernick is on the field or not.[16] In other words, politics and sport are not as separate as many may want to think.

Indeed, for the millions of Americans who watch, follow, and discuss sports, sports aren't just a source of leisure and entertainment; sports are also a source of social identity that provides belonging and acts as a civic anchor. Eric Dunning argues that sport offers individuals "we feelings," particularly important in a contemporary world that moves at a "bewildering pace of change" and offers a range of isolated existences.[17] Examining the Husker football fan community, Roger Aden offers support for Dunning's theoretical arguments. Aden argues that the Husker fan identity provides what Giddens calls ontological security, providing Husker fans with an anchor, a unifying experience, and a "stable sense of self-identity."[18] Gary Crawford argues that sport may be replacing older, more traditional sources of belonging, like church.[19]

This chapter builds upon these notions, agreeing with scholars like Dunning, Aden, and Crawford that sport fandom can serve as a source of belonging with the same power and importance as traditional sources of belonging like churches, unions, and political parties. This chapter investigates the civic implications of moving our sources of belonging to fan identities and communities. In what ways can we draw upon sport as a collective identity, civic association, and source of belonging in order to do public engagement, and with what implications? In this chapter I take up this concern. I argue that Husker football can provide an important entry to public culture for Nebraska citizens when TeamMates unpairs the Husker ethical framework from the Husker football ethical modality in order to pair the Husker ethical framework with a mentoring ethical modality through a strategy of *connecting*.

Contextualizing Husker Football Fandom: A Championship Team in a Unified State

For Nebraska, a state of 1.8 million people, football at the University of Nebraska–Lincoln (UNL) is important. There are no professional sports teams in Nebraska, and the University of Nebraska–Lincoln is the only university in the state playing Division I football.[20] While other states often have major state school rivalries, like Michigan State and the University of Michigan or Iowa State and the University of Iowa, Nebraska has only one major football program. Both scholars and fans argue that this creates a kind of unity within the state of Nebraska: Nebraska football fans all cheer for the same team.[21]

Despite a small population base, Nebraska has built a remarkably successful football program. Nebraska has won a total of five national titles in 1970, 1971, 1994, 1995, and 1997.[22] Only two other schools have won five national titles since 1970.[23] Head football coach Bob Devaney won Nebraska's first national championships in 1970 and 1971 and stayed on as head coach just one more year before becoming Nebraska's athletic director and handing over the football program to Tom Osborne.[24] Osborne had been an assistant coach and offensive coordinator under Devaney since 1967. As head coach from 1973 to 1997, Osborne won national championships in 1994, 1995, and 1997.[25] After stepping down as head coach in 1997, Osborne was elected congressional representative for the Third District of Nebraska, ran for Nebraska state governor, and worked as the University of Nebraska–Lincoln athletic director.[26] Under Tom Osborne's leadership as athletic director, UNL moved from the Big 12 conference to the Big 10 conference in 2011, a football powerhouse second only to the Southeastern Conference (SEC).

With "one team in town" (and a successful team at that), Nebraska football takes on great importance in the state. Every home game has been sold out since 1962, giving Nebraska the national record for the longest sellout streak. Only the University of Michigan comes close, and their streak is thirteen years shorter. On game day, the Nebraska football stadium itself becomes the third-largest city in Nebraska.[27] That means that one in every twenty-five residents attends the game.[28] Thousands of others tailgate outside the stadium, watch the game on television, or listen to the game on the radio. On game day, local grocery stores and other businesses often play a radio or TV broadcast of the game.[29] For Nebraskans, Husker football is important and pervasive.

The History of TeamMates and the Coaches Challenge

While the Husker fandom is pervasive, the idea for TeamMates didn't originate in Husker football. Rather, the idea came from Nancy Osborne, Tom Osborne's wife, and a *60 Minutes* episode. In 1991, Nancy saw a *60 Minutes* segment about Eugene Lang, a wealthy businessman who visited his former Harlem elementary school and saw more poverty than ever before.[30] Lang wanted to provide an opportunity for higher education as a way to support and enable students' academic achievement. So, he offered to pay for the college education of a group of sixth-graders if they graduated from high school. Inspired by Eugene's story, Nancy turned to her husband and said, "Is there anything we can do?" The next day, Tom went to his players and asked for volunteers to mentor seventh- and-eighth-grade boys in Lincoln public schools. Twenty-two football players volunteered, and out of their twenty-two mentees, twenty-one graduated from high school on time and eighteen went on to postsecondary education.

Encouraged, Tom and Nancy expanded their efforts, eventually establishing TeamMates as the leading mentoring nonprofit in Nebraska, providing youth with adult mentors. Now, Suzanne Hince, Tom Osborne's daughter, leads the organization as the executive director. The organization uses a one-on-one school-based approach to mentoring in which each adult mentor meets with his/her youth mentee at school once each week, usually at lunch.[31] During a mentoring session, a mentor might help his/her mentee work on homework, play a board game, work on a hobby, or talk about school, family, and the future.[32] The TeamMates mentoring philosophy does not place mentors in the role of a parent. Rather, TeamMates asks that mentors be a "positive role model" for a young person and be a consistent person in his/her life. TeamMates explains on their website, "Mentors help identify the gifts and talents of young people that provide them a sense of hope and vision for their life."[33] Indeed, TeamMates has found that 82 percent of the young people who have a TeamMates mentor have improved attendance at school, 76 percent have fewer disciplinary referrals, and 49 percent experience academic improvement.[34] Currently, TeamMates provides mentors for more than eight thousand youth in Nebraska, Kansas, Iowa, and Wyoming[35] TeamMates hopes to increase that number to twelve thousand by 2020.[36]

TeamMates raises money and recruits mentors through a number of campaigns and events, including its annual gala called the Tail Gate, mentor meet-ups, trips to the Husker football spring game and a Creighton University basketball game in Omaha, Nebraska, as well as many other events organized by local TeamMates chapters.[37] But among all these events, the Coaches Challenge is the biggest and most visible event used to recruit new mentors. In 2008, Ellen Hod, executive director of Kansas Mentors, a statewide mentoring partnership, called Suzanne Hince, the executive director of TeamMates, and proposed a "fun challenge between the state of Kansas and state of Nebraska to recruit mentors."[38] Hince quickly agreed. Hince and Hod developed the idea of using a scoreboard on their websites to show how many mentors have been recruited.[39] During the challenge, Coach Schneider from Kansas State led the Kansas recruiting effort for Kansas Mentors, while Tom Osborne from the University of Nebraska–Lincoln led the recruiting effort for TeamMates. At the Kansas State–Nebraska football game, the winner of the mentor recruiting challenge was announced.[40] In 2011, Nebraska left the Big 12 and joined the Big 10, taking Kansas State off their 2011–12 season schedule.[41] So, TeamMates reached out to Iowa, and the contest expanded to three states. During the 2012 Coaches Challenge, the three states recruited more than seven thousand new mentors.[42] In 2013, Minnesota and Michigan joined as well. With five states involved in the campaign in 2013, nearly nine thousand new mentors were recruited, almost 1,300 of those in Nebraska.[43] The Coaches Challenge is poised to become a Big 10 conference event and has caught the interest of MENTOR, the national mentoring partnership in the US. In 2014, MENTOR helped organize and create media materials for the Coaches Challenge campaign.

The Husker Ethical Framework

In the Coaches Challenge, TeamMates draws on a well-developed Husker ethical framework. In this section, I articulate what that ethical framework looks like and how it emerges from the Husker football fandom. In *Huskerville: A Story of Nebraska Football, Fans, and the Power of Place*, Roger Aden offers the definitive study of Husker football fandom.[44] Through systematic phone surveys of Nebraska residents, paper surveys completed by Husker fans living outside of Nebraska, participant observation at a number of watch parties around the country, and personal stories submitted by Nebraska fans from around the world, Roger Aden argues that the Husker fan identity is defined through three central values: (1) working hard, (2) being neighborly, and (3) staying down-to-earth. Aden argues that these Husker fan values also come to signify a Nebraskan state and cultural identity. Here I argue that these Husker fan values can also function as the basis of an ethical framework that can be applied to civic actions. In this section, I examine how working hard, being neighborly, and staying down-to-earth emerge as a Husker ethical framework, supplementing Aden's findings with my own participant observations and interviews as well as data collected from books, YouTube videos, and music since the publication of Aden's book in 2007.

WORKING HARD

Huskers value hard work, toughness, and determination. Aden argues that this work ethic emerged from a tradition of prairie homesteaders in which it took hard work just to survive the winter. Nebraska football's early nickname, the Bugeaters, comes from this tradition.[45] During droughts, people would eat bugs to stay alive, refusing to give up on their dream of homesteading. In this sense, the name Bugeaters demonstrates determination—a willingness to make any sacrifice to achieve one's goal. Nebraska today is still largely agricultural, and farmers and blue-collar workers continue to espouse a commitment to hard work.[46]

Fans see their own work ethic reflected in the play of the team. Fans commonly assume that the football team will succeed when they work as hard as the farmers do in the fields.[47] Huskers attribute football wins to working hard and blame losses on not working hard enough. Aden summarizes the hard work value this way: "When hard-working, dedicated people are given a fair chance to prove themselves, they will succeed."[48] Tom Osborne, too, views this ethic as central to the football program and its success: "We've been able to attract players who not only have ability but who also have excellent character and work habits. I've often felt that our players have outworked opponents more than they have outshown them with talent."[49] To Nebraska fans, Nebraska football wins by working hard.

Husker fans are also proud of the football players' hard work off the field. Nebraska has the highest number of Academic All-Americans in the nation, beating out schools like Notre Dame, MIT, Penn State, and Stanford.[50] Indeed, within the first five minutes of the very first watch party I attended, one Husker fan turned to me and reminded me of this statistic. It seemed that if I was going to learn what it was like to be a Husker, this was one of the most important things I needed to know. The University of Nebraska proudly displays its Academic All-American record in the football stadium, framing it in big white text that is easily seen during the game from any seat. A former Husker track athlete explained the importance of Nebraska's Academic All-American record to me in an interview in Omaha: "Growing up, going to Nebraska [football] games I was always on the side of the stadium where Nebraska places how many Academic All-Americans they received. . . . So, growing up, going to football games, that was something I always thought I wanted to do was, was be one of those numbers on the side of the stadium. It's highlighted, you know, in a very big way."[51] Fans see both the Academic All-American statistic and Nebraska athlete graduation rates as proof that Huskers work hard. Nebraska graduates 80 percent of the athletes who complete their eligibility.[52] This is particularly important considering the increasing concern that college athletics exploits athletes by promising them an education but casts them aside when their eligibility is used—African American athletes in particular.[53] Indeed, one of the other prominent Division I universities in Nebraska, Creighton University, has struggled significantly with this problem. In the 1980s, Kevin Ross played basketball for Creighton but ultimately finished his four years of eligibility and coursework unable to read more than his name.[54] Despite a widespread pattern in which athletic departments and sports fans at other universities devalue academic achievement, Husker fans value the hard work athletes put into their academics and play on the field.

In addition to wins on the field and academic records, Husker fans point to the success of the football team's walk-on program as evidence that hard work matters. The Nebraska football walk-on program gives men who were passed over for a scholarship a chance to try out for the team and, through hard work, eventually earn playing time or scholarships. Most of the walk-on players are men from rural Nebraska towns. Indeed, for the 2014 season, only five out of eighteen walk-on players were from either Omaha or Lincoln (the two metropolitan areas in Nebraska), and only two walk-on players came from outside of Nebraska.[55] The remaining eleven players were from towns with populations ranging from 342 to 31,000. These rural towns are places where hard work is especially valued. Roger Aden quotes one Husker fan as saying: "Most of the players are Nebraska high school athletes: they walk onto the program and bring with them the hard work ethic that is characteristic of people who make their living farming. Having grown up in the state and realizing how many would like to be NU athletes, but so few actually make it, they understand just how much of a privilege it is to wear the Nebraska jersey."[56] Nebraskans see walk-on players as the epitome of hard work.

The importance of the Husker football walk-on program was demonstrated when former head football coach Bill Callahan (who took the reins after Osborne stepped down) significantly reduced the size of the walk-on program. Husker fans were disappointed and hurt.[57] His action cut at a program that rewarded Nebraskans who worked hard, a key value of Nebraskan fan culture. Eventually, Callahan was fired. After that, Bo Pelini, the coach hired to replace Callahan, restored the walk-on program. For Huskers, working hard plays a key role in their football fan and state identity.

At the same time, the walk-on program and the discourses surrounding it function as a way to admit more white men to the team (in an increasingly black sport) and function as a way to value those white players by praising their hard work. Sport sociologist Mary McDonald explains, "Contemporary racist binary thinking reduces black athletes to their physicality while white athletes are praised as hard working and intellectually superior."[58] This emerges in Nebraska's football program through the walk-on program. The predominantly white native Nebraskans who walk on are valued for their hard work, while scholarship players, who are often people of color, are valued for their talent. As the vast majority of walk-on players come from small towns in Nebraska, "small-town Nebraska" comes to function as code for a "white football player from a rural Nebraskan town." It is these walk-on players who are deeply valued in Husker fandom. As Randy York puts it in his column, the N-Sider, for Husker athletics: "Nebraska fans never tire of storybook scripts written by walk-ons."[59] Unfortunately, these storybook tales center around white players. As a result, discourses around the walk-on program serve to position white men as ideal Huskers and ideal citizens in Nebraska.

STAYING DOWN-TO-EARTH

The second tenet of the Husker ethical framework is remaining down-to-earth. In remaining down-to-earth, Huskers avoid bragging or flaunting. Husker fans believe it might be OK for the group to stand out for its successes, but individuals should not. Aden found that Husker fans describe being down-to-earth as being "straightforward, genuine, well-rounded, honest, trustworthy, fundamental, and plain."[60] Huskers see these qualities in fans from all parts of the state and all walks of life. Aden quotes one fan explaining the kinds of people attending football games at Memorial Stadium: "Ranchers from Kimball and Chappell. Stockbrokers from Papillion and Millard. Teachers from Columbus and Clatonia. Farmers from Gothenburg and Indianola. Realtors from Chadron and Alliance. . . . Families from three-generation season-ticket holders. Couples who plan all year for six weekends. Retirees who are taking the grandkids."[61] In an interview with me, Jim Pillen, TeamMates board member, University of Nebraska regent, and former Husker football player, emphasizes the wide reach of Husker fandom, saying, "So it [Husker football] is the thing that can draw East to West, North to South no matter what background anyone comes from."[62] Husker fans believe it doesn't take anything special to be a Husker.

Aden points out that being down-to-earth emphasizes process, not product. He quotes a Husker fan as saying, "If you do things the right way, you don't need to tell everybody about it; they will see it for themselves."[63] This sentiment is reinforced by a sign above the southwest corner of Memorial Stadium that says, "Not the victory but the action; Not the goal but the game; In the deed the glory."[64] This remains an important mantra for Husker fans. Rapper and University of Nebraska–Lincoln student Ramon Brown included it in his 2011 song "Big Red Anthem," played regularly in Memorial Stadium at football games.[65] For Huskers, how you win is more important than whether you win. The Husker Prayer, too, emphasizes process: "If we should win, let it be by the code, faith and honor held high." Suzanne Hince, executive director of TeamMates, explained in an interview with me that this is one of the defining features of Husker fans: "An appreciation of a game well played"—whether Huskers win or lose.[66] Tom Osborne's coaching philosophy specifically decentered a focus on winning at all costs. In his book, Osborne explains that for him, success isn't measured in terms of wins or losses. Rather, success is measured "in terms of how closely a team has come to realizing its potential."[67] He goes on: "As a result, I've almost never talked to a team about setting a goal of winning a particular football game but of getting into position to win the game. The important thing is to play the best we are able to play. If we do that, we should be able to live with the consequences."[68] Husker fans tend to reject a winning-at-all-costs philosophy in favor of staying down-to-earth and valuing the process.

However, Osborne's not-winning-at-all-costs philosophy has limits. One of the most well-known examples is Osborne's lenient treatment of Lawrence Phillips, a star running back for the Huskers. On September 10, 1995, Lawrence Phillips assaulted his ex-girlfriend, Kate McEwen, and dragged her down three flights of stairs. Despite Phillips's plea of "no contest," Tom Osborne allowed Phillips to stay on the team, only suspending him for six games. Osborne framed his decision as a way to give Phillips a second chance and thought that football and the structure of the college sport would help. Osborne said: "The easy thing would have been to dismiss him, probably permanently. But, basically, after examining all the factors involved . . . we simply didn't feel it was the right thing to do."[69] But in reality, Osborne's decision meant that Phillips would play in the 1995 national championship game, ultimately prioritizing winning football games over justice for domestic violence victims. Even with Osborne's leniency, Phillips continued to commit major crimes. Phillips played for four years in the NFL, but in 2008 he began serving a thirty-one-year prison sentence and eventually committed suicide in 2016.[70]

Osborne's decision was controversial even across the sports community, which routinely sees team owners prioritize winning over all else, including sexual assault and domestic violence, often letting players off the hook with minor suspensions. Mike Lopresti, writer for *USA Today*, says Osborne's decision "had the strong whiff of cutting corners on principle, to be ready for the big game."[71] This is a major contradiction for Osborne, who defined his career and the Husker identity by those principles. This contradiction strikes at the heart of what it means to be a Husker fan, and as such, it lingers in Husker collective memory. Dirk Chatelain, writer for Nebraska's *Omaha World Herald*, adds that "to this day, [it] taints Osborne's national reputation."[72] ESPN writer and Husker fan Mitch Sherman said that, even twenty years later, "Lawrence Phillips continues to cast [a] shadow over Nebraska."[73] While being down-to-earth and rejecting a winning-at-all-costs strategy may define what it means to be a Husker, Huskers do not enact that value consistently—important ruptures occur.

BEING NEIGHBORLY

The third central tenet of the Husker ethical framework is being neighborly. Aden explains that for Huskers, being a good neighbor means being helpful, loyal, respectful, and friendly. Aden quotes one Nebraska fan as saying: "I grew up in the Husker tradition. My family taught me to be helpful and give a hand when someone needed it."[74] I saw this neighborly tradition in action when I tailgated at a Nebraska home game in November 2013. The friends I was tailgating with brought their elaborate big-screen TV and satellite connection to allow us to watch the game while tailgating, a common practice for fans who don't have tickets to the game. But we were struggling to get the satellite connection to work. The people tailgating next to us offered to run a cable over from their satellite to our TV. As a result of neighbors helping neighbors, we were able to watch the game.

Huskers are neighborly not only when they are helpful but also when they are loyal. Husker fans pride themselves on being loyal to their team through national championships, coaching transitions, and moves to new conferences. Husker fans distinctly declare themselves as *not* fair-weather fans.[75] In his book, Tom Osborne writes, "There's also tremendous loyalty surrounding Nebraska, not just by the coaches, but by the fans as well."[76]

Indeed, this is demonstrated in part by how hard it can be to get tickets to Nebraska football games. Since 1962, all Nebraska football games have been sold out.[77] In total attendance at home and away games during the 2013 season, Nebraska ranked as the fifth-highest in the nation.[78] Simply put, the loyalty and devotion of Husker fans make getting tickets to football games in Nebraska difficult: tickets are in high demand.

Just as fans support their team, members of the football team support each other. During Tom Osborne's tenure as coach, he created a culture that put the team above individuals. Roger Aden quotes Osborne as saying: "We tried to cultivate an attitude of unselfishness, to realize that if the team won on the field, then we all won. We tried to move players from a self-centeredness to a team-oriented concept. We tried to teach that if you sacrificed personal goals for team goals, it would benefit everybody in the end."[79] In an interview with me, TeamMates board member and former blackshirt (starting defensive player) Jim Pillen explained that learning to put the team above himself was the most memorable part of his Husker experience: "I wanted to wear a blackshirt worse than anything else in my life. . . . [O]nce I got my blackshirt, I did everything to help the guy below me win it, and take it from me because that was best for the team. So that was a great thing to be part of. There's nothing better."[80] Pillen shows a loyalty to the team that extends to helping players take his starting position away from him.

In addition to being helpful and loyal neighbors, Husker fans value being respectful and friendly neighbors. Aden quotes one fan as saying, "Being a good neighbor . . . means welcoming, helping, and respecting those who visit your home—even if they are different from you."[81] This is evident in the Husker Prayer that the Husker football team chants together in a call-and-response fashion before every game. It states, "If we should lose, we'll stand by the road, and cheer as the winners go by." Husker football players and fans alike are expected to respect the other team and praise them for their skilled win. Fans enacted this value after the Nebraska vs. Northwestern University football game on November 5, 2011. Fans responded with the respect of true neighbors after Northwestern University beat Nebraska at home.[82] Morty Schapiro, the president of Northwestern University, described what he saw in an interview for a documentary on Husker fandom:

I've never in my life before seen better fans than Nebraska fans. When we came in, they were unbelievably gracious. And we were lucky enough to escape with a victory. I went into the locker room at the end of the game, and the Nebraska fans were lining the walkway as the team went through and they were clapping. They were clapping. Our coach looked at them. We all looked at them. And we just clapped back. I've never in my life seen anything like that. I'm a Nebraska fan forever. I've never seen nicer fans in my life.[83]

Husker fans work hard to maintain a tradition of respect, particularly when interacting with the opposing team. Indeed, Shapiro's surprise at seeing Nebraska fans clapping even after losing the game indicates the exceptional nature of Nebraska's tradition of respect and friendliness compared to other Division I football programs. I saw this exceptional tradition of respect firsthand when I attended Nebraska's away game at the University of Michigan. While Nebraska fans traditionally clap for the opposing team even after losing, Michigan fans didn't even wait until they lost to boo Nebraska, their opposing team. Michigan fans booed when the Huskers ran out onto the field at the beginning of the game and booed every time Nebraska made a good play. Michigan fans directed their frustration at the Nebraska players on the field as well as Nebraska fans in the stands. As people were entering the stadium, one Michigan fan on his way down the stairs to his own seat passed by me, marked as a Nebraska fan with my red-and-white Nebraska hat, scarf, and sweatshirt, and said, "Fuck you, Nebraska!"

Nebraska fans take great pride in how they treat opposing teams and fellow fans. In Ramon Brown's rap song titled "This Is Nebraska," he frames Nebraskans as "friendly people and we love the game" and says that "the team is playin hard but is respectful to all the rivals." He ends the song by saying, "Thank you for coming out and chillin at Memorial, and come again we really aren't that territorial. You got a good team, we just had a better one."[84] Nebraska's tradition of respect and friendliness continues to be upheld in homegrown, student-produced media.

Women off the field also play a key role in "being neighborly." This point is especially important because "working hard" and "staying down-to-earth" are largely defined through the players and coaches on the field,

Figure 2. A screenshot from the University of Nebraska Athletic Department's video *Nebraska Football 2014—Be Ready*.

excluding women from the picture nearly entirely, except for the "being neighborly" tenet. Football is a predominantly male sport, and few women play or coach the sport. This keeps women out of the most powerful positions in Husker fandom and defines the ideal Husker and Nebraskan as a man. For example, in 2014, the University of Nebraska Athletic Department posted a promotional video titled *Nebraska Football 2014—Be Ready* on their YouTube channel. In the video, the voice-over from Nebraska football players argues that Nebraska football is "built on 125 seasons of stories we were told growing up."[85] This line is paired with the image of a father and son watching the Husker football game together (fig. 2). While the "we" in these lines refers to "Huskers" broadly, the video footage paired with this voice-over specifies just what kind of Huskers they really mean: white men.[86]

Because men are valued as ideal Huskers, women have little visibility in the community. However, women manage to assert some, though severely limited, visibility by performing the third Husker value: "being neighborly." Through my fieldwork at watch parties in Madison, Wisconsin, it was clear that within the Husker football fan community in Madison, women played an important role. Out of four watch-party organizers who scheduled the viewing, set up decorations, organized raffles and scholarship funds, and kept track of attendance, two were women. At this local level, women had assumed leadership positions within their fan community. Both Husker watch parties and tailgating were anything but opportunities for men-only bonding. Rather, these were family affairs: kids, babies, and extended relatives all attended.

Anne Osborne and Danielle Sarver Coombs point out that female fans are often severely restricted in their performance of fandom by contradictory expectations for the multiple roles and identities they may hold.[87] For example, being a football fan may mean sitting and watching the entire game at home without missing a minute, while being a housewife may mean starting to cook dinner even if the game goes into overtime. For female Husker fans, roles like "hostess" and "family leader" that are already coded feminine can be performed as a way to meet the Husker obligation of "being neighborly." This gives women an important, though extremely limited, entrance to Husker fandom. By attending and organizing Husker watch parties and tailgating events, women Husker fans assert their Huskerness, their visibility, and their Husker belonging. By being neighborly, women are able to perform their roles as wives and hostesses while also performing a Husker identity. While men are routinely granted visibility and priority as Huskers within the Husker fan community, women contest this overvaluing of men by using watch parties and tailgating as ways to assert their own visibility in Husker football fandom. However, this performance of Huskerness is deeply tied to heteronormativity and offers limited roles for women.

While both men and women Husker fans routinely profess a commitment to being neighborly by being respectful, Husker football players and men fans struggle to enact that value when it comes to domestic violence, showing little respect for the humanity of their wives and girlfriends. One of the most famous cases is Christian Peter's 1991 rapes of Nebraska student Kathy Redmond.[88] After Redmond reported the rapes, Peter received little discipline from Osborne—Peter played in all his football games except one exhibition spring game. Today, Redmond advocates for domestic violence victims through her nonprofit, the National Coalition Against Violent Athletes, which works to educate athletes and support victims. But Nebraska's problem with domestic violence isn't confined to its players—it extends to Husker fans as well. A national study found that after major losses and major wins in football, domestic violence incidents tend to spike.[89] For some Huskers, football losses are enough to not only forget an ethic of neighborly care and respect but enough to trigger domestic abuse.

CREATING AND MANAGING POPULAR CULTURE:
DEFINING THE ETHICAL FRAMEWORK

While the tenets of the Husker ethical framework are shaped by Husker fans and Husker coaches both, the coaches have significantly more institutional power. This is especially important given that Husker coaches are mostly white men. Indeed, scholars across media, sports, and popular culture have long pointed out that the people who create, control, and profit from popular culture (producers, directors, writers, and actors) are often straight white men, resulting in disparate representation of people of color, women, and LGBTQ people.[90] Inclusion at the level of creation and management of popular culture is important in its own right: better representation on production crews, writing teams, and coaching staffs results in better circulation of the voices of marginalized people and often helps creates popular culture that is less racist, sexist, and homophobic. But for fan-based citizenship performances, inclusion at the level of creation and management of popular culture is also important because it determines who has the most power to shape ethical frameworks drawn from popular culture artifacts.

This is particularly striking in the case of Husker football. While the Husker football team has many players who are people of color and while many Husker fans across the state are women, the people who control and manage the Husker football team are almost exclusively white men. In particular, the Nebraska head football coach exercises both institutional and cultural power in defining what it means to be a Husker and a Nebraskan. As at many other Division I universities, the University of Nebraska–Lincoln's head football coaches and athletic directors are predominantly white men.[91] These are the people who have the most power to shape the Husker football fan-object and the Husker ethical framework.

Out of all football coaches and athletic directors, Tom Osborne possesses the most cultural and institutional power to shape Nebraska football and the Husker identity. As head coach from 1973 to 1997, as athletic director from 2007 to 2013, and as a winner of three national titles, Tom Osborne possesses great cultural and institutional power in Nebraska. Put frankly, Osborne's voice is heard and privileged throughout Husker fandom. According to TeamMates board member John Northrop: "The man is a legend in this state. Wherever he goes, he does not have a problem getting people to listen to him. And once they listen to him, the majority of those people will buy into what his story is."[92] Osborne has not only visibility but also a different burden of proof than other citizens in the state. Fans joke that Tom Osborne is considered a "god" in Nebraska. Northrop explains: "Tom Osborne is probably the greatest individual that I have met in my life. I've met several presidents, numerous senators—I've been to the White House, to the Oval Office. But, there is no greater experience than being able to sit down with Tom Osborne in his office and be in his presence."[93] Osborne has significantly more power than anyone else in Nebraska to define what it means to be a Husker and how those characteristics fit into a Husker ethical framework.

Indeed, Osborne has exercised such power. As head football coach, Osborne instituted character development during practice and emphasized academic achievement, both of which came to become defining tenets of the Husker ethical framework. Osborne also shaped who would be defined as a Husker. When he recruited players and hired coaches, Osborne literally chose who would embody the definition of "Husker."

While the institutional and cultural power of the head coaches and athletic directors at the University of Nebraska–Lincoln leaves little room for fans who are people of color or women to shape the ethical framework of the Huskers, such action is not impossible. In 2011, Ramon Brown, a UNL student and a person of color, wrested some of that power for himself and contributed to the shaping of the Husker ethical framework through his fan-made music. Brown was born in Monterrey, Mexico, but moved to Lincoln, Nebraska, as a child.[94] An accomplished rapper in Nebraska, Brown has recorded more than seven studio albums. In 2011, Jason Dunn, president of the UNL student movement known as Take Back Gameday, approached Brown about writing a song to be used at student pep rallies held before home football games.[95] Brown wrote and recorded "Big Red Anthem" and then filmed a music video for YouTube.[96] The YouTube video received more than 370,000 views, and the song is played in Memorial Stadium during all home football games. In 2012, Brown recorded a second rap song about Husker football called "This is Nebraska (Big Red Anthem 2)," donating profits from the iTunes sales of the song to TeamMates.[97]

Through his popular rap songs about Nebraska football, Brown plays a significant role in shaping the Husker ethical framework. He retells the history of Husker football by referring to important games like the 1996 game against the Florida Gators and rehearsing important records like three undefeated seasons in the Missouri River Valley Conference. Brown articulates what it means to be a Husker by referring to important values like loyalty when he describes Huskers as the "most loyal fans in the world of college football," and friendliness when he says, "Thank you for coming out and chillin' at Memorial and come again we really aren't that territorial."[98] In the music videos for both songs, Brown raps while surrounded by important Husker fandom members like cheerleaders, mascots, the marching band, and football players in uniform, which provides a kind of institutional authorization for his visibility, belonging, and voice. However, most of Brown's songs reinforce the Husker ethical framework created by Tom Osborne, Bob Devaney, and their staff. Brown's voice may be permitted because he reinforces the ethical framework already created by the institutional actors at the University of Nebraska–Lincoln. The case of Husker football demonstrates that inclusion at the level of creation and management of the popular culture affects who has power to shape ethical frameworks.

Defining the *Connecting* Rhetorical Strategy

Most frequently, the Husker ethical framework is used at football games: it governs action on the field, interaction with the other team, and participation in fan practices like chants or cheers. Sometimes the framework may be extended to everyday situations, in which fans find themselves giving someone a ride after their car breaks down. Most often, Husker values dictate action through fan practices or everyday actions that define relations between neighbors. So how does TeamMates make the Husker ethical framework applicable to civic action like volunteering for a charity? How does TeamMates pair a noncivic ethical framework with a civic ethical modality? I argue that TeamMates uses a strategy of *connecting* in their Coaches Challenge campaign.

Early on, research on fan activism identified "metaphor" as key to the relationship between fandom and politics. Henry Jenkins offered an early definition of fan activism that stated that it is "often framed through metaphors drawn from popular and participatory culture."[99] Indeed, some of the first cases to be studied as fan activism used metaphors heavily, including the Harry Potter Alliance, *Star Trek,* and *X-Files,* though research didn't identify the cases as using a similar rhetorical strategy.[100] These examples were all narrative-based, betraying fan studies' tendency to study television fans. As narrative structures, television is well suited to the metaphors used in the *connecting* strategy. Here, I expand on this notion, theorizing fully what it means to call fan activism metaphorical by articulating *connecting* as a rhetorical strategy.

Connecting, as a strategy, is characterized by parallels and links. As such, it is fundamentally metaphorical in nature. Metaphor has long been studied as an essential part of communication. Aristotle includes discussions of metaphor in both *Rhetoric* and *The Poetics,* explaining, "Midway between the unintelligible and the commonplace, it is metaphor which most produces knowledge."[101] Contemporary scholars George Lakoff and Mark Johnson argue that metaphor is central to the very way we think, act, and talk. In fact, metaphor is embedded in our conceptual system for everyday interaction and is central to the ways in which we make sense of our world and communicate that sense to others.[102] Like metaphors, *connecting* brings two things together and frames them as the same or similar. I. A. Richards refers to the two parts of a metaphor as the tenor and the vehicle.[103] When the tenor is used along with a vehicle in a metaphor, they interact. In doing so, the vehicle emphasizes some details of the tenor, while deemphasizing others, and ultimately conveys new meaning.[104] Rhetoricians have attended to this process, examining a wide range of metaphors, including metaphors of light and dark, metaphors of war, metaphors used to describe threats, etc.[105] In each case, the metaphor presents two dissimilar images as the same (the tenor and the vehicle), and the audience is forced to reconcile the two normally conflicting images. Ultimately, their meaning becomes interdependent.

While rhetoricians have focused on how metaphors have been used in public contexts toward political ends, literary scholars have focused on how metaphors have been used in narratives. Indeed, allegory has sometimes been called "extended (or continued) metaphor" within a narrative.[106] Allegory describes narratives in both prose and in poetry, "in which the agents and actions, and sometimes the setting as well, are contrived by the author to make coherent sense of the 'literal,' or primary, level of signification, and at the same time to communicate a second, correlated order of signification."[107] Literature scholar Angus Fletcher puts it this way, "In its simplest terms, allegory says one thing and means another."[108] Examples include Chaucer's *House of Fame*, Plato's "Allegory of the Cave," Dante's *Divine Comedy*, book 2 of John Milton's *Paradise Lost*, Jonathan Swift's *Gulliver's Travels*, and John Bunyan's *The Pilgrim's Progress*. These examples illustrate the wide range of topics allegory can take on, including religion, philosophy, and, most relevant to fan-based citizenship, politics.[109] Allegory, as a term, helps us understand the metaphors contained within a narrative text like Harry Potter. Indeed, Harry Potter has many allegorical elements, including a parallel between Voldemort's ideology and Nazi Germany's. At an event at Carnegie Hall, J. K. Rowling was asked: "Many of us older readers have noticed over the years similarities between the Death Eaters' tactics and the Nazis from the 30s and 40s. Did you use that historical era as a model for Voldemort's reign, and what were the lessons that you hope to impart to the next generation?"[110] In her response, Rowling says explicitly, "It was conscious." She goes on: "I think most of us, if you were asked to name a very evil regime, we would think Nazi Germany. There were parallels in the ideology. I wanted Harry to leave our world and find exactly the same problems in the wizarding world."[111] Allegory functions as a theoretical tool to help us understand extended metaphors lurking within narrative texts.

Connecting borrows from both traditions of metaphor and allegory. *Connecting* draws from the rhetorical functions of metaphor, using parallels and links to make arguments about public issues. While studies of metaphor have examined metaphors like disease and enemy, they have almost never considered metaphors originating in particular books, movies, or television shows—they are ill-equipped for the kind of extended metaphors popular culture offers. To fill that gap, *connecting* also draws from the literary tradition of allegory, offering complex extended metaphors, stacked upon and within one another. Yet, allegory alone is insufficient. While allegory takes better account of the relationship between a metaphor and a narrative-based entertainment text, it doesn't extend to the use of that metaphor in public communication. Rather, allegory, as a theoretical concept, helps scholars attend to the dynamics of literature—the narrative or the fan-object, not the use of that metaphor in public discussions about political issues or invitations to participate in civic activities. Blending the rhetorical functions of metaphor with the extended metaphors of allegory, the *connecting* strategy draws a series of parallels and makes one-to-one equivalencies between a fan-object and a public issue.

While *connecting* highlights similarities, it doesn't elide or evacuate differences. Isaac West argues that analogical reasoning, including the reasoning that emerges in the use of metaphors, invites consideration of both similarities and differences. Comparisons of differences through analogical reasoning can be "generative" and "inventive," functioning as "resources, not roadblocks, to building alliances between discrepant cases."[112] In the case of fan-based citizenship, this means that fans don't literally believe that Warner Brothers is the *Daily Prophet* like in the case of the Not in Harry's Name campaign in chapter 1. They see the similarities but also the differences: Warner Brothers does not produce a magical newspaper. Fans are not delusional—even though they draw parallels and make metaphors between their fan object and a public issue. Rather, those moments of both similarity and difference between fan-objects and public issues are productive and generative.[113]

Pairing through a Strategy of *Connecting*

I argue that TeamMates pairs Husker football with mentoring through *connecting*. In doing so, it draws two parallels: (1) inviting fans to join the team, and (2) asking fans to help Nebraska beat their opponents. By doing so, TeamMates gives Nebraskans a way to demonstrate their commitment to the Husker football team: mentoring.

JOIN THE TEAM

One of the ways in which TeamMates connects Husker football and mentoring is inviting Nebraska citizens to "join the team." In the official press releases for the 2013 Coaches Challenge campaign, the mentoring partnerships for each state are introduced as "The Teams."[114] Iowa, Kansas, Nebraska, Minnesota, and Michigan each has its own team, led by the head football coaches of each state. This is reinforced in the 2013 Coaches Challenge poster, shown in figure 3. The Coaches Challenge poster also appeared on the Coaches Challenge webpage, was printed as postcards and a poster, and was used as an image on the TeamMates Facebook page. On the right side of the poster, white outlines of each state and team identify the opponents, while the red, filled-in image of the state of Nebraska identifies the home team. While the teams are the states and the football coaches retain their role as leaders, the statewide nonprofit mentoring partnerships take on the role of the university—sponsoring, fielding, and supporting the players in each state. The mentoring partnerships train mentors, pay for mentors' background checks, match mentors with mentees, and otherwise organize the mentoring process.

With states as teams, coaches as leaders, and mentoring organizations as universities, state citizens become football players in the Coaches Challenge materials. Text in the center of the poster says, "JOIN THE TEAM. BE A MENTOR." Here, TeamMates explains that citizens can sign up for the team by becoming a mentor. The image shows a football coach wearing his red-and-white sweat suit, looking toward the field, and watching his team huddle up to get ready for the game. While the coach is a generic image, chosen because the national mentoring nonprofit MENTOR wanted to coordinate media materials and widen the appeal beyond Nebraska, it is easy for Husker fans to read either former head coach Tom Osborne or then current head coach Bo Pelini into the picture. Both coaches have a similar build to the one included on the poster, and the sweat suit fits what head coaches typically wear. The presence of the head coach on the poster (either as Tom Osborne or as Bo Pelini, the head coach in 2013) adds power to the call to join the team: this invitation to join TeamMates' Nebraska team becomes particularly attractive because the team is led by the head coach. Through the Coaches Challenge, TeamMates gives Nebraskans a way to join Osborne's or Pelini's huddle. By pairing the Husker ethical framework with a civic ethical modality of volunteering through a strategy of *connecting*, TeamMates transfers the prestige, importance, and value of joining the Husker football team to volunteering to mentor.

Figure 3. The poster TeamMates used for the 2013 Coaches Challenge.

But Tom Osborne and Bo Pelini aren't the only people inviting Nebraskans to join TeamMates' team: Former Husker Chad Kelsay, too, delivers this message in his radio public service announcement. Kelsay addresses Nebraskan citizens, saying: "I'm recruiting for the team. I'm looking for someone like you to be a TeamMates mentor. Someone who is willing to reach out to a child and make a difference in their life." Kelsay is a former

Husker blackshirt who played on both the 1995 and 1997 national championship teams and was later drafted into the NFL. Kelsay graduated with a degree in finance and took a job with an Omaha financial firm after his two-year professional football career. Having grown up in Auburn, Nebraska, Kelsay is in many ways "the story of traditional Nebraska football": a small-town kid who made the team, helped the team win national championships, graduated with a college degree, played in the NFL, and then came back to Nebraska to start his second career.[115]

Husker fans highly value being asked to join the team by Osborne, a renowned coach, and Kelsay, a representative of traditional Nebraska football. Indeed, the invitation to join the Husker team is a great honor. As one native Nebraskan and former Husker athlete explains in an interview: "For me being a Husker is very special. . . . Just putting on that red you know and competing. . . . It's something that you aspire to as a child [being from Nebraska]. Being such a big fan of football and Husker sports and when you actually get there, it's such a special life-changing moment I would say."[116] The TeamMates Coaches Challenge campaign gives Nebraskans a way to put on that red uniform and join the Husker team: by volunteering to mentor, you can join the team and join the huddle.

By *connecting* "citizens" to "players" and calling Nebraskan citizens to join the team, TeamMates invokes Husker ethical obligations. An invitation to join the team carries with it an obligation to be a helpful neighbor. As a Husker, when someone asks for help or asks you to join the team, you agree to help your neighbor. TeamMates board member and former blackshirt Jim Pillen explains: "Nebraskans are gracious, generous, helpful people and so if your chips are down, you know there's always going to be somebody to help you. We care about each other. We care about mankind. I mean there's—people go out of their way to help other people. That's why there's no other place like Nebraska. That's what makes it special."[117] To be a Husker and Nebraskan, one must provide help when asked. That makes turning down Osborne and Kelsay's offer to join the team difficult. To be a Husker is to join the team whenever asked. Kelsay himself is proof of the value of being neighborly and contributing to the team or community: Kelsay was willing to join the Nebraska football team, and his contributions helped win national championships. By connecting players and citizens, TeamMates presents a strong call for civic action. Volunteering to mentor becomes an attractive and prestigious choice when imbued with the same importance as joining the football team; it becomes a necessary choice when the neighborly ethical obligation is invoked.

TeamMates also paired Husker football with volunteering by drawing a parallel between beating football rivals and beating the mentor gap. First, beating rivals requires a winning score. In their official press releases, TeamMates explains, "Any new mentor application that is received between August 1 and November 30, 2013 will count toward the 'score' of the respective state."[118] Citizens can give their state a point by volunteering to mentor. The press release goes on, "By signing up to be a mentor, fans can not only show their state/team pride, but can help improve the life of a child!"[119] In this way, TeamMates *connects* volunteering to mentor with helping Nebraska beat their rivals.

TeamMates reinforces this connection by prominently displaying the number of recruited mentors in the form of a scoreboard posted on its website (fig. 4). By framing the number of mentors recruited as a "score," TeamMates imbues it with all the cultural significance and importance of a Husker football game score and its resulting statistics. Indeed, Husker football scores and statistics carry great significance within the Husker fan community. Fans discuss, reminisce, and replay important Husker football games, both the surprising wins and the devastating losses. In Ramon Brown's rap song, he says, "Remember '95 against the Florida Gators?" During the 1995–96 season, Brown was only three years old, but the 1996

Figure 4. A screenshot of the scoreboard from the front page of the TeamMates website.

Fiesta Bowl, in which Nebraska won the national championship by a 38-point margin, is remembered throughout the Husker fan community.[120] The University of Nebraska points to the importance of retelling these stories in a 2014 promotional video posted on YouTube. Voiced by current Nebraska football players, the video argues that "this is our time . . . built on 125 seasons of stories we were told when growing up."[121] The background for this voice-over is a set of clips of historical and well-remembered Nebraska plays.

For Husker fans, remembering Nebraska scores and statistics forms an important part of what it means to be a Husker. This importance is transferred to the number of mentors recruited through the use of a Coaches Challenge scoreboard that tracks a changing score across September, October, and November. While Husker scores are always printed prominently in Nebraska newspapers, the number of mentors recruited is not usually granted such visibility and importance. But the TeamMates Coaches Challenge campaign changes that. By making the number of mentors recruited a matter of winning or losing a game, the issue of youth mentoring gains social and cultural importance.

Second, the "beating rivals" parallel connects the mentoring gap to a difficult matchup on the field. Text at the top of the Coaches Challenge poster reads: "15 million youth need a mentor. Which state will rise to the occasion?" "Rising to the occasion" is a common phrase used in sports analysis to draw attention to a shift in position for a team.[122] This may come in the form of high rankings, moves to a new conference, or a challenging matchup, particularly in bowl games. These shifts in position point to the difference between potential or hype and actual game performance. Analysts and fans alike speculate whether their team can live up to expectations and rise to the occasion. The TeamMates poster frames fifteen million youth in need of a mentor as a particularly difficult matchup. Not every team could beat such a formidable opponent—not every team could rise to the occasion. Whether playing against a regional rival like Kansas State or closing the mentoring gap, Huskers will have to rise to the occasion in order to win. By drawing a parallel between the mentoring gap and challenging opponents, TeamMates makes the mentoring gap an important problem worth working to solve. Just as challenging long-standing rivals like Oklahoma were the opponents Huskers most wanted to beat during the 1980s and 1990s, the 2013 Coaches Challenge campaign argues, the mentoring gap ought to be the social problem Huskers most want to solve now. Rivals (like Oklahoma and Kansas State) and the mentoring gap are significant opponents that require Huskers to rise to the occasion.

In inviting Nebraskans to beat rivals/beat the mentoring gap, Team-mates invokes two important ethical obligations of the Husker ethical framework. First, it calls Huskers to work hard. Tom Osborne explains that the football team won the games it did because they worked hard, not because they had more talent than Oklahoma. The TeamMates Coaches Challenge campaign calls Huskers to work hard against a formidable opponent, the mentoring gap. Thus, TeamMates recognizes that mentoring is not easy and that it takes commitment and hard work. But because the Husker ethical framework calls on Nebraskans to work hard for their big wins, volunteering to mentor becomes a matter of being a good Husker.

Second, the TeamMates Coaches Challenge campaign invokes the Husker ethical obligation to be neighborly. Tom Osborne routinely asked his Husker football players to sacrifice individual goals for the good of the team. Osborne believed that putting the team above the individual was the only way to beat their toughest opponents. If fifteen million youth in need of mentoring is the equivalent of Oklahoma's football team, Huskers must put the team above the individual to have any chance of winning. In the Coaches Challenge, putting the team above the individual means giving up some of one's own time to mentor. Denny Walker, a TeamMates board member, explains that the most common concern holding people back from volunteering to mentor is "their fear of not being able to live up to one hour a week. They think that they're too busy already."[123] But Walker calls Nebraskans to make an individual sacrifice to benefit the team: "I try to talk to them about spending less time at Starbucks or you know [mentoring] can sometimes be over your lunch."[124] By giving up one hour a week, Huskers can make an individual sacrifice to help the team achieve its goal: beating Kansas. Solving big problems by coming together as a team is a key part of the Husker ethical framework. As Roger Aden explains, Nebraskan homesteaders used to depend on a tradition of neighborly help. When a neighbor got sick, the whole town came together to plant the neighbor's crops.[125] For Huskers, a town or a team must make individual sacrifices for the good of the whole. Just like Oklahoma, the mentoring gap is a formidable opponent that can be beaten not only through hard work, but also through neighborly teamwork.

Conclusion: Civic Community in Nebraska and New Resources for Citizenship

The 2013 Coaches Challenge, infused with Husker values, illustrates that football fandom can function as a key source of belonging and can be used to invite citizens to participate in civic engagement.[126] The TeamMates Coaches Challenge campaign invited Husker fans to engage in fan-based citizenship performances—to volunteer to mentor out of a commitment to the Husker football team. The Husker ethical framework emerges from social practices, traditions, discourses, and media in which fans, players, and coaches articulate why Huskers win, why Huskers lose, and what qualities define the greatest Huskers of all time. In this way, Husker fans constructed an ethical framework of working hard, being neighborly, and staying down-to-earth. The TeamMates Coaches Challenge used a strategy of *connecting* to pair a noncivic Husker ethical framework with a civic ethical modality—volunteering to mentor. In calling Nebraskans to "join the team," TeamMates draws connections between states and football teams as well as players and citizens. In doing so, Teammates invokes the Husker ethical obligation to be neighborly and provide help when asked. In calling Nebraskans to "beat rivals," TeamMates draws connections between the mentoring gap and a formidable opponent like Kansas State or Oklahoma as well as football scores and mentor recruitment. These connections help transfer importance from football scores to mentor recruitment and from major rivals to the mentoring gap. These connections also activate Husker obligations to work hard and to sacrifice individual goals in order to beat challenging opponents.

The rhetorical strategies that the 2013 TeamMates Coaches Challenge used point to the potential to unite Nebraska as a civic community at a time when political parties are deeply divided. Jim Pillen calls Husker football a "unifier" and a "connector."[127] Suzanne Hince explains that Husker football provides a "unity of purpose" for the people of Nebraska, giving them direction and coordinating actions and goals.[128] Huskers are knowledgeable, actively engaged, and care deeply about their team and their state. Perhaps the Husker football ethical framework offers an opportunity to bridge political divisions beyond mentoring, enacting a unified, connected, and engaged Nebraska civic community. At the same time, utilizing a Husker ethical framework carries particular limitations. Because football players and coaches are valued as ideal Huskers and Nebraskans, straight white men exert enormous power over how to define Husker and Nebraskan identity. Ultimately, TeamMates and its Coaches Challenge campaign demonstrate that sport fandom can provide a rich resource for productive citizenship performances.

EXPANDING

The Nerdfighters' YouTube Project for Awesome

In January 2007, brothers Hank and John Green decided to communicate with one another through only vlogs for one year, eliminating all textual communication including email, instant messages, and texts. They called their YouTube channel The VlogBrothers. By the end of 2007, John and Hank had accrued such a following that they decided to continue to make videos, though they lifted their personal ban on textual communication. As of 2018, their YouTube channel had more than three million subscribers, and their videos had accrued more than 725 million views.[1]

In their four-minute videos, Hank and John draw on their respective expertise to engage what they call "nerdy" topics. John is a young-adult novelist whose books have topped the *New York Times* best-seller list.[2] Movies based on his books *The Fault in Our Stars* and *Paper Towns* were released in 2014 and 2015. Hank is an entrepreneur and content creator who produced an Emmy-winning web series, founded and manages a record label for YouTube music artists, created a crowd-funded platform for educational YouTube videos, founded and runs the website EcoGeek, recorded and released four of his own music albums, created his own science-focused YouTube channel, and published a novel.[3] John's love of books and the humanities and Hank's love of environmentalism and science allow the pair to cover a wide range of topics including NASA and Kurt Vonnegut. As John and Hank talk about their nerdy passions, they also debate politics, discuss the news, and reflect on the world, all while offering lots of silliness along the way.[4]

Between their nerdy topics and their silly performance style, John and Hank have cultivated a following of dedicated fans who have come to call themselves "nerdfighters." Nerdfighters create communal space for their fan community mainly in the comments of VlogBrothers YouTube videos, in fans' own YouTube videos, on Tumblr, in the Nerdfighter Ning (a social network site), and on subreddits (discussion forums). Drawing fans from fandoms like Harry Potter, *Sherlock* (2010–present), and *Doctor Who* (1963–89 and 2005–present), nerdfighters are well versed in fan practices like fan art and fan music, and nerdfighters have applied these fan practices to the VlogBrothers videos. Fans leave comments on YouTube, post on forums, create tumblr blogs, post GIFs, make art, and attend VlogBrothers live performances and YouTube fan conventions. The VlogBrothers fandom, what fans have come to call "Nerdfighteria," has become a rich online fan community.[5]

In addition to rich fan practices like fan art, civic engagement has emerged as an important aspect of the Nerdfighteria fandom. Between 2011 and 2015, nerdfighters loaned more than $5.3 million to entrepreneurs through Kiva, a microfinancing organization.[6] VlogBrothers fans have also planted trees, adopted green environmental practices, and donated money to political campaigns. But the largest and most well-known VlogBrothers civic project is the Project for Awesome. During the annual December 17–18 event, YouTube users post YouTube videos in which they advocate for their favorite charities, an action that benefits charities and makes charity visible and important on YouTube. YouTube users can donate money directly to the charity of their choice or donate money to the Project for Awesome fund. At the end of the Project for Awesome, the money in the fund is divided among the top vote-getting charities.

Each year, the Project for Awesome has become larger and more successful. During the first year, users made more than three thousand Project for Awesome videos that had a total running time of more than forty hours and more than ten million views, resulting in $130,000 being donated that year.[7] Four years later in 2014, nerdfighters raised more than $1.25 million. By 2016 and 2017, they were consistently raising more than $2 million.[8] The nerdfighters' Project for Awesome is a compelling case of fan-based citizenship performances in terms of civic participation, demonstrated through the number of videos made and watched, the number of comments made, and the amount of money donated to charity. These fans are engaging public culture in a significant way.

Like the Harry Potter Alliance and TeamMates, the VlogBrothers anchor their civic appeal in a fan identity. But whereas the Harry Potter Alliance drew upon the fictional Harry Potter story and TeamMates drew upon success on the football field to create an ethical framework, the VlogBrothers have neither available to them. Instead, the VlogBrothers create a coherent content world out of fragmented videos that span fictional and nonfictional topics, genres, and traditions by using a framing narrative and intertextual references. This rhetorical work creates a content world that is rich, coherent, and compelling, and thus able to serve as a foundation for the nerdfighter ethical framework. By drawing on the VlogBrothers' videos and fan survey and interview responses, I find that the nerdfighter ethical framework is comprised of five values that all "increase awesome" in the world. I argue that the VlogBrothers and their fans often perform their nerdfighter ethical framework through fan-based ethical modalities—that is, fans increase awesome by singing along at Hank's concerts or doing collaborative art projects.

The VlogBrothers fandom offers an important contrasting case to the Huskers football fandom, offering differences in terms of history, demographic composition, and fan practices. Whereas the Huskers are rooted in a geographic location (Nebraska), the VlogBrothers are rooted in a digital platform (YouTube). The Husker fandom shares ties with larger sports cultures, shaping fan practices like tailgating. On the other hand, the VlogBrothers fandom shares ties with larger geek cultures, shaping fan practices like fan art. Further, the fandoms are quite different demographically. While the Husker football fandom is predominantly adult white men, the VlogBrothers fandom is predominantly white women in high school or college. By examining cases that have vastly different fan-objects, fan practices, and fan membership, we can begin to understand how fan-based citizenship performances occur across a wide variety of fandoms.

But the VlogBrothers fandom does not only serve to point out the wide variability of fan-based citizenship performances across fan communities. Rather, the case of the VlogBrothers' Project for Awesome demonstrates different strategies for pairing ethical frameworks with ethical modalities. So while TeamMates paired their ethical framework with civic modalities through a strategy of *connecting,* the VlogBrothers utilize a strategy of *expanding.* John and Hank expand the nerdfighter ethical framework to include not only fan-based ethical modalities, like posting in discussion forums, but also civic ethical modalities, like donating to charities. By *expanding* the nerdfighter ethical framework to also include a civic ethical modality, the VlogBrothers invite nerdfighters to participate in charity work because of their fan identifications. As a fan-based civic project, the Project for Awesome functions to open up new entries to public culture and create a new kind of civic space online, departing from problematic sexist norms and practices of internet culture. I begin by turning to the literature on vlogs before contextualizing the VlogBrothers fans. I then articulate their ethical framework and examine how it is paired with fan-based ethical modalities, and then how it is *expanded* to also include civic ethical modalities in the Project for Awesome.

Vlogs and Online Video

Vlogs are defined as video blogs, video versions of the diary-like entries that are posted online with the most recent entry at the top.[9] In this sense, they can be thought of broadly as a genre of online video.[10] In their survey of the most popular videos on YouTube in 2009, internet studies scholars Jean Burgess and Joshua Green found that almost 25 percent of the most popular content on YouTube were vlogs. Most of these vlogs feature one speaker, almost exclusively shown through extreme close-up shots and jump-cut transitions.[11] In a content analysis of a random set of vlogs in 2010, internet studies scholars Maggie Griffith and Zizi Papacharissi found that the majority of vloggers were men between twenty and fifty years old. Frequently, vlogs are personal and diary-like.[12] But that does not mean that vloggers discuss only personal issues. Indeed, many vloggers also discuss news, technology, and travel, perform comedy, share makeup tips, and talk back and forth with other vloggers.[13]

The VlogBrothers are one of the most well-known vlogging channels on YouTube. By 2015, they had more than 2.5 million regular subscribers. John and Hank started uploading videos in 2007, only two years after YouTube was launched and at a time when YouTube culture was still largely being built by a handful of creators for small audiences. Since then, John and Hank have played a key role in shaping the culture of online video and YouTube fandom by organizing YouTube-wide projects like the first fan convention for online video in 2011 and the Project for Awesome, which invites all YouTube creators and viewers to participate and enjoys sponsorship from YouTube itself. Fan studies research has considered the role of YouTube as a platform for fan communities to share content and maintain community. But fan studies has yet to consider fans *of* new media, not just fans who *use* new media for fan practices.[14] My study of the VlogBrothers in this chapter helps to fill that gap by exploring YouTube fandom and its use in civic contexts.[15]

Context: Who Are Nerdfighters?

While John and Hank did not necessarily set out to create videos appealing primarily to nerds, their own definitions of themselves as nerds shaped their topics and shaped their audience. Only one month after they began their project, John developed the term "nerdfighter." While in an arcade at the Savannah, Georgia, airport, John stumbles upon a videogame, and says to the camera: "This game seems to be called Nerd Fighters. That's my favorite kind of fighters!"[16] It is not discovered until much later that John simply misread the title of the game; the game is actually called "Aero Fighters."[17] John continues talking to the camera: "Here's my question about Nerd Fighters: Is Nerd Fighters a game about people who fight against nerds, or is it a game about nerds who fight against other people?"[18] John pauses, and then continues: "I've come to believe that Nerd Fighters is a game about nerds who fight; nerds who tackle the scourge of popular people."[19] While in subsequent videos John quickly leaves behind the oppositional definition of nerdfighters as people who fight against popular people, the other aspect of the definition of nerdfighters, as nerds who fight, comes up over and over again in John and Hank's videos and in fan discussions.

In these first videos in 2007, John and Hank further develop the contours of the "nerdfighter" identity by defining nerdfighter as an empowered fan. John says: "Because nerds like us are allowed to be unironically enthusiastic about stuff. We don't have to be like, 'oh yeah, that purse is ok,' or like, 'yeah, I like that band's early stuff.' Nerds are allowed to love stuff, like jump-up-and-down-in-the-chair-can't-control-yourself, love it. Hank, when people call people nerds mostly what they're saying is 'you like stuff' which is just not a good insult at all, like, 'you are too enthusiastic about the miracle of human consciousness.'"[20] According to John, being a nerd is being a dedicated fan and is certainly not an insult. This rhetorical move is not unprecedented. Indeed, it draws upon the "Star Trek nerd" and the "Dungeons and Dragons nerd" of popular culture imaginaries, though John also attempts to recoup this identity. He emphasizes enthusiasm as the defining aspect of the superfan nerd, notably rejecting lack of social skills or athletic ability. For John, the important part of the definition of "nerd" is really, really liking media, culture, and ideas. John's rhetorical move to define "nerd" as an enthusiastic fan also serves to unite multiple definitions of nerd. By defining "nerd" as a dedicated fan, John is able to include people who really, really love math as well as the people who really, really love Harry Potter. Consequently, broadening the definition of "nerd" also broadens the VlogBrothers audience.

By providing these broad contours of what it means to be a "nerd-fighter," John and Hank provide a shared identity for VlogBrothers fans.[21] However, these characteristics are defined in a way that avoids excluding potential fan community members. John and Hank explain that there is no minimum threshold a nerdfighter must meet—no criterion that limits access to the Nerdfighteria fandom. John says, "If you wanna be a nerdfighter, you ARE a nerdfighter!" All it takes to become a nerdfighter is opting in.

So, who are the fans that take up the nerdfighter identity in the Vlog-Brothers' fandom?[22] I used interviews and a set of open-ended online surveys to answer this question. By comparing my survey results with a 2014 survey organized by Hank Green that he termed the "nerdfighter census," we can gain an approximate understanding of who comprises the nerd-fighter community. First, most nerdfighters are women. Of the fifty-two nerdfighters who completed my survey, 76 percent of respondents were women, 18 percent were men, and 6 percent self-identified with other terms. Similarly, Hank found that 72 percent of respondents were women, 26 percent were men, and approximately 2 percent identified as questioning, genderqueer, gender fluid, androgynous, transgender, trans man, trans woman, transsexual, or intersex. Both my survey and Hank's found that the majority of nerdfighters are women. Second, most nerdfighters are also teenagers and young adults. While most of my respondents were between eighteen and twenty-four years old, it is likely that the additional parental consent required for minors to participate in my survey turned away nerdfighters under eighteen years old. Hank's census data shows that 18 percent of nerdfighters are thirteen to fifteen years old, 32 percent are sixteen to eighteen years old, 26 percent are nineteen to twenty-two years old, and 15 percent are twenty-three to thirty. About 94 percent of all nerdfighters fall within the thirteen to thirty-year-old range.

Third, nerdfighters are overwhelmingly white (92 percent of my respondents and 85 percent of Hank's respondents identified themselves as white), and they live mostly in the United States (82 percent of my respondents and 59 percent of Hank's respondents). However, even in my data, which skew heavily to the US, I still have participants from the UK, Australia, Croatia, and the Netherlands. Hank's census data show that after the US, the country with the highest percentage of nerdfighters is the UK with 13 percent, then Canada with 8 percent, then Australia with 5 percent, then Germany with 2 percent, and then Ireland, New Zealand, and Sweden each with about 1 percent. Approximately 10 percent of nerdfighters live outside of these eight countries. They live in countries like the Philippines, India, Mexico, Israel, Argentina, Poland, Lebanon, Morocco, Bahrain, Bangladesh, El Salvador, Cambodia, Iraq, Nigeria, Libya, Haiti, Afghanistan, and many more.

Last, the respondents to my survey demonstrated that nerdfighters may be quite diverse in their sexuality. Only 54 percent of my respondents identified as heterosexual, while other nerdfighters identified as bisexual, gay, asexual, demisexual, panromantic, or asexual. Unfortunately, Hank did not include a question on sexuality in his survey, and thus I can't compare my results with his. Overall, nerdfighters are largely young white American women who may be more diverse in terms of their sexuality.

EXCLUSION AND FAN COMMUNITY BOUNDARIES

Even though the Nerdfighteria fandom may be an inclusive community for women, it implicitly excludes people of color. When asked, "What is your least favorite aspect of Nerdfighteria?" some nerdfighters pointed toward these exclusions and expressed hope that Nerdfighteria could change. One nerdfighter said: "Diversification and boundaries! There's been a lot of talk about the lack of racial diversity in Nerdfighteria, as well as flat out racism on the part of individual nerdfighters. Looking at Hank's latest census breakdown, Nerdfighteria is very, very predominantly white. That needs to change. This community needs to be more open to diversity."[23] Other nerdfighters noted that Nerdfighteria had exclusions beyond racial exclusions. One nerdfighter said: "It's [Nerdfighteria] very cis/het/white oriented. I think the community could open up to people who don't fall under the previous labels."[24] Another nerdfighter noted, "I think Nerdfighteria could work on intersectionality,"[25] while another added, "I think we need to be very conscious about being inclusive, especially with regard to socioeconomic status, religion, and sexuality. The community can feel homogeneous, so we need to celebrate and welcome diversity."[26] Even for a community that routinely proclaims, "If you want to be a nerdfighter, you are a nerdfighter," exclusions still persist, particularly along racial lines.

At the very least, nerdfighters appear to be somewhat aware of the implicit exclusions in their community and to be somewhat troubled by those exclusions. However, nerdfighters seem to be unsure of how to tackle the problem beyond calls for more inclusion and more intersectional thinking. The nerdfighter fan community will have to take more substantial steps if it wants to see its community become more inclusive. John Green's December 30, 2014, video was one example of a good first step. In the video, John explicitly tackles the question of racism, but he does so with the purpose of demonstrating that structural racism exists. In this way, John targets his video for a predominantly white audience who need to be persuaded that racism exists at all. While John works against racism by discussing it in his video on the main VlogBrothers channel, he also reinforces a view of the nerdfighter community as white. A video like this would be unimportant or uninteresting to people of color who feel the effects of racism every day. Examples like this demonstrate how Nerdfighteria can be a community explicitly focused on inclusion while also maintaining implicit exclusions in their media and social practices. Importantly, such exclusions at the level of fan community belonging are not inherent to any fan community or fan mode of engagement with popular culture. Fan communities *can* become more inclusive, but achieving such inclusivity will take significant work.

The Nerdfighteria Fandom and the Nerdfighteria Content World

Fans in the nerdfighter fan community come together around the Vlog-Brothers vlogs. Like the Huskers, these vlogs don't have a narrative structure that can give way to an ethical framework in the same way Harry Potter does. Rather, vlogs stride the line between fiction and nonfiction: vloggers may make up silly and impossible songs while also telling stories about their daily lives. Additionally, vlogs are fragmented: the content world of vlogs is spread out across thousands of short videos that do not necessarily have a linear structure or single through-line. Yet, John and Hank have created a rich content world for their fans through a framing narrative and intertextual references.[27]

One way in which John and Hank have brought coherence to their content world is through their use of a framing narrative that provides a context through which smaller narratives can be told.[28] In their first video, posted on January 1, 2007, John and Hank present their framing narrative to their audience: the brothers have agreed to stay in touch with each other through vlogs, eliminating all textual communication. In this framing narrative, John and Hank invoke the genre of family communication: letters or phone calls among family members, talking about their days, reflecting on life, and making each other laugh. The framing narrative is invoked across almost all of their videos, primarily through direct address. John and Hank begin most of their videos by saying, "Good morning, Hank" or "Good morning, John." Additionally, John and Hank often justify their videos by framing them as communicative responses to the other brother. At the end of 2007, John and Hank revised their framing narrative by removing their personal ban on textual communication but left the rest of the narrative intact.

John and Hank use this narrative of brotherly conversation to frame the rest of their communication, which typically includes five types of videos: discussions, conversations, songs, games, and what they term "punishments." Punishment videos depict John or Hank performing some sort of physical or emotional challenge, like waxing one's chin. This punishment is warranted because of some violation of the "no textual communication" rule or because of a loss of an agreed-upon game or challenge. In other videos, John and Hank play games with nerdfighters. The most well-known game is Truth-or-Fail, in which John and Hank give the viewer a series of four to six statements and viewers are asked to decide whether or not the statement is true. In song videos, Hank plays songs he has written about a variety of topics, including Helen Hunt, Harry Potter, and monster-truck rallies. In discussions, Hank and John consider current events and world news, including the "political situation in Nepal."[29] In still other videos, John and Hank engage in a kind of conversation about their own daily lives, including news of adopting a puppy and buying a new house.

The five video types are not independent of the others. Indeed, throughout their videos, John and Hank engage in complex intertextual references to past videos. Media studies scholar Jonathan Gray defines intertextuality as the "interdependence of all textual meaning upon the structures of meaning proposed by other texts."[30] John and Hank make intertextual references when they refer to the topics or jokes from earlier videos. By referring to fictional songs during political discussions, they blend discussions of real-world situations with fictional stories and songs. This is seen most obviously in John and Hank's definition of a nerdfighter as both someone who is made of awesome instead of bones and organs, which is a fantastical joke, and as someone who takes real-world action, which is a realistic imperative. In 2009, Hank recorded a song that mixed both real actions and fictional jokes. Hank sings about a Nerdfighteria Island where "the roads are paved with peeps and there are no perverted creeps." He says, "There is no place I'd rather be / than living with my nerdy friends; making videos, happily / On Nerdfighteria Island."[31] Hank mixes real-world actions, like making YouTube videos, with elements of fantasy, like roads paved with peeps. Here, real-world actions are integrated into a fictional song about a utopian island. Ultimately, the Nerdfighteria content world is created through intertextual references that blend real concerns with imaginary circumstances.

For nerdfighters, John and Hank have created a rich content world, one that enables and encourages traditional fan practices. Nerdfighters create fan art, discuss the videos in YouTube comments and in the nerdfighter forums, and buy T-shirts and posters proclaiming their nerdfighter identity. Nerdfighters also attend the fan convention for YouTube, VidCon, attend Hank's concerts and John's readings, and organize their own local meet-ups with other nerdfighters. Enabled by a coherent content world, nerdfighters have created a rich fan community. The VlogBrothers demonstrate that rich fandoms can be built around vlogs as well as television shows and movies.

The Nerdfighter Ethical Framework: Increasing Awesome

Drawing upon the Nerdfighteria content world, John, Hank, and their fans have constructed a nerdfighter ethical framework centered on "being awesome." For nerdfighters, being awesome is one of the defining features of being a nerdfighter. In fact, "increasing awesome" has become a central slogan within the fan community: John and Hank sign off their videos with the slogan, "Don't forget to be awesome," and nerdfighters use the slogan as a sign-off in emails, videos, and face-to-face greetings. The slogan is often abbreviated to "DFTBA" and is printed on T-shirts, coffee mugs, and posters. While "being awesome" is certainly vague enough to be defined in many ways, the Nerdfighteria community has come to define awesome through five main tenets: enthusiasm, intellectual engagement, silliness, empathy, and community. These five values form the nerdfighter ethical framework.[32]

First, nerdfighters define being awesome as being enthusiastic or passionate. For fans, this means being excited about things you like. John Green defends enthusiasm in a video he made after the sixth Harry Potter movie premiered, when he says, "Nerds like us are allowed to be unironically enthusiastic about stuff."[33] One nerdfighter explains how important this aspect of the nerdfighter ethical framework is to her: "Everyone is so passionate in Nerdfighteria. You can talk to almost anyone and they are so open about their love of things, which I rarely find in others."[34] For nerdfighters, being awesome is being enthusiastic and showing your passion to others.

Second, nerdfighters define being awesome as being intellectually engaged. This includes curiosity, critical thinking, and an openness to learning new things. John and Hank's videos often take on topics like net neutrality and health-care costs and in the process invite nerdfighters to intellectually engage these concepts and topics.[35] One respondent explained that Nerdfighteria has an "appreciation for art/literature/knowing stuff."[36] But Nerdfighteria isn't focused on accumulating facts; they take on difficult questions. One respondent explains that Nerdfighteria has a "focus on complex thinking."[37] Another respondent added, "I like how I learn more by being a part of it [Nerdfighteria]."[38] Being intellectually engaged is a key tenet of the nerdfighter ethical framework.

Third, increasing awesome means being silly and having fun. One respondent said, "My favourite aspect [of Nerdfighteria] is the amount of fun and humor Nerdfighteria has even when dealing with serious issues or discussion."[39] Another respondent explains that Nerdfighteria does important things but also does "things that are fun and things that are silly and happy and wonderful."[40] Silliness and fun are valued alongside other more "serious" outcomes.

Fourth, nerdfighters define awesome as showing empathy for others. This includes everyday kindness as well as a kind of openness necessary to viewing other people "complexly."[41] When asked what their favorite aspect of Nerdfighteria is, respondents frequently mentioned the kindness of the group. One nerdfighter explains that Nerdfighteria is "all about helping each other and being friendly."[42] But being empathetic doesn't stop at being kind or nice. For nerdfighters, being empathetic means "seeing lives and perspectives other than mine."[43] Another nerdfighter adds, "I increase awesome when I help expand what it means to be human in ways that [are] freeing for other people."[44] One nerdfighter explains that "decreasing world suck" means "help[ing] groups of people who are marginalized."[45] For nerdfighters, empathy, kindness, and openness represent a key tenet of their nerdfighter ethical framework.

Last, for nerdfighters, being awesome is creating community and connecting to other people. Hank praises the nerdfighter community for this particular value in the nerdfighter ethical framework. He says that nerdfighters are "extremely good at being a tight-knit community that is very geographically disparate, which is not something that a lot of other communities are good at being."[46] Nerdfighters work hard to build and maintain that community, to support community members, and to take time to enjoy the feeling of connectedness and belonging. Indeed, for many nerdfighters, their sense of community is their favorite aspect of Nerdfighteria. One nerdfighter explains, "I've made my best friends here, I've met my significant other here, this is my place, my community, my home."[47] Another says that Nerdfighteria means "having a place where I feel like I belong. I feel a part of something that stands for the things I believe in. I am Nerdfighteria and Nerdfighteria is me. (But the cool thing is that everyone in Nerdfighteria can say this!!)."[48] Still another nerdfighter argues that Nerdfighteria is a particularly strong community, even though it is online: "The collaborative nature. All the modern philosophers talk about how technology is making us distant, but Nerdfighteria disproves that."[49] Recognizing that this kind of community is difficult to maintain, one nerdfighter cautions: "I think that it's easy to get wrapped up in the idea that Nerdfighteria is about Hank and/or John (and their respective media accomplishments), when it's really not. It's about the community of people with shared values who formed around Hank and John."[50] Nerdfighters appreciate, cultivate, and work hard to maintain a feeling of connectedness in their large online community. Nerdfighters increase awesome through their fan practices, being enthusiastic, being intellectually engaged, being silly, showing empathy, and creating community.

The Nerdfighter Fan Ethical Modalities

Most often, nerdfighters perform the nerdfighter ethical framework through their everyday fan practices grounded in the nerdfighter content world. They show membership in the fan community by increasing awesome in various ways. These everyday fan practices can be understood as noncivic ethical modalities, particular actions grounded in the fan community that allow nerdfighters to enact the nerdfighter ethical framework.

Nerdfighters enact the first tenet of the nerdfighter ethical framework, enthusiasm, through discussion of VlogBrothers videos in forums, creating and contributing to a wiki about nerdfighter videos, attending VidCon, buying, making, and wearing T-shirts with nerdfighter references and jokes, and attending concerts and readings hosted by John and Hank. By doing so, fans engage the VlogBrothers videos enthusiastically and passionately, sharing their love of videos with others.

Nerdfighters enact the second tenet of the nerdfighter ethical framework, intellectual engagement, through nerdfighter ethical modalities like watching SciShow and CrashCourse. Hank started SciShow, a YouTube channel focused on explaining scientific concepts and history, in 2011.[51] The ten-minute videos cover biology, chemistry, genetics, and the history of science, with topics like "The Science of Lying" and "What You Need to Know about Ebola."[52] CrashCourse is a series of videos that Hank and John have created together.[53] Hank and John are joined by other hosts, each taking up a different discipline and creating a series of videos before moving on to a new topic. They have made videos on world history, US history, literature, psychology, chemistry, ecology, and biology. CrashCourse has more than seven million subscribers and SciShow has another four million.[54] Both CrashCourse and SciShow's videos regularly garner between one hundred thousand and seven hundred thousand views. CrashCourse and Sci-

Show invite nerdfighters to be curious, ask questions, and explore interesting topics even when they aren't assigned for school. In addition to these educational videos, John periodically organizes a nerdfighter book club. Nerdfighters read the same book, John makes videos discussing the book, and then nerdfighters continue the discussion themselves in the forums. The nerdfighter book club has read books like Ray Bradbury's *Fahrenheit 451* and Katherine Boo's *Behind the Beautiful Forevers*.[55] In the nerdfighter book club, John leads nerdfighters through an exercise in intellectual engagement, asking nerdfighters to find meaning in the books they read and to articulate their arguments and opinions. John and Hank encourage nerdfighters to enact the intellectual engagement portion of the nerdfighter ethical framework by enacting ethical modalities like watching SciShow and CrashCourse and participating in the nerdfighter book club.

Nerdfighters enact the silliness tenet of the nerdfighter ethical framework through a variety of noncivic, fan-based ethical modalities, often adding an element of silliness to practices that enact other tenets like community building. One of the most significant ethical modalities used to meet the silliness tenet of the nerdfighter ethical framework is the "stuff on heads" practice. In 2007, Hank put a gift bag on his head to be silly, have fun, and be weird on purpose.[56] When John was in the hospital, Hank created a montage video of nerdfighters putting things on their heads to cheer John up.[57] Now, nerdfighters will put things on their heads while creating videos to add some silliness and fun to the world. Putting stuff on their heads is just one ethical modality nerdfighters use to enact the silliness tenet of the nerdfighter ethical framework. Nerdfighters also listen to Hank's silly songs like "People Who Love Giraffes" and make silly jokes about things like puppy-sized elephants. John and Hank give nerdfighters many possible ethical modalities that can be used to enact the silliness tenet of the nerdfighter ethical framework.

Nerdfighters enact the empathy tenet of the nerdfighter ethical framework through a number of ethical modalities anchored in a fandom context. In some cases, nerdfighters use random acts of kindness as an ethical modality to enact the empathy tenet of the nerdfighter ethical framework. Nerdfighters listed "making your friends brownies,"[58] "smiling at more strangers and holding more doors open,"[59] and "telling a stranger (or someone you know) that you like their outfit"[60] as examples of awesome. One nerdfighter adds: "One of my students had been spending all day studying in my building on campus. She broke for an afternoon snack and the vending machine ate her money. I gave her my last soda I had stashed in my desk drawer. Very small act, huge impact on her stress level decreasing."[61] For nerdfighters, empathy includes random acts of kindness as well as social justice. When asked to name examples of world suck, one nerdfighter offered, "The bias that led TIME not to include Laverne Cox on its list of 100 influential people is a manifestation of world-suck."[62] Nerdfighters discuss social justice issues, increase awareness, and organize projects to take action on social justice issues. Groups like FemmeFighteria provide a place for nerdfighters to discuss issues from feminist perspectives, pushing each other to view others in complex, humanizing ways. The empathy tenet of the nerdfighter ethical framework demands random acts of kindness and social justice work.

Nerdfighters enact the community tenet of the nerdfighter ethical framework through a fan group gathering ethical modality. This includes VidCon, which was launched in 2010 as a convention for fans of online video. It provides an opportunity for fans to gather IRL (in real life) to enjoy panels, keynotes, demonstrations, concerts, games, and more. In 2016, more than twenty-six thousand attendees met in Anaheim, California, for the convention, while many others watched livestreams online.[63] VidCon is the only annual gathering of nerdfighters face-to-face, offering a unique opportunity for community building. Additionally, nerdfighters often meet up with other local nerdfighters, organizing trips to bookstores, hanging out in a park, or watching *The Fault in Our Stars* (2014) or *Doctor Who* (1963–89 and 2005–present). For nerdfighters, the value of community is so important that they support other projects that locate power in grassroots communities, like the AFC Wimbledon Club.[64] Nerdfighters also create community by collaboratively working on projects. One nerdfighter explains, "In the nerdfighter community we increase awesome though supporting other members of our community and working together to create awesome things."[65] For example, in 2007, nerdfighters worked together to find ten red weather balloons released by DARPA (Defense Advanced Research Projects Agency) for a chance to win forty thousand dollars. Nerdfighters reported sightings, sorted through reports, and dispatched other nerdfighters to confirm sightings. Even though nerdfighters came together as a community to achieve a single goal, they ultimately lost to a group from MIT. But for nerdfighters, it's not about the red balloons. One nerdfighter points out: "It's about making connections—whether in a joke or through an academic investigation—that enrich my sense of joy and connectedness and understanding in and of the world."[66]

Expanding the Nerdfighter Ethical Framework

Most of the time, nerdfighters enact the nerdfighter ethical framework through fan practices, or noncivic, fan-based ethical modalities. But in order to encourage participation in the Project for Awesome, John and Hank rhetorically *expand* the nerdfighter ethical modality to include not only fan-based ethical modalities (like fan conventions, discussion boards, etc.) but to include civic ethical modalities as well.[67] In this way, the charity ethical framework is unpaired from its charity ethical modality; the nerdfighter ethical modality is then paired with the charity ethical modality. While Nerdfighteria has a number of civic projects that rely on *expanding* the nerdfighter ethical framework to civic ethical modalities, the Project for Awesome is the civic project that is the largest and, perhaps, most well-known. In this section, I argue that John and Hank frame the Project for Awesome as a way to enact a charity ethical modality that meets the requirements of the nerdfighter ethical framework, *expanding* the nerdfighter ethical framework to a charity ethical modality. John and Hank achieve this by framing the Project for Awesome as a way to meet all five tenets of the nerdfighter ethical framework: empathy/social justice, enthusiasm, intellectual engagement, community, and silliness.

PERFORMING AWESOME THROUGH CHARITABLE WORK

John and Hank frame the Project for Awesome as a way to make the world more "awesome" through empathy, achieved by helping people, enabling people to help themselves, and ending some of the institutional and systemic problems that are responsible for "world suck." While the nerdfighter ethical framework tenet of empathy for others regularly requires fans to create a kind and accepting community for one another online, when paired with a civic ethical modality, the empathy tenet of the nerdfighter ethical framework requires nerdfighters to take on world problems and social justice issues. John points out in a 2014 video that the Project for Awesome resulted in money "going to fight disease and poverty and illiteracy and injustice"[68] and in 2013 explains that the Project for Awesome money went to "organizations fighting, among other things, illiteracy and domestic violence and global poverty."[69] Nerdfighters "decrease suck" and "increase awesome" through a civic ethical modality of creating videos advocating for their favorite charity, promoting videos by commenting, liking, and sharing, and donating money to the Foundation to Decrease World Suck.

Across their videos discussing the Project for Awesome, John and Hank invite nerdfighters to "make a video about a charity that you feel passionately about,"[70] upload videos about your "favorite charities,"[71] and use the video to "show us charities you care about in action."[72] Nerdfighters are invited to bring the same enthusiasm they show for VlogBrothers videos and Doctor Who to the charities they are advocating for. Nerdfighters also listed enthusiasm and passion in their survey responses as characteristics that make a good Project for Awesome video. One nerdfighter explains that "being enthusiastic about the cause that you are talking about and finding ways to get the viewers excited about it as well" is important for Project for Awesome videos.[73]

Enthusiasm also guides nerdfighters' choices of which Project for Awesome videos to watch out of the thousands of choices available. Nerdfighters explained in the survey that they watched videos made about issues they deeply care about, like clean water, microfinancing, literacy, or charities they are passionate about, like the Harry Potter Alliance, the Red Cross, or the This Star Won't Go Out Foundation. Nerdfighters also use their enthusiasm for particular YouTubers as a way to choose which Project for Awesome videos to watch. Nerdfighters frequently responded that these were the two most prominent ways they filtered the Project for Awesome videos. As one nerdfighter put it: "I watch those from my favorite YouTubers and those about causes I'm passionate about."[74] While these aren't the only ways nerdfighters choose which videos to watch (they also follow the videos highlighted on the livestream and watch YouTube's recommended videos in the sidebar), this is one way in which nerdfighters pair the enthusiasm tenet of their nerdfighter ethical framework to charity, a civic ethical modality.

John invites nerdfighters to apply the same intellectual engagement and careful thinking that they use to discuss the exploration of Mars to the Project for Awesome. In a 2013 video, John explains how important the discussion and the voting components of the Project for Awesome are: "We raise money for the Foundation to Decrease World Suck, and then, as a community, we decide where to donate it, which helps us to think about our priorities and our values and the importance of being thoughtful philanthropists."[75] In a 2014 video, John says, "I'm so grateful to everyone who donated and also to everyone who took the time to vote so that we could be good stewards of this money."[76] Nerdfighters too recognize this as a central goal of the Project for Awesome. One nerdfighter explains that the Project for Awesome is about "raising a discussion about how the money we raise should be spent/distributed. i.e., what, as a community, should we prioritize?"[77] Nerdfighters see the Project for Awesome as identifying "mutually agreed-upon causes"[78] and "charities that are important to the community" through intellectual engagement.[79]

Nerdfighters frequently identified "informative" as an important characteristic that makes good Project for Awesome videos. Nerdfighters look for videos that identify the mission of the charity, include statistics about the problem, and evidence of the charity's effectiveness in solving the problem (often photographs). One nerdfighter said good Project for Awesome videos should be "thought provoking,"[80] and another said they must use "good information."[81] Indeed, nerdfighters view learning about and increasing the awareness of public issues and charities as an important goal that defines the Project for Awesome. One nerdfighter explained that the Project for Awesome "gets more people thinking and talking about ways to help others,"[82] and another adds, "It makes people aware of problems and sollutions [sic] (and attempts to solve them)."[83] Another nerdfighter adds that the Project for Awesome does good in the world when nerdfighters are "seriously considering world issues and credibility of organizations."[84] Still another nerdfighter asserts that this is what the Project for Awesome is all about: "The Project for Awesome i[s] about spreading the word about charities that people may have heard of or about charities that just need more help."[85] Increasing awareness of issues and charities is one way of "increasing awesome" in the world through an intellectual engagement with information about public issues and global problems.

John and Hank routinely frame the success of the Project for Awesome as reflective of the power of the Nerdfighteria fan community. The Project for Awesome works because everyone can "work together to make the world suck less."[86] John went so far as to say that "a lot of life is about doing things that don't suck with people who don't suck. That's why I enjoyed the Happy Dance Project and the Project for Awesome so much. All these people who don't suck came together to do something that doesn't suck."[87] Hank argues that the Project for Awesome is powerful because of nerdfighters' community ties: "The nerdfighters wield great power because they are many and they work together to do things like this [the Project for Awesome]."[88]

During 2007 and 2008, when the Project for Awesome was largely a subversive project that tried to hack YouTube's algorithms, the success of the project really did depend on the community exerting great power together. Without thousands of comments, likes, and views, the Project for Awesome videos would never have made it to the front pages of YouTube. Indeed, on December 17, 2007, a video about Mike Huckabee's presidential run was the only non–Project for Awesome video on YouTube's most discussed page. Now, however, YouTube works closely with John and Hank to support the project, providing them with resources like a studio for the livestream event or visibility on their homepage. Hank argues that the power of the nerdfighter community is exactly why YouTube was so interested in supporting the event: "Really the obvious and real reason why YouTube wants to be involved in this is because they see how powerful this community is and how much more powerful it could be if we all shared these resources and used the power of our community and of their platform and mixed it together for true epicness."[89]

John and Hank try to enable this community aspect of the Project for Awesome, even as the Project for Awesome is spread out over thousands of videos uploaded within a single day. To facilitate this, they have organized communal spaces in which nerdfighters can gather together to talk about the Project for Awesome videos while also commenting, liking, and sharing them. Through BlogTV and then through a livestream, John and Hank, along with other vloggers, highlight particular videos, discuss particular issues, and make jokes along the way. For nerdfighters, feeling like they are part of the nerdfighter community can be a central goal of participating in the Project for Awesome. One nerdfighter writes in the survey, "The project for awesome is about taking pride in that community and feeling that the community is a force for good."[90]

Even though the Project for Awesome is centered on a discussion of serious public issues, John and Hank still invite nerdfighters to make videos that are fun and silly, pairing the silliness tenet of the nerdfighter ethical framework to the charity ethical modality of the Project for Awesome. Across their videos, John and Hank consistently frame the Project for Awesome as fun. In a 2008 video, Hank encourages nerdfighters to join him at BlogTV live: "We'll be there talking about whatever it is we're doing, and helping people out with their Project for Awesome videos, and generally discussing the awesome. . . . I'm actually really, really, really, really, really, really, really excited about this because last year I just remember how much fun it was. I mean, it was like this huge YouTube–wide party in which people were all hanging out in the comments."[91]

For Hank, commenting on Project for Awesome videos is as fun as "hanging out."[92] In a 2009 video, John says: "So come and spend as much of your Thursday and Friday as possible with Hank and me. I promise it'll be fun. If you like nerdy fun, which . . . let's face it . . . you do." Hank adds, "And it's a very fun way to spend a Thursday!"[93] This was as true in 2008 and 2009 as it was in 2013. Hank explains, "The livestream is basically everybody hanging out."[94] Through their discussion of the Project for Awesome, Hank and John explicitly and routinely frame the Project for Awesome as "fun" and "a good time."

John and Hank's invitation to have fun and be silly is reflected in nerdfighters' expectations for Project for Awesome videos. Nerdfighters expect good Project for Awesome videos to be not only informative and accurate but also entertaining and funny. One respondent defined what a good Project for Awesome video looks like: "It is short, informative, funny, and makes a good point on why that charity in particular is worth donating to."[95] Another respondent made a similar point: "It should be entertaining but informative, short enough to keep someone's attention, and should address why the cause is important and/or why the organization is important."[96] For nerdfighters, the Project for Awesome videos shouldn't sound like UNICEF commercials or news broadcasts. Project for Awesome videos balance fun and entertaining silliness with well-researched information.

By extending the nerdfighter ethical framework to include a civic ethical modality of charity, John and Hank invite the nerdfighters to participate in fan-based civic engagement. For nerdfighters, participating in the Project for Awesome is a way to meet the ethical requirements of being a nerdfighter and a way enact that fan identity. For these fans, donating to charities and advocating for public issues isn't a matter of being a Democrat, meeting Christian ethical obligations, or responding to UNICEF's civic appeals. These YouTube fans discuss public issues and donate to charities because of a commitment to their fan-object, their own fan identity, and the values that emerge from their participation in fandom (enthusiasm, intellectual engagement, silliness empathy, and community). For nerdfighters, discussing public issues on YouTube is a matter of being a good nerdfighter.

IMPLICATIONS FOR WOMEN'S VOICES ONLINE

Fan-based citizenship performances like the nerdfighters' Project for Awesome and the TeamMates Coaches Challenge help to create new pathways for entries to public culture and new kinds of civic spaces for citizens. We can see this most radically in the nerdfighters' Project for Awesome in part because of the particularly problematic context in which it occurs. While internet culture disciplines women severely for discussing politics, the nerdfighters' Project for Awesome creates a powerful space for women's political voices online.

The 2014 Gamergate controversy demonstrates just how dangerous political participation online is for women. Created by male video game players, Gamergate movement members issued misogynistic threats to women and people of color who called for better representation and inclusion in video games and asserted their own visibility.[97] But these threats were not restricted to Gamergate or to video game players and video game culture. Across the internet in many online communities and digital cultures, women's voices are routinely met with severe criticism and violent threats.[98] In an article for the *Pacific Standard* magazine, journalist Amanda Hess details the consistent and persistent threats she receives online, like, "Happy to say we live in the same state. im [sic] looking you up, and when I find you, im going to rape you and remove your head."[99] Hess argues that these kinds of threats are not unique to her as a journalist who covers women and sexuality: "None of this makes me exceptional. It just makes me a woman with an Internet connection."[100] Hess points to other women who have discussed the death and rape threats they often receive, like Alyssa Royse, who blogs about sex and relationships; Kathy Sierra, who writes about technology; and Lindy West, who writes for *Jezebel*. Cultural studies scholar Emma Alice Jane argues that these threats and name-calling are in fact the "*lingua franca* in many sectors of the cybersphere."[101] Women's voices online, particularly in spaces like YouTube, are often met with derision and threats of violence.

It is this kind of context that makes the Project for Awesome somewhat remarkable in its ability to create a space for women's voices in public advocacy. The Project for Awesome has resulted in thousands of videos being made and thousands of dollars being raised, all accomplished by a community that is 70–75 percent female. By creating a fan culture that welcomes women and by extending that fan-based ethical framework to civic ethical modalities, John and Hank's Project for Awesome functions as a space in which women's political voices are permitted, protected, and even welcomed in ways they are not across the rest of the internet. As a fan-based citizenship performance, the Project for Awesome offers a new entry to public culture and functions as a different kind of civic space, inviting women to discuss politics in ways they cannot in other online parts of public culture. However, Nerdfighteria's whiteness means that the Project for Awesome may help white women voice themselves online, but not women of color, who face additional threats.

Conclusion: YouTube Fandom as a Source of Civic Identity & Community

The Project for Awesome has become a remarkable success in recent years. Most people might be skeptical at the prospect of trying to convince YouTube creators to make videos that discuss public issues and then trying to convince YouTube viewers to watch those videos. In a culture where videos about cats or injuries gain the most attention and visibility, it is somewhat remarkable that the Project for Awesome succeeds in organizing discussions of public issues on YouTube's platform. But, by utilizing fan-based civic appeals, the Project for Awesome succeeds where presidential candidates and nonprofit organizations on YouTube largely flop. By taking the nerdfighter ethical framework and extending it to encompass charitable giving, advocacy, and discussion, the Project for Awesome deploys all of the power of the fan community toward a civic action. For fans who deeply love the VlogBrothers, participating in the Project for Awesome by discussing and donating to charities is an easy choice. The Project for Awesome offers fans a way to enact the nerdfighter ethical framework while also enacting a civic ethical modality. The case of the nerdfighters' Project for Awesome has found immense success in terms of participation and money raised and has created a protected space for women's political voices in digital culture.

The Project for Awesome completely upturns some of our most fundamental assumptions about citizenship and civic organizations. It puts an online fan community at the center, rather than a geographic local community or a civic institution. Civic participation isn't predicated on any kind of perception of duty to a government or imagined nation-state but rather on being a member of a fan community—a nerdfighter can perform their nerdfighter fan identity by participating in the Project for Awesome.[102] Further, the rhetorical and communication processes through which civic performances are invited and emerge are a significant departure from traditional means. While traditional nonprofit organizations benefit from the Project for Awesome, the Project for Awesome envisions a new process of drumming up those donations and inviting participation far different from nonprofits' traditional mailing campaigns, news coverage, and gala events. Rather, the Project for Awesome occurs completely on YouTube, inviting deliberation as a way to garner participation and commitment, all centered around public values emerging from the Nerdfighter fan community. Indeed, the strategy of *expanding* points to the importance of fan communities in civic culture—membership and participation in a fan community first can enable those rich fan values to be expanded to other contexts beyond fan practices, including civic engagement. The Project for Awesome demonstrates that ethical frameworks for civic action can begin in noncivic places. Ultimately, the Project for Awesome envisions a new kind of citizenship anchored in fan identities and relationships, grounded in online communities, and enabled by digital platforms.

RETELLING
Greenpeace's #SavetheArctic #BlockShell LEGO Campaign

In 2014, LEGO became the biggest toy company in the world.[1] LEGO sells seven LEGO sets every second, and its brand is worth $4 billion.[2] One commentator called LEGO "nothing less than the Apple of toys."[3] LEGO has framed its remarkably successful interlocking bricks as educational, facilitating unlimited play, the growth of the childhood imagination, and robust creativity. But LEGO has also expanded well beyond the educational toy market to become a major media franchise in its own right. LEGO produces television shows like *Ninjago* (2011–present) and *Legends of Chima* (2013–present) and released the hit *The LEGO Movie* (2014), in addition to numerous best-selling video games.[4] LEGO has become one of those toys that seems ubiquitous in children's playrooms and their media worlds.

While LEGO bricks dominate the children's toy industry, some of LEGO's biggest fans aren't children at all but rather adults. These folks call themselves "adult fans of LEGO," or AFOLs, for short. And while most LEGO sets may be primarily designed for children, AFOLs believe LEGO bricks hold remarkable potential for complex builds and artful designs that go well beyond the capabilities of a child. For AFOLs, building with LEGO bricks as adults becomes a way to continue an activity they enjoyed deeply as children. Like all fans, AFOLs have a deep love for their fan-object. In the case of AFOLs, that love for their fan-object doesn't fade with age. AFOLs share their love of LEGO and interact with other LEGO fans through websites, discussion boards, image-sharing sites, and fan conventions. While some estimates of AFOL's share of LEGO purchases put the group at only 5 percent of LEGO's yearly sales (around $115 million), AFOLs play a key role in building the LEGO brand through public exhibitions while also building their own rich fan community through fan conventions, events, and websites.

In 2014, Greenpeace targeted AFOLs and parents who buy LEGO bricks for their children as audiences for an activist campaign against Shell Oil. Greenpeace's #SavetheArctic #BlockShell campaign aimed to convince LEGO to end its partnership with Shell, a partnership reportedly worth $116 million.[5] Since 1966, Shell's logo has appeared on gas stations and gas trucks across more than 16 million LEGO sets sold globally.[6] Greenpeace's campaign asserted that Shell's partnership with LEGO was bad for children and bad for the environment. Greenpeace explained, "But when LEGO's halo effect is being used to sell propaganda to children, especially by an unethical corporation who are busy destroying the natural world our children will inherit, we have to do something."[7] Shell's deal with LEGO, Greenpeace argues, has two types of consequences. First, it advertises to children, convincing them that Shell is a good company that poses little threat. Greenpeace sums up this claim by asserting, Shell is "polluting our children's imaginations."[8] Second, Shell's deal with LEGO helps Shell at a corporate level. LEGO gives Shell "respectability"—respectability that would enable Shell to court investors and public support for its drilling practices. Greenpeace hoped that by ending LEGO's partnership with Shell, Shell would be less able to continue drilling in key environmental areas like the Arctic.

Greenpeace's #SavetheArctic #BlockShell campaign consisted of a fifteen-page report, numerous tweets and blog posts, a petition with more than seven million signatures, a YouTube video, a street performance in Toronto, and numerous other media stunts and performances.[9] The most visible part of the campaign was the YouTube video. Produced by the London-based creative agency Don't Panic, the video garnered more than 8.3 million views and earned coverage from major news outlets like *CNN*, *Forbes*, the *Huffington Post*, the *Christian Science Monitor*, *Mashable*, and others.[10] Greenpeace called the LEGO video the "most viral in Greenpeace history."[11] In the end, Greenpeace's campaign succeeded: three months after Greenpeace released its video, LEGO announced that it would not renew its contract with Shell.

Greenpeace's campaign takes an approach different from TeamMates and different from the nerdfighters. Rather than *connecting* fan ethical frameworks to civic ethical modalities or *expanding* fan ethical frameworks to include civic ethical modalities, Greenpeace *retells* the story depicted in a seminal LEGO fan-object, *The LEGO Movie*. Greenpeace's video reimagines the LEGO content world as experiencing an extensive oil spill. By depicting a fictional LEGO world that is flooded with oil, Greenpeace shows viewers the threat Shell poses to their beloved fan-object, fan culture, and the ethical framework LEGO fans uphold. Greenpeace's video retells the story from *The LEGO Movie* in order to pair an AFOL fan ethical framework with a Greenpeace civic ethical modality of signing a petition and boycotting LEGO, all in support of the Arctic.

Greenpeace's #SavetheArctic #BlockShell campaign succeeded, though not because of AFOLs. In my fieldwork with AFOLs, they largely reported ignoring or disagreeing with the Greenpeace campaign. For many AFOLs, it came down to Greenpeace's targeting of LEGO. The Greenpeace #SavetheArctic #BlockShell campaign demonstrates how the love of the fan-object is necessary to undergird any pairing between a fan-based ethical framework and a civic ethical modality. While Greenpeace successfully paired an AFOL ethical framework with a Greenpeace civic modality, Greenpeace threatened LEGO, and AFOLs largely rejected the campaign. On the other hand, Greenpeace's criticisms of LEGO as being in bed with Shell likely played well with parents of children who play with LEGO. For parents without the total fan devotion of AFOLs, the decision to boycott a seemingly bad toy company because it supports Shell Oil may be a much easier one. Thus, Greenpeace's case is complex: Greenpeace successfully paired fan-based ethical frameworks with civic ethical modalities, which would have made the campaign a rhetorical success, but Greenpeace offended fans in the process. This would have made the campaign a rhetorical failure if not for an alternative audience of parents of kids who play with LEGO, who were able to make the campaign a success. Greenpeace's #SavetheArctic #BlockShell case is not a clear-cut case of a successful or failed fan-based citizenship campaign. Rather, it is a case filled with abundant caveats and complexities. The advantage of this is that the Greenpeace case teases out characteristics of fan-based civic appeals that wouldn't be visible in clear-cut cases. The Greenpeace #SavetheArctic #BlockShell campaign illustrates a necessary element for fan-based civic appeals, love of the fan-object, while also demonstrating how multiple audiences may respond and interact differently with fan-based civic appeals.

I begin this chapter by contextualizing LEGO and AFOL fan culture as based around building "my own creations" (MOCs) and sharing both images of those MOCs and the strategies used to build them. Next, I identify the major demographic characteristics of participants in the AFOL fan community, exploring the ways in which boundaries are constructed that exclude women and people of color. After explaining who AFOLs are and what their fan community and its practices are like, I outline the three tenets of the LEGO ethical framework: creativity, support, and public outreach. Then, I turn to the Greenpeace video, exploring how it *retells* the story from *The LEGO Movie*. By inserting Shell Oil into the LEGO content world and rewriting the ending of *The LEGO Movie*, Greenpeace invokes the AFOL ethical framework and pairs it with Greenpeace civic ethical modalities of signing petitions and boycotting LEGO. Last, I examine how this rhetorical strategy plays out differently across two central audiences: AFOLs and parents of kids who play with LEGO. To begin, I turn to the history of LEGO and AFOL fan culture.

Contextualizing LEGO and AFOL Fan Culture: MOCs and LUGs

In 1932, Ole Kirk Kristiansen founded LEGO in Billund, Denmark. Trained as a carpenter, Kristiansen initially used wood to build children's toys, including animals like the famous LEGO duck and, later, their stacking bricks.[12] Emphasizing Kristiansen's commitment to toys that enable high-quality play, Kristiansen named his business LEGO: a combination of the Danish words "leg" and "godt," which translate to "play well." In 1947, Kristiansen began experimenting with plastic injection molding, and by 1953 the company's best-selling toys were its plastic LEGO bricks.[13] Over the years, the LEGO Group continued to develop sets that would extend the building capacity of its LEGO bricks. The LEGO Group developed DUPLO blocks for young children, the TECHNIC series with electronic movement, and the BIONICLE series with socket types of connections for action-figure building.

In 1998, LEGO launched its first licensed sets for major media franchises. These sets were released in conjunction with *Star Wars I: The Phantom Menace*. Since then, LEGO has designed sets for *The Simpsons, Lord of the Rings, Ghostbusters, Disney Princesses*, DC and Marvel superheroes, and Harry Potter. In 2003, LEGO began making films and TV shows about their LEGO products starting with *BIONICLE* (2003) and *LEGO: The Adventures of Clutch Powers* (2010).[14] In 2014, the LEGO Group released their first feature-length film in theaters: *The LEGO Movie* (2014).[15] The film was a wild success. It grossed more than $460 million worldwide, giving it a higher domestic gross than *Cars* (2006), *Toy Story 2* (1999), and *Harry Potter and the Prisoner of Azkaban* (2004).[16] LEGO followed up its 2014 hit *The LEGO Movie* with two more movies in 2017: *The LEGO Batman Movie*, an offshoot of *The LEGO Movie* based on its Batman minifigure character, and *The LEGO Ninjago Movie* based on its Ninjago television series and LEGO line. LEGO and Warner Brothers plan to release two more films in *The LEGO Movie* series in 2018 and 2019.[17]

While LEGO may be the biggest toy company in the world, it's not just for kids. In fact, LEGO has found a significant following of adults who call themselves AFOLs. The long history of LEGO means that generations have grown up with the toy. Children who played with the sets in the 1970s are now forty-five to fifty-five years old. Even millennials who played with the sets as children in the 1990s are now approaching their thirties. Most AFOLs played with LEGO as children but stopped building as teenagers or young adults—this is what many AFOLs call their "dark age," which ends after AFOLs rediscover LEGO as adults. AFOLs return to LEGO for a host of reasons. Frequently, AFOLs describe returning to LEGO when they have children of their own. Other times, AFOLs return to LEGO to buy and build the sets they never could afford as kids. For other AFOLs, it's just a rediscovery of something they had previously loved. Few AFOLs pick up LEGO as adults without having played with it as children. In *The Cult of LEGO*, Bryce McGlone explains adults' attraction to LEGO this way: "Adults tend not to 'play,' so toys like action figures fall away. LEGO allows adults to create while still providing that childlike outlet."[18]

For many AFOLs, their love of LEGO is anchored in nostalgia. Lincoln Geraghty asserts, "Memories of having Lego as a child, and what that represented on a personal level, merge with the corporate history of the toy to become a nostalgic framework for conversation and new productions, new creations, new images and new fans."[19] Geraghty goes so far as to claim that "memory and nostalgia are also inherent qualities of the Lego experience."[20] The quality of the plastic brick and the consistency of its building system over the years has meant that adults can pull out the tubs of bricks they played with as children and continue to use them with today's sets. John Baichtal and Joe Meno, authors of *The Cult of LEGO*, point out that "a LEGO set becomes an heirloom: A tub of bricks can be passed down from child to child and even from generation to generation."[21] For many AFOLs, LEGO has powerful, enduring qualities.

As adult fans, AFOLs build MOCs ("my own creations"). That is, they build things out of LEGO without depending on the instructions for individual sets created by the LEGO Group. MOCs are often organized into popular categories like city, trains, castle, great ball contraptions, and minilanders.[22] Most AFOLs adhere to a few basic rules for MOCs: First, don't use the off-brand Mega Bloks—use only LEGO-brand bricks. AFOLs view Mega Bloks as inferior in quality to LEGO and have a fierce brand loyalty and love for LEGO. Second, don't use superglue to hold your bricks together—the structure should be able to hold together using only the clutch power of the bricks (superglue would be viewed as cheating).

AFOLs share their MOCs in a number of ways. AFOLs share their MOCs digitally on social media platforms like Flickr and Facebook, in magazines like *BrickJournal* and *Bricks*, on popular websites like the Brothers Brick, and on discussion forums like EuroBricks. AFOL fan conventions give AFOLs an opportunity to show off their MOCs and look at other fans' new MOCs in person. AFOLs also use conventions to talk with other fans about building techniques and brainstorm new ideas. Between BrickFair, Brick Universe, and others, there are more than a dozen AFOL fan conventions each year in the US alone.

But AFOL fan conventions typically occur once a year—and even for the most active AFOL, attending more than two or three fan conventions a year can be time-consuming and expensive. Between fan conventions, many AFOLs spend time building and sharing their MOCs with other AFOLs locally through LEGO user groups known as LUGs. In 2012, there were seventy-six LUGs in North America and 160 LUGs around the world.[23] LUGs may build together, participate in fan conventions, organize public exhibitions, and put on community events.[24] LUGs function as one of the central organizing mechanisms in the AFOL community by functioning as a public face of the AFOL fandom in local communities.

LUGs and fan conventions give AFOLs a chance to share their MOCs with fellow fans. But AFOLs work hard to reach the broader public as well, sharing their MOCs with community members, especially children. AFOLs do this by organizing local public exhibitions, which are often put on by LUGs. In 2012, there were approximately three hundred of these events in North America alone.[25] For example, the Cincinnati-based LUG, OKI LUG, organizes their own Kentucky Brick Expo and a Christmas-themed Brick-Mas event, in addition to participating in the local Cincinnati Comic Con. At these public exhibitions, AFOLs put their MOCs on display along with activities aimed at engaging kids with LEGO, including LEGO scavenger hunts and DUPLO building areas. For AFOLs, public exhibitions are an important way to share the joy of LEGO with the public.

Who Are AFOLs?

While LEGO fans are quick to point out that anyone can build wonderful things with LEGO, fan researchers like Jennifer Garlen point out that the LEGO fan community is made up almost entirely of men who are middle-aged and white.[26] My own fieldwork, interviews, and open-ended online survey revealed similar demographics. These demographics indicate the primary ways in which boundaries are set up in the AFOL community, sometimes constructed through the LEGO Group's own branding and marketing and sometimes constructed through AFOL fan practices.

First, the AFOL fan community appears to be mostly men. Of the participants who completed my survey, only 14 percent identified themselves as women, and only 2 percent identified themselves as transgender. Within the past thirty years, the LEGO Group has made a conscious choice to frame their bricks as "toys for boys" in an effort to capture the coveted four- to twelve-year-old boy demographic.[27] This is clear in LEGO's marketing materials (which feature almost exclusively boys or boys and fathers), in the themes for its sets (which, particularly since 2004, have been hypermasculinized), and in the very presence of the characters included in the sets (most minifigures are men or are gender neutral—women are nearly absent from the main LEGO line).[28] Indeed, LEGO has courted that four- to twelve-year-old boy demographic with fervor and has done so quite successfully. A recommitment to marketing exclusively to boys in the 2000s helped bring the company back after near collapse in 2004.[29]

In 2012, LEGO launched its biggest product line made exclusively for girls: LEGO Friends. But consumers and activists criticized the LEGO Group's move for its pink colors, stereotypically feminine themes, minifigures that were incompatible with the main line of LEGO products, and the gender-based marketing that invited girls to play with the LEGO Friends sets and excluded them from the main LEGO line. In creating separate lines of LEGO sets for girls, LEGO attempted to gain girl consumers without threatening its coveted four- to twelve-year-old boy demographic in the main LEGO line. This is a signal that the LEGO Group sees girls as a less valuable secondary market, capable of threatening their primary market of boys four to twelve years old. LEGO puts boys at the core of the company, valuing them as the ideal consumer.[30]

The gendered boundaries around LEGO as a children's toy have significant implications for the gendered boundaries around AFOL fandom. For many AFOLs, their love of LEGO begins as children. Indeed, LEGO's marketing toward boys means that later on in life most adult LEGO fans are men. This is demonstrated clearly with the popular AFOL phrase "1×5" meaning "a hot girl."[31] As an AFOL explains in *A LEGO Brickumentary* (2014), the 1×5 brick doesn't exist, and neither do hot girls at LEGO conventions—just men (or women who don't satisfy the male gaze). The AFOL fan community is largely a male-oriented space.

Second, most AFOLs are middle-aged, though some are young adults. The average age of my survey participants was thirty-nine years old. AFOLs work against the LEGO Group's marketing of LEGO as toys for children. Here, AFOLs explicitly frame LEGO bricks as appropriate for adults and frame the AFOL community as a place for adults. Indeed, this definition and its corresponding boundary are institutionalized through the LEGO Group's formal requirement that all members of LUGs be at least eighteen years old. This average age also reflects the high cost of building with LEGO. AFOLs regularly warn newcomers like me that the hobby can be expensive. It makes sense that adults would pick it up in their thirties and forties when they might have more disposable income than they did in their twenties.

Third, AFOLs are almost exclusively white. All but one of my survey participants identified themselves as white. This is true not just in my online survey of AFOLs but also at fan conventions like BrickCon and in documentaries like *A LEGO Brickumentary*.[32] The LEGO Group's own marketing and corporate values contribute to the remarkable whiteness of the AFOL fan community. Derek Johnson argues that the LEGO Group has an investment in whiteness that is shown through the "normative whiteness of its yellow minifigures and the invisibility of blackness in its 'core' construction toys."[33] Blackness is "buildable" only through specifically licensed minifigures like NBA players and Marvel's Nick Fury.

This investment in whiteness is strengthened through LEGO's connections to science, technology, engineering, and math (STEM). LEGO is routinely framed as (and bought and sold as) a building toy, one that asks children to pay attention to the number of studs in each block, connections that enhance stability, and relationships between component bricks, all of which are enhanced by the LEGO TECHNIC line, which combines building with programming. This kind of thinking is at the core of STEM. Indeed, LEGO explicitly places STEM at the center of its education efforts. On the LEGO Education website, LEGO says, "Through real-life STEM challenges and engaging physical and digital creation, encourage your students to develop 21st century skills through coding as they program solutions in a real-world context."[34] The LEGO lesson plans for elementary school children range from lessons about spinning tops to robust structures to wearables. Further, the official LEGO League Jr. competition program is centered on science and technology rather than art or storytelling.[35] The only age group that features non-STEM learning areas is preschool, in which playing with LEGO bricks is framed as an opportunity to learn social skills and develop character.[36] This focus on STEM is reflected in AFOLs' career choices: many AFOLs reported entering STEM careers after playing with LEGO as children.

LEGO's close association with STEM means that it also has a close association to STEM's discourses of whiteness. Indeed, STEM fields are notoriously white. *Science* magazine reports that African Americans and Hispanics are remarkably underrepresented in science and engineering jobs.[37] And this gap isn't getting smaller. France Cordova, director of the National Science Foundation, argues that "with the country's changing demographics, one could argue that the gap between those with access to STEM and those who don't is actually increasing."[38] In an op-ed in the *New York Times*,

Daniel Colón Ramos and Alfredo Quiñones-Hinojosa write: "Our minority trainees are exhausted. Training in biomedical research is taxing, but that is not what tires them. They are drained by the constant bombardment of narratives and stereotypes that compromise their ability to focus on their training. The prejudice is crushing their creativity and stifling their innovation. It is suffocating a generation of biomedical researchers."[39] The kind of prejudice and racism Ramos and Quiñones-Hinojosa describe in their op-ed has well-documented effects. Studies have found that black grant applicants are significantly less likely than white grant applicants to receive National Institutes of Health (NIH) R01grants, even after controlling for confounding factors like training, publication records, institution, etc.[40] Similar racial disparities were found in the NIH's Small Business Innovation Research program.[41] STEM fields are dominated by white men, and that shows up in STEM education at universities, STEM institutions like the NIH, and STEM culture in research labs. When LEGO is aligned with STEM, the whiteness of these STEM fields reinforces LEGO's own investment in whiteness.

LEGO's close association with STEM has implications for girls and women as well. STEM is well-known for its overrepresentation of men. In engineering, women make up only 12 percent of the workforce.[42] In computing, women make up an even smaller percentage of the workforce today than they did thirty years ago. For women of color, the statistics are even more troubling. Only 6 percent of the bachelor's degrees in computing and 3 percent of the bachelor's degrees in engineering are awarded to women of color.[43] The women who do manage to find their way into STEM degree programs often face harassment: a 2014 study of female science professors found that one in three of the professors surveyed reported experiencing sexual harassment.[44]

Government agencies, private companies, and nonprofits have begun to shift attention to the question of girls and women in STEM, but little progress has been made, and in some cases backlash occurs. For example, only a few weeks after Danielle Brown began work as Google's vice president of diversity, integrity and governance, James Damore, then an employee at Google, posted an essay on Google's internal forums reacting to Google's increased efforts to talk about implicit and explicit biases in the tech workplace. Damore claimed that "the distribution of preferences and abilities of men and women differ in part due to biological causes and that these differences may explain why we don't see equal representation of women in tech and leadership." Damore went on to say, "We need to stop assuming that gender gaps imply sexism." While Google later fired Damore, his memo and his sexist view of women in tech have far-reaching implications.[45] In the *Washington Post*, Cleve Wootson worried that "the engineer's words reflect the unspoken thoughts of many others in an industry dominated by white men," while also "reflect[ing] a tech company culture that's unwelcoming or even hostile to women and minorities."[46] STEM and LEGO, by association, get framed as "for white boys"—not for girls, and not for people of color.

For AFOLs, the demographics of their community as mostly white, middle-aged men are common knowledge. One participant explained, "AFOLs tend to be middle-class male Caucasians."[47] Even AFOLs who fit those descriptions can see that most of the AFOLs around them look the same. One AFOL explained, "As a white, reasonably well off, intelligent, heterosexual, atheistic male, I pretty much fit the stereotype of a LEGO hobbyist."[48] Another added, "I'm an educated, middle-class white male and it seems like many other AFOLs fit this description."[49] Many LEGO fans maintain these gendered and racialized boundaries at least in part through a blindness to social identity built through privilege. When asked, "How does your social identity affect your experience in LEGO fandom? That might include your gender, race, sexuality, disability, age, or religion," AFOLs routinely asserted that social identity doesn't matter. One AFOL said, "I don't think it makes any difference."[50] One fan framed LEGO as a tool, rejecting any connection to social identity at all: "It plays no meaningful role in my experience. The brick has no gender, race, sexuality, disability, age, and certainly no religion, aside from sorting."[51] One fan dismissed common criticisms of LEGO, saying:

> As we are just playing with bricks and figures with jaundice skin, there is no issue within the community for gender, race, disability, age or religion. The big uproars that happen over sets not containing girl figures, the Friends line being too girly, not enough black minifigures, no gay couples, etc, are almost always coming from people who

wouldn't have touched a brick in their fickle lives. It's hilarious how people swing such non-problems and they have no grounds or authority to speak on the matter.[52]

Most AFOLs were quick to assert that their social identity doesn't affect their participation in the AFOL community at all, ignoring the privilege that places them at the center of this community. This blindness reinforces the racialized and gendered boundaries already in place.

The LEGO Ethical Framework: Creativity, Support, and Public Outreach

AFOLs draw on a content world comprised of both narrative-based media like television shows and films and the nonnarrative-based LEGO bricks to create their ethical framework. The LEGO bricks are centered, while the films and television shows function in secondary, supporting roles. Like the Husker football fandom and the VlogBrothers vlog fandom, the LEGO ethical framework emerges in a way that is slightly different from the content worlds of narrative-based fandoms like Harry Potter or Star Trek. For LEGO fans, an ethical framework emerges from community-defined proper uses of the bricks. That is, fans come to articulate what makes "good" LEGO builds—what kinds of uses of the bricks are desirable and what kinds of uses of the bricks are to be avoided. Fans work to interpret and poach ethical tenets from official communication from the LEGO Group, including company interviews, marketing, press releases, and factory tours. Fans also draw on LEGO narrative-based media, like television shows and movies, as sources that come to define LEGO use and play.[53] Fans discuss, critique, and enact these evaluations, interpretations, and definitions through blogs, Flickr, magazines, videos, and conventions. In doing so, a LEGO ethical framework emerges. In this next section, I outline the LEGO ethical framework drawing on fan interviews, participant observation, and LEGO's biggest film, *The LEGO Movie*. I argue that the LEGO ethical framework consists of three main tenets: (1) creativity that uses one's imagination, (2) kind support for fellow AFOL builders, and (3) public outreach that builds interest and love of LEGO.

AFOLs explain their love of LEGO by pointing to the ways in which LEGO enables creativity fueled by one's imagination. In the 2010 documentary *AFOL: A Blockumentary*, AFOL Tom Rafert explains: "What defines us? Our love for the brick. We are just fascinated with the amazing possibilities and the chance to get our imagination in tangible form."[54] When asked what makes a good AFOL, participants responded with answers like, "A good AFOL is a creative builder,"[55] and "I think a good AFOL is someone who thinks outside of the box."[56] For AFOLs, their MOCs are concrete demonstrations of their own creativity and imagination. One AFOL explained, "The best MOC's are made from imagination." Another AFOL said, "Creativity" makes the best MOC."[57] The participant goes on, "A good MOC can incorporate simple pieces to create something that looks complex and can make you forget that it's a toy model."[58]

For AFOLs, MOCs are so interesting, inspiring, and impressive because they don't involve following directions. This openness is what makes room for creativity and imagination. Faye Rhodes, a LEGO builder, explains: "Also, I'm primarily interested in the creative process. I like to create robots and program them. I rarely build someone else's design—admire them, yes, learn from them, yes."[59] MOCs not only demonstrate creativity and imagination, but they also inspire those qualities in others. One AFOL explained that this is why public showings of LEGO MOCs are so important: "It inspires the imagination of others."[60]

Creativity in the AFOL community is a matter of creating clever, unusual, unique, and innovative builds. There are typically four ways to do that: through size, recognizability, detail, and parts usage. AFOLs can show creativity in building something really big or really small and overcoming the challenges that arise when building at those extreme scales. AFOLs recognize that while really big MOCs might be impressive, not many AFOLs have the financial means to build on that scale. Thus, AFOLs are quick to see creativity in other aspects of MOCs besides size. One of those aspects is the creative use of parts. LEGO offers only a limited number of brick types. Thus, AFOLs are challenged with finding new ways to use LEGO parts to create things the LEGO designers never intended. One AFOL explained that the best MOCS are defined by "clever use of pieces to be as faithful as possible to the prototype or original idea."[61] Another AFOL explained, "If the builder uses a part in a new inventive way, that is always a plus."[62] AFOLs might also enact the creativity tenet by building a MOC that is easily recognizable. AFOLs explain that these MOCs are closely modeled after well-researched objects and have "realism." Last, AFOLs might show off their creativity by building models that have impressive details integrated throughout. One AFOL explains: "I look for detail. It might be the way the flowers are created and disbursed. It might be an action or activity a minifig is doing. It might be the detail you can see through a window."[63] Another AFOL explains why details are so important: "A good MOC is all about the details you can see everywhere. A wall shouldn't be flat in one colour; neither should a piece of landscape look the same nearly everywhere. Everything is different! If used, give the minifigs the right expressions, [it] makes a MOC so much better!"[64] Most MOCs can't be impressive in all four criteria at once. It is difficult to build a MOC that is huge, while featuring impressive recognizability and detail and also using parts in innovative ways. Most MOCs will feature one or two of these criteria.

Creativity exercised through one's imagination was also a central theme of *The LEGO Movie*. *The LEGO Movie* traced two story lines—one that followed a young boy named Finn and his interactions with his father and another story line imagined by Finn and acted out through LEGO bricks. In Finn's life, his father prohibits him from playing with his expensive and elaborate LEGO displays, carefully organized by theme and built according to the instructions. In Finn's imagined LEGO world, Lord Business uses superglue to terrorize the LEGO people, restricting their movement between themed worlds and requiring them to live lives according to the instructions. Ultimately, the LEGO characters defeat Lord Business, and Finn talks with his father. No superglue is used, and Finn is free to imagine space astronaut minifigures living in the Old West while building LEGO creations creatively without the use of instructions. In this way, the central conflict of the movie is resolved when Finn is able to use LEGO to play in creative and imaginative ways. The writers and directors of the film, Phil Lord and Christopher Miller, openly talked about creativity being at the center of *The LEGO Movie*: "We made something that uses LEGO as a medium to tell a story, rather than a story to sell LEGO. We saw it as a way to talk about creativity."[65] For Lord and Miller, creativity was about "innovation," "ingenuity," and "making mistakes."[66] Even in making a film about LEGO, Lord and Miller sought to retain some of the challenges LEGO bricks have. "We were making a movie about a toy that inspires creativity," they explained. "And we thought if we embraced the limitations of the medium, it would inspire creative solutions."[67] Like AFOLs, using pieces in clever ways is part of the joy of LEGO for Lord and Miller.

For many AFOLs, their valuing of creativity is modeled after the LEGO Group's own corporate values. And for the LEGO Group, creativity is central to its mission: LEGO's website states, "The company is committed to the development of children and aims to inspire and develop the builders of tomorrow through creative play and learning."[68] The LEGO Group's vision of creativity is one that is anchored in childhood purity, innocence, and racelessness, making it a kind of creativity that is raced as white. Derek Johnson argues that this value undergirds a preracial corporate identity: "innocent as a child, pure at its core, and non-complicit in the racial order."[69] Minifigures raced as black didn't appear until 2002, and only then were brought about as part of a licensing deal with the U.S. National Basketball Association (NBA). Even then, LEGO maintained a sharp differentiation between its licensed sets with raced minifigures and its other sets with yellow minifigures that LEGO maintained were race-free, designed to accommodate children's pure imaginations. The LEGO Group's corporate value of creativity is complicit with its "corporate claims to racelessness."[70] This enables the LEGO Group to deny "their continuing investment in whiteness" and allows LEGO to "absolve the company of any complicity in the politics of racial representation past, present, or future."[71] The LEGO Group advocates a childhood creativity tied to whiteness.

SUPPORT

The second tenet of the AFOL ethical framework is kind support for fellow AFOL builders. Often this support emerges in the back-and-forth conversations between fans discussing building techniques, strategies, and implementation. Being able to do this generously and in a kind way is important for AFOLs. One AFOL said that all AFOLs should "support other builders the best you can" and "be willing to take and receive critiques from others that are trying to help."[72] Another AFOL phrased it this way: "Be supportive of everyone's creations and always be willing to help."[73] In the AFOL community, good AFOLs are "informed, informative, encouraging, and constructive" in their conversations with other fans.[74] One fan summed it up by saying, "Be gentle, be honest, be helpful."[75]

While critique of MOCs might be the central form of support in the AFOL community, it is not the only form. Support for many AFOLs is defined as supporting each other in one's goals of building and sharing LEGO MOCs. AFOLs can support the community by setting up for shows or "helping run LEGO fan websites."[76] Indeed, one AFOL says that being a good AFOL is about "being a friend to the other AFOLs."[77] For this participant that meant "attending meetings, helping with shows, building for show, [and] helping others with their builds."[78] Only at the end of this AFOL's list did they say, "Sometimes it can be a suggestion which may improve the build."[79]

But AFOLs' support doesn't always have to be instrumental. This support can come in the form of "admiring the work of others."[80] It might also involve an openness: One AFOL explained that good AFOLs are "always open and accepting of each other's creative contributions."[81] This AFOL calls others to "build from the heart, mind, soul, and spirit."[82] One AFOL defined the most important qualities of good AFOLs as "a sense of community spirit, tolerance, and helpfulness."[83] To be a good AFOL, one ought to support others through instrumental MOC critique and interpersonal support.

The LEGO Movie envisions a kind of support for fellow builders that is characterized by teamwork rather than isolated building. After Lord Business nearly arrests the group of Master Builders that had been working to end his evil plans, the Master Builders are at a loss, not sure what to do next. Emmet turns to the Master Builders and says: "Guys you're all so talented and imaginative, but you can't work together as a team. I'm just a construction worker but when I had a plan and we were all working together, we could build a skyscraper. Now, you're Master Builders. Just imagine what could happen if you did that. You could save the universe."[84] Emmet suggests that the only way to defeat Lord Business and save the LEGO world is by supporting each other's builds through teamwork. Even Master Builders working creatively and independently wouldn't be enough to defeat Lord Business. Ultimately, *The LEGO Movie* asserts that building

LEGO in the most imaginative ways happens when people build together in supportive ways.

The last component of the AFOL ethical framework is public outreach that shares the love of LEGO. This occurs most often in the form of public exhibitions at which AFOLs set up their MOCs. AFOLs often stand nearby their MOCs to talk with children, parents, and other adults. This kind of public engagement is a key part of what it means to be an AFOL. One AFOL explains, "Personally, I appreciate AFOLs who share, teach, and in general reach out to other LEGO fans and the general public."[85] While some AFOLs may not participate in LUGs or public exhibitions, good AFOLs are still "willing to talk about it [LEGO] to anyone who asks"[86] and "have fun with Legos and share with others."[87]

Public outreach that shares the love of LEGO serves a number of functions: building interest, normalizing the fandom, and providing recognition to builders. First, it builds interest in LEGO in both kids and adults. AFOLs explain that public exhibitions "broaden the fan base"[88] and "get kids involved."[89] One AFOL fan says that public exhibitions are "a great way for kids and adults to come out and see what's possible and that they could be capable of doing something just like it."[90] Public outreach encourages kids to get involved in LEGO, which enhances their creativity and imagination. For many AFOLs, public outreach "inspires the imagination of others."[91] But public outreach also recruits new AFOLs. One AFOL said that they "also open up the idea of LEGO as a hobby to adults who might otherwise dismiss it."[92] Another put it this way: "I believe it also shows others that there [sic] not the only one. Some people just take a little encouragement and support to see that they aren't the only ones out there tha[t] like this kind of thing and it's perfectly ok, there is nothing wrong with being a[n] AFOL, no one is there to judge you, be yourself and do what you enjoy!"[93] For AFOLs, building interest in kids and adults isn't just about recruitment—it's also about supporting the LEGO brand. Public exhibitions promote the LEGO brand. One AFOL explains, "As far as the LEGO Company is concerned, public exhibitions of LEGO are the best advertising they have."[94] Ultimately, public exhibitions build interest and "inspire people to build" with LEGO.[95]

Public outreach also helps normalize AFOLs, who are sometimes accused of "just playing with children's toys." Public exhibitions help "show the world how LEGO can be used. Many people only think it's a kids toy, but it's far from that!"[96] Another AFOL says that public exhibitions "help explain that LEGO can be an art medium, not just a kids' toy."[97] Public outreach frames AFOLs and their serious LEGO building as interesting and acceptable. One AFOL put it this way: Public exhibitions help show people that "it isn't as weird as most people think when the[y] picture adults playing with children's toys."[98]

Public outreach also provides recognition of the hard work AFOLs put into their MOCs. One AFOL said public exhibitions provide "visibility!" They explain, "This is a great way for the average person to get their work out there."[99] AFOLs note that it's always nice to feel that your work is appreciated and that members of the public are impressed with what you have built. It is this public recognition that drives many AFOLs to continue to build new MOCs. One AFOL explains that "recognition of hard work is important, and the public displays encourage people to be involved (purchasing and building) with perpetuating the Lego brand."[100] Public outreach shares the love of LEGO, builds interest, provides recognition, and normalizes the fandom. One AFOL summed up public outreach like this: "It's fun to talk to people about your hobby!"[101]

In *The LEGO Movie*, the builds that the main characters create serve to inspire each other just like the AFOLs' public exhibitions do. After Wyld Style inspires everyone in the LEGO world to build things from their imagination rather than from Lord Business's instructions, Emmet confronts Lord Business. "Look at all these things that people built. You might see a mess," Emmet asserts, but "What I see are people—inspired by each other, and by you. People taking what you made and making something new out of it."[102] In the end, people of the LEGO world not only built what was in their imaginations but also built creations inspired by other people's creations. The writers and directors of *The LEGO Movie* hoped that the movie would "inspire creativity in viewers."[103] They explain, "We wanted to make a movie that made you feel more creative when you walked out than when you walked in."[104] Indeed, for AFOLs, LEGO creations inspire other people.

Parts of the public outreach tenet of the AFOL ethical framework are contradicted by the power and privilege in the AFOL fandom. While white male privilege functions to *limit* membership, the public outreach tenet aims to *expand* membership. This tension largely remains hidden in the fandom, though it bubbles to the surface at times. For example, when AFOL City displays use only yellow minifigures at public exhibitions, they are simultaneously enacting the public outreach tenet while enacting white privilege—excluding people of color from their LEGO worlds even as they try to include more people within their memberships. Public outreach (and its aim at inclusion) and white and male privilege (and its resulting exclusion) at times contradict one another.

ALL TENETS INFLUENCE EACH OTHER

Of course, the three components of the AFOL ethical framework (creativity, support, and outreach) aren't so discrete in practice—they all connect to and reinforce one another. As one AFOL (LEGO Participant AD) put it in an online survey, "A good AFOL furthers the creativity of themselves and others using LEGO by coming up with new and innovative building techniques on subject matters that interest them and shares the result with others, so they and the community might become better builders with a wider range of techniques at their fingertips." AFOLs value creativity and work to support that and share it with others. For AFOLs, it may be difficult to imagine one part of the ethical framework without the others.

Defining the *Retelling* Rhetorical Strategy

Typically, the AFOL ethical framework requires hundreds of bricks for AFOLs to enact as they build MOCs that are creative, express support for other AFOLs, and connect with the broader communities around them. So how does Greenpeace pair the AFOL ethical framework with its environmental activism ethical modality? How does Greenpeace make the AFOL ethical framework tenets of creativity, support, and public outreach relevant to civic action? In this section, I argue that Greenpeace uses a strategy of *retelling* to pair an AFOL ethical framework with a civic ethical modality.

Founded in 1971 by a small group of activists who wanted to prevent the US from testing nuclear weapons near the Alaskan island Amchitka, Greenpeace has become one of the largest and most visible environmental organizations in the world in large part through its innovative media-centered communication strategies.[105] Environmental communication scholars Merav Katz-Kimchi and Idit Manosevitch call Greenpeace "the most prominent and media savvy environmental group" and "a trailblazer in its innovative usage of digital media."[106] Rhetoric scholar Kevin DeLuca argues that Greenpeace's primary rhetorical strategy has been staging image events, defined as "staged acts of protest designed for media dissemination."[107] Image events are spectacles designed for mass media coverage. When Greenpeace activists take actions like placing their boats between whaling ships and whales, activists create events that are designed to meet the logics of image circulation on both mass media and networked media.[108]

Many aspects of Greenpeace's #SavetheArctic #BlockShell campaign function as image events. For example, activists dressed as LEGO minifigures held protest signs outside of a LEGO store in New York City, and in Toronto activists handed out fake "Shell Oil Spill" LEGO sets. But the central part of Greenpeace's campaign represents a departure from its image events strategy. Greenpeace embraces a strategy anchored in fan identities: fan-based civic appeals. In this section, I argue that Greenpeace's video pairs the AFOL fan ethical framework with a Greenpeace ethical modality by *retelling* the story of *The LEGO Movie*.

Retelling as a rhetorical strategy is characterized by a blend of the parody and remix video genres. Parody works by creating a new text/artifact that textually references another, pointing to strategically placed similarities and differences.[109] Television shows like *Saturday Night Live* (NBC, 1979–present), *The Simpsons* (Fox, 1989–present), and *The Colbert Report* (Comedy Central, 2005–14) are well known for their parodies.[110] Parody is not only entertainment; parody also functions to expose the limits of dominant discourses and constitute public culture through the construction of public identities and agencies.[111] In doing so, parody can sometimes have a biting edge, mocking the source text it references. For example, *The Colbert Report* criticized, poked fun at, and destabilized the conservative news show genre it imitated through exaggeration. While parody may mock its source text, the *retelling* rhetorical strategy retains a love of and appreciation for the source text. In doing so, retelling blends the textual references of parody with the source text appreciation of fanfiction and fan vids.

The *retelling* rhetorical strategy also draws heavily from fan communities' long histories of retelling the stories of their fan-objects through fanfiction and fan vid remix videos. In fanfiction, fans write out new stories in narrative form. Fans imagine "alternate point-of-view or alternate-ending retellings" while exploring "what-ifs, could-have-beens, or (more often) should-have beens."[112] Fan studies scholars Karen Hellekson and Kristina Busse describe fanfiction as the "rewriting of shared media" and note that it often involves "a specific amateur infrastructure for its creation, distribution, and reception."[113] Sites like LiveJournal and Fan-Fiction.net serve as repositories for fanfiction: fans write fanfiction, post it online, and read fanfiction written by others. Fan vid remixes reimagine the shared fan-object too but use film and video as the mode for its retelling, creatively cutting footage together in new ways. Similarly, fan vid remixes make arguments about what should or could be, or what is actually lying underneath the original video.[114] For example, Edo Wilkins's remix rearranged footage from George W. Bush's State of the Union address.[115] Rather than allow Bush to proudly describe the ways in which the country was combatting terrorism, Bush proudly describes the ways he is committing terrorism. Wilkins retells Bush's original story and in doing so critiques Bush's policies. Other remix videos retell the original story not only to critique the source text but also to imagine the desired alternative. For example, the remix artist Killa critiqued the heteronormativity of television by reimagining the platonic friendship between Spock and Kirk in *Star Trek: The Original Series* as romantic with her fan vid remix *Perhaps Perhaps Perhaps*.[116] By cutting together knowing glances and intimate touches between Spock and Kirk and by adding a romantic song as a backdrop, Killa presents a compelling vision of Kirk and Spock as lovers.

While the AFOL fan community doesn't have the same tradition of fanfiction or fan vid remixes that television and book fan communities do, the AFOL fan community developed a tradition of brickfilms instead. Brickfilms are videos that use stop-motion animation to tell a story using only LEGO bricks. Brick films are sometimes replicas of existing movie or television scenes played out with LEGO and the original audio laid over. Other times brick films tell original stories, using LEGO instead of live actors. Like brickfilms, Greenpeace's video tells this story using only LEGO bricks; however, it doesn't utilize stop-motion animation like brickfilms do.

Greenpeace's retelling strategy blends elements from brickfilms, fanfiction, and fan vid remix traditions with elements from parody. Like parody, *retelling* uses extensive intertextual references from a source text to create a new text that makes a new point. Like fanfiction and fan vids, *retelling* retains the love of the source text while it uses the characters and content world from the fan-object (in this case, *The LEGO Movie*) to imagine a new story. Ultimately, the *retelling* strategy creates new stories by making intertextual references and using original source material in new ways that maintain a love of the source text, which functions to pair a fan-based ethical framework with a civic ethical modality.

Pairing through a Strategy of *Retelling*

Greenpeace's campaign asserts that Shell is a threat to LEGO's ethical framework by *retelling* the story depicted in *The LEGO Movie*. Greenpeace's video opens by showing us an Arctic world. Greenpeace's Arctic world theme fits easily into the content world of *The LEGO Movie*, which is made up of themed areas like the Old West, Pirates Cove, and Bricksburg. Greenpeace's video appears to begin after *The LEGO Movie* has ended and all of the LEGO minifigures are able to live and build together without oppressive rules from Lord Business. Like many children's movies, *The LEGO Movie* gives its audience a happy ending. As moviegoers we are left confident that creativity will thrive unimpeded in the LEGO world. In a world after Lord Business is defeated, LEGO minifigures can build whatever their imaginations envision and can visit any of the themed lands freely, not only the pieces from the corresponding themed sets. The Greenpeace video shows us this happy ending. In the Greenpeace video, we see minifigures that might match Arctic-themed sets like polar bears, hockey players, and an Eskimo fisherman. But we also see *Game of Thrones* characters, Santa Claus, and WyldStyle and Emmet from *The LEGO Movie*. Anyone can visit the Arctic world, not just the pieces from the LEGO Arctic sets. The happy state of the Arctic world is reinforced by the smiles on the faces of the

Figure 5. A screenshot showing oil enveloping LEGO minifigures. © Greenpeace/ Don't Panic.

minifigures. The Greenpeace video shows us *The LEGOs Movie*'s happy ending: an Arctic world thriving after the defeat of Lord Business.

But this happy ending doesn't last long. Indeed, the Greenpeace video retells the story of *The LEGO Movie* by rewriting its happy ending. Even though Lord Business was defeated, and even though LEGO pieces are no longer restricted by rules and instructions, the LEGO world, according to Greenpeace, is neither happy nor safe. Twenty seconds into the video, the video begins to show Shell's presence in the Arctic world. Construction equipment is lined up on the land and an oil rig is just offshore. Minifigures of scientists and construction workers all bear Shell's logo. These Shell logos were most likely added by Greenpeace. LEGO has produced Shell gas stations (which are now out of production) and Formula One racing cars with Shell's logo, but never construction equipment or oil rigs.

Shell's presence in the Arctic world threatens the happy ending of *The LEGO Movie*. The video shows the oil rig springing a leak. Soon, oil spills into the ocean and across the Arctic world. The LEGO animals and minifigures that were so happy at the beginning of the video are enveloped in oil (fig. 5). Greenpeace's video emphasizes this dramatic change in the LEGO Arctic world by repeating some of the same shots the video opened with. At the beginning of the video, the camera zooms in on an Eskimo minifigure fishing in the ocean. After the oil rig springs a leak, the camera again

Figure 6. Screenshots of the end of the Greenpeace video. © Greenpeace/Don't Panic.

zooms in on the Eskimo minifigure fishing—the only change is the oil that is slowly creeping up the minifigure's leg. The repetition of this shot with only one change serves to direct blame toward Shell for the destruction of the LEGO Arctic world. The LEGO Arctic world was living *The LEGO Movie*'s happy ending until Shell entered the picture. Eventually, the entire LEGO Arctic world is enveloped with oil. Greenpeace's video traces the flood of oil, zooming in on each minifigure as they are slowly enveloped (fig. 6). The video ends by panning up from below the oil to show that the only thing that survived the oil spill is a flag with the Shell logo. Greenpeace's video shows the destruction of the LEGO Arctic world by the oil leaked from Shell's offshore oil rig.

By *retelling* the story depicted in *The LEGO Movie*, Greenpeace pairs the LEGO ethical framework with civic action to protect the environment. Greenpeace envisions an ending drastically different from the one depicted in *The LEGO Movie*: Lord Business may have threatened imaginative and creative play by freezing the LEGO world with superglue, but Shell threatens imaginative and creative play by burying it under oil spills. The LEGO world becomes a stand-in for LEGO values. Greenpeace's video shows that the LEGO world, and the values it represents (creativity, support, outreach), is not safe at all but is instead destroyed by Shell. No bricks are left to play with at the end of Greenpeace's video. LEGO fans cannot build in creative ways using their imagination, cannot support each other in their builds, and cannot do public outreach by sharing their builds and inspiring others. Shell threatens all aspects of the AFOL ethical framework.

"EVERYTHING IS AWESOME!!!" SONG

Greenpeace pairs these camera shots of LEGO bricks and minifigures with the central song from *The LEGO Movie*, which functions to emphasize the threat Shell poses to the LEGO ethical framework. In *The LEGO Movie*, the "Everything Is Awesome!!!" song draws attention to the threat Lord Business poses. The song becomes an anthem for the LEGO minifigure people who follow the rules: everything is awesome if you do what Lord Business says, follow the instructions, and do what you're told. The lyrics proclaim: "Everything is Awesome, everything is cool when you're part of a team / Everything is awesome, when you're living out a dream."[117] The song is poppy with a quick tempo, energetic electronic beats, and happy vocals. But in the film, there is a nagging feeling of contradiction between the happy vocals and the actual lyrics like, "We're the same, I'm like you, you're like me, we're all working in harmony."[118] It feels a little too restrictive—the happiness is a little too easy. Indeed, the "Everything Is Awesome!!!" song functions to direct our attention to the threat Lord Business poses to creativity and imagination in the film. Lord Business maintains authoritarian control over the LEGO minifigure people, convincing them they're happy when they follow the directions. It is only after Emmet and Wyldstyle convince the LEGO minifigure people to build with their own imaginations that the LEGO minifigure people become truly happy.

In Greenpeace's video, the "Everything is Awesome!!!" song is rewritten but still relies on a nagging feeling of contradiction and functions to direct our attention to the central threat. Greenpeace had the song rewritten, slowing down the tempo, using only piano accompaniment, and using slower, sadder, lower vocals. In the video, the lyric "Everything is awesome" seemingly contradicts both the emotion conveyed in the performance of the song and the depiction of what is happening in the LEGO land. In fact, this juxtaposition is jarring and uncomfortable to watch. The "Everything Is Awesome!!!" song draws attention to LEGO's performative contradiction: LEGO's professed values contradict its enactment of those values. While LEGO may assert that it values creative building through imagination, supporting fellow builders, and inspiring other builders through public outreach, the inclusion of the Shell Oil bricks actually threatens that creative, supportive, and social play. The "Everything Is Awesome!!!" song represents another way in which the ending of *The LEGO Movie* is retold in Greenpeace's video. The song is reenvisioned as sad and tragic but still represents contradictions between professed and actual values. Ultimately, Greenpeace makes a civic argument grounded in a commitment to the LEGO ethical framework.

GREENPEACE'S ETHICAL MODALITY

Pairing the AFOL ethical framework with a Greenpeace ethical modality is an important move. Typically, the AFOL ethical framework is enacted by building with LEGO, participating in LUGs, posting images on Flickr, and attending fan conventions. But Greenpeace pairs LEGO fan values to a Greenpeace civic ethical modality comprised of civic actions like signing Greenpeace's petition, making donations, and boycotting LEGO. The last seven seconds of the video emphasize this call to action by embedding a link to the petition right in the video with the text: "Sign the petition!" After oil covers the last bit of the LEGO Arctic world, text appears that summarizes Greenpeace's claim that "Shell is polluting our kids' imaginations" before moving on to a call to action: "Tell LEGO to end its partnership with Shell." The petition is housed on the webpage for Greenpeace's Save the

Arctic campaign. The user can sign the petition there while also reading the report on Shell Oil and LEGO. By *retelling* the story in *The LEGO Movie*, Greenpeace makes the AFOL fan ethical framework relevant to environmental actions. When Shell Oil is allowed in the LEGO world, the entire LEGO world is destroyed, along with its corresponding values. Greenpeace shows what LEGO fans can do to prevent it. To save LEGO creativity, fans must petition, boycott, and donate money. Greenpeace's ethical modality is unpaired from its ethical framework of conservationism and environmentalism and re-paired to a LEGO ethical framework. To support creativity, fans must sign the Greenpeace petition. Ultimately, Greenpeace's video calls fans to protect their LEGO values by opposing Shell's deal with LEGO and Shell's drilling in the Arctic.

Greenpeace's Criticism of LEGO

So far, I have argued that Greenpeace successfully paired an AFOL ethical framework (creativity, support, and outreach) to a Greenpeace ethical modality (petition, boycott, and donate). But Greenpeace's successful pairing was undermined by its criticism of LEGO. AFOLs love LEGO deeply, and thus, many found it very difficult to carry out Greenpeace's call to action: boycotting LEGO. Greenpeace's argument was consistent with the AFOL ethical framework of creativity, support, and public outreach, and it invoked those values in powerful ways. But the call to action contradicted a defining feature of AFOL culture: love of LEGO.

Indeed, in my online surveys, many AFOLs indicated that Greenpeace's boycott appeared as an attack on LEGO itself. In fact, to many AFOLs, Greenpeace appeared to be a bigger threat to LEGO fan values than Shell. Most AFOLs agreed that Shell's drilling in the Arctic could be problematic. AFOLs expressed some broad support for the environment, recognizing that disastrous oil spills like the 2010 Deepwater Horizon disaster are clearly bad for the environment. But few AFOLs expressed strong support for the actions that Greenpeace asked them to take. Rather, AFOLs waivered, stuck in the contradiction between supporting their fan-object, LEGO, and recognizing that oil spills are bad and oil dependence will likely have significant consequences for the planet. One AFOL explained the internal dialectic this way: "I think it [Greenpeace's video] activates people thinking about environment and pollution. But I don't think it was a good idea to associate Lego and fun with Pollution and Lego."[119] AFOLs criticized Greenpeace's choice to target LEGO. "I think it made LEGO out to look like more of a bad guy than Shell, which (I presume) was the target of Greenpeace."[120] AFOLs like this one directed blame at Shell rather than LEGO: "I find the campaign uses TLG [the LEGO Group] as a proxy victim to reach its goal, causing collateral damage to a fairly innocent company. The resources could have been used directly against Shell instead."[121] AFOLs saw that Shell was the source of the problem.

Many LEGO fans dismissed the video's assertion by pointing out LEGO's own relationship with the environment. Some fans saw a contradiction between the plastic in LEGO's bricks and Greenpeace's targeting of Shell gas station bricks used for marketing: "In any case plastic is a by-product of petroleum, and everyone who watched that video is heavily reliant on fossil fuels for transportation, energy, and the by-products. I strongly disapprove of Greenpeace's tactics and actions in many situations."[122] Other AFOLs defended LEGO by pointing out the very real steps the LEGO Group is taking to reduce its impact on the environment: "I liked the video and understand the message. I know that Lego is looking into more sustainable ways to produce their bricks, but I'm concerned over quality too."[123] One fan explained: "LEGO is one of the few consumer products that can be easily recycled and repurposed immediately and on-site by the consumer. It is the wrong target for militant environmentalists."[124]

Greenpeace's campaign indicates that criticism of the fan object can threaten a successful pairing of a fan-based ethical framework and a civic ethical modality. In other words, it makes little sense to predicate a civic argument on love of a fan-object (by anchoring it in a fan-based ethical framework) and then turn around and criticize that fan-object. This poses a contradiction for fans—one that they are likely to work through by prioritizing love of the fan-object above all else. Of course, this is not to say that fans themselves never criticize their fan-object. Indeed, groups like the Harry Potter Alliance called Warner Brothers to bring the production of its chocolate frogs in line with the ethics of the Harry Potter story.[125] In the end, the Harry Potter Alliance succeeded in convincing Warner Brothers to use fair-trade chocolate in its Harry Potter candy. Similarly, Greenpeace could have retained its *retelling* strategy but reframed the civic action as making LEGO even better. Rather, Greenpeace tried to pressure LEGO into changing its partnership through bad publicity and consumer boycotts. For AFOLs, that contradicted their foundational commitment to LEGO.

Even without AFOLs' support, Greenpeace's campaign still found success. Three months after Greenpeace's video was uploaded, LEGO announced that it was ending its partnership with Shell. While AFOLs largely rejected Greenpeace's campaign, Greenpeace's simple assertion that LEGO was bad for associating itself with Shell was likely better received by parents of kids who play with LEGO than by adult fans of LEGO. For middle- and upper-class parents who can afford to buy their children LEGO sets, it's easy to sign the petition and boycott LEGO while substituting other toys for their children. For these parents, the choice between protecting their children's imaginations and supporting LEGO is an easy one. Thus, for an audience of parents of kids who play with LEGO, the video's call to protect their children's imaginations at all costs plays well.

In the end, Greenpeace's video likely prompted change based on the public relations cost of the wide circulation of Greenpeace's campaign video rather than actions taken by AFOLs. This has emerged as a winning strategy for Greenpeace in recent years.[126] Greenpeace's campaigns have increasingly circulated images structured around encouraging consumers to demand that companies take better environmental actions. The public relations cost of these campaigns is high for the companies targeted—they question consumers' brand loyalty and muddy companies' hard-earned brand identities. Transnational corporations like LEGO have been quick to act to minimize the effects of these campaigns.

Conclusion: Retelling as a Rhetorical Strategy and Protecting the Fan-Object

The case of Greenpeace's #SavetheArctic #BlockShell campaign demonstrates that maintaining the love of the fan-object is necessary to undergird any pairing of a fan-based ethical framework with a civic ethical modality. While Greenpeace may have successfully paired the AFOL ethical framework with Greenpeace's civic modalities, Greenpeace did so in a way that asked fans to criticize, target, and hurt the LEGO Group. For AFOLs, love of LEGO comes even before the LEGO ethical framework. Any action that would hurt or publicly shame the LEGO Group would contradict the love of LEGO that undergirds the AFOL ethical framework. For fans, that meant Greenpeace's video carried little power. Greenpeace's case demonstrates that appeals must be carefully constructed. For fans, civic action must be in line with their commitment to their fan-object. If it is not, fans face the choice between supporting their beloved fan-object or taking civic action. For highly dedicated fans in well-developed fan communities online, commitment to a fan-object comes first. But when civic actions are in line with fan commitments, fan-based civic appeals can be powerful.

Further, Greenpeace's video demonstrates another way in which public engagement can be anchored in fan identities, fan values, and fan-based civic appeals. The case of Greenpeace's LEGO campaign shows us how a strategy of *retelling* can pair fan ethical frameworks with civic ethical modalities. By retelling the story of *The LEGO Movie*, Greenpeace framed Shell as a threat to creativity that uses imagination, support among fellow AFOLs, and public outreach. Thus, Greenpeace called parents and fans to engage in civic acts like signing their petition, making donations, and boycotting LEGO. Like the Huskers' *connecting* and the nerdfighters' *expanding*, *retelling* pairs fan ethical frameworks with civic modalities, inviting fans to take civic action out of a commitment to their fan values, identities, and communities. After examining three ways in which fan-based civic appeals can be constructed (connecting, expanding, and retelling), chapter 5 looks at a case in which ethical frameworks and civic ethical modalities are not successfully paired, mitigating any impact fan-based civic appeals might have on public culture, political issues, and citizen's political commitments.

ABSENT PAIRINGS

Disney, UNICEF, and the Star Wars Force
for Change Campaign

In the late 1970s, George Lucas dreamed of creating an epic space opera that would tell a story of adventure, romance, and moral lessons with some of the most innovative special effects of the age. After finishing *American Graffiti* (1973), Lucas spent four years working on *Star Wars* before it premiered in 1977. The film was a resounding success, making more than $450 million domestically, the second-highest ever adjusted for inflation.[1] The film was also critically acclaimed, winning Academy Awards for art direction, sound, costume design, visual effects, music, and film editing.[2] The success of what was originally known as simply *Star Wars* and later became known as *Star Wars Episode IV: A New Hope* led to two more films in what has become known as the original trilogy: *Episode V: The Empire Strikes Back* (1980) and *Episode VI: The Return of the Jedi* (1983). It would be more than fifteen years before Lucas would release any new Star Wars films, but finally, in 1999, Lucas released three new films that told the story of the Star Wars universe before Luke, Han, and Leia. After thirty-five years and six Star Wars films, George Lucas sold Lucasfilm and the rights to the Star Wars story to Disney for more than $4 billion. Disney quickly announced three new Star Wars movies: Episodes VII, VIII, and IX. Disney's purchase meant that fans' ten years of waiting since the last Star Wars film would come to an end. Indeed, Disney delivered on its promise, and more. It released *Episode VII: The Force Awakens* in 2015, *Rogue One: A Star Wars Story* in 2016, *Episode VIII: The Last Jedi* in 2017, and *Han Solo: A Star Wars Story* in 2018. Episode IX, still untitled, is set for release in 2019.

Over the years, the Star Wars films have garnered a large fan following: thousands of kids played Star Wars games on the playground and fought with pretend lightsabers in bedrooms and later grew up to be adults who analyzed the minutiae of the Star Wars world online and built their own movie-accurate lightsabers. Many of these fans cannot remember a time in their lives before Star Wars. For more than forty years, Star Wars fans have been lining up outside of movie theaters for the premieres of Star Wars films, a quintessential Star Wars fan experience that has been immortalized in novels like Rainbow Rowell's *Kindred Spirits* and television shows like ABC's *The Goldbergs* (2013–present). Between film release dates, Star Wars fans discuss and celebrate Star Wars at fan conventions like the annual Star Wars Celebrations hosted in cities across the world like Orlando and London. In 2017, the Star Wars Celebration Orlando drew more than seventy thousand attendees.[3] Star Wars fans are just as dedicated online. A search in iTunes reveals more than one hundred podcasts about Star Wars, including the popular *Full of Sith* and *Coffee with Kenobi* podcasts. Indeed, Henry Jenkins argues that before Star Wars, "no other science-fiction property had so totally saturated a generation's media experiences. No previous science-fiction film had gained this kind of blockbuster status."[4] The Star Wars fandom is more than forty years old and still a rich culture and community.

In preparation for the first post-Lucas film, *The Force Awakens*, Disney launched the Star Wars Force for Change in 2014.[5] The charity campaign raised money for UNICEF by holding a sweepstakes raffle for the chance to win a role in Episode VII. The raffle would be organized and run by Omaze, a company that specializes in celebrity charity campaigns by focusing on unique once-in-a-lifetime experiences for fans. In the end, the campaign raised more than $4 million. The success of the first Force Awakens campaign led to many others. Since 2014, Disney and Lucasfilm have auctioned off a chance to attend a red-carpet premiere of *Star Wars Episode VII: The Force Awakens*, a visit to Skywalker Ranch, and a visit to the Han Solo movie set. Across campaigns running from 2014 to 2017, the Force for Change has raised more than $10 million for charities, including UNICEF, Make-a-Wish, the American Red Cross, Boys and Girls Clubs, and others.

In this chapter, I examine the first campaign in the Force for Change project. The first campaign came at a difficult time for Disney. The threat of fan reactions after the prequel trilogy hung over Disney while Disney faced additional concerns from fans who didn't trust the corporation—best known for children's animated princess movies—with their beloved adult science fiction adventure films. Disney needed to win over Star Wars fans, and the Force for Change gave them an opportunity to do that before the first movie was even released. I focus my analysis on the first Force for Change campaign because it was critical to Disney's relationship with fans and its success led to additional campaigns being launched over the next three years.

Here, I argue that the 2014 Force for Change campaign was a monetary success but a civic failure. While the Force for Change may have called upon fans to take civic action, it failed to construct a compelling pairing of a Star Wars ethical framework with a civic ethical modality. Instead, I argue that the Force for Change relied on noncivic appeals for donations, inviting fans to participate in the campaign not out of a commitment to a public issue or civic action but simply in order to be a good fan. By failing to pair a Star Wars ethical framework with a civic ethical modality, the Force for Change does little to engage public culture.

The Force for Change is an important case study because of the way it draws our attention beyond the act of citizenship to the process of citizenship. More than any other case study in this book, the Force for Change campaign demonstrates the difference between the "what" of citizenship (the donations) and the "how" of citizenship (the process of performance). Just as voting can be performed in a variety of ways that engage public culture differently, so too can donating money to charity. If we look at the Force for Change only as an act of citizenship, looking only at the "what" of citizenship, we ought to assume the campaign was a resounding success, raising a significant amount of money for an important charity. But if we look at the "how" of citizenship, we can begin to see the ways in which charity donations were divorced from public culture and grounded instead in fan culture, ultimately making the campaign a rhetorical failure. This case demonstrates that not all campaigns that raise money for charity invite engagement with public issues and other citizens. It demonstrates what happens when a pairing of a fan-based ethical framework with a civic ethical modality is absent. In the case of the Force for Change, purchases of Star Wars T-shirts with proceeds going toward UNICEF functioned like purchases of a Star Wars T-shirt rather than a donation to UNICEF, making the Force for Change campaign civically bankrupt even as the campaign was financially successful. I begin by contextualizing Star Wars fandom before turning to the question of who Star Wars fans are and what kind of boundaries are created in the Star Wars fan community. Next, I argue that a strong Star Wars ethical framework exists, before exploring the components of possible Star Wars ethical frameworks. I then argue that the Force for Change campaign is a case of an *absent* pairing, utilizing fan-based, non-civic appeals for donation.

Contextualizing Star Wars Fandom: Generations and Schisms

The Star Wars fandom is big in two senses. In one sense, it's a large fandom because three trilogies have been released, spanning across Generation X, millennials, and Generation Z, and each trilogy has achieved some degree of mainstream success.[6] In another sense, Star Wars is an especially large fandom in terms of the texts within its universe. While each of the Star Wars films holds a kind of gold-star status, there are also hundreds of Star Wars novels and comics, making it nearly impossible for most fans to have read and watched all the Star Wars material. Until 2014, the comics, novels, games, and television shows made up the Expanded Universe (EU), material that lay outside of the films but was consistent with the films' story and universe. In 2014, after Disney acquired Lucasfilm, Disney announced that all of the previous Expanded Universe novels and comics would be known as Star Wars Legends and would no longer be considered canon, or consistent with the film stories. In fan terms, the announcement meant that "the Expanded Universe would be retconned."[7] Disney reserved the right to use story lines, characters, or plots from Legends but absolved itself of the responsibility of maintaining consistency moving forward. Instead, Disney now maintains consistency in the new canon, in particular across its films and its animated television shows, *Star Wars: The Clone Wars* (2008–15) and *Star Wars: Rebels* (2014–18).

The long history of Star Wars (from 1977 to 2018) shapes the fandom in a number of significant ways. First, this long history reflects varying cultural positions of Star Wars fans. The first Star Wars movie, *A New Hope*, was released in 1977 at a time when science fiction, fandom, and geek culture was culturally devalued and largely relegated to the freaks, geeks, and nerds. In 2017, at the time of the release of the eighth Star Wars movie, *The Last Jedi*, science fiction and geeky fandom have found a more valued place within mainstream culture. For better or worse, Star Wars and its fandom are now mainstream and enjoy the benefits and the drawbacks that position carries. As a major mainstream media franchise, Star Wars has many novels, comic books, and television shows all exploring the Star Wars universe alongside matching merchandise readily available at major stores ranging from Target to the Gap. Over the years, the Star Wars universe has grown substantially, and the media and merchandise that make up that universe have become more accessible.

Second, Star Wars' long history means that the Star Wars fandom is largely intergenerational. The release of three trilogies (the original trilogy in the late 1970s/early 1980s, the prequels in the 2000s, and the new trilogy in the 2010s) means that fans have different entry points to Star Wars fandom and different childhood memories of Star Wars. The fans who were kids during the original trilogy were young adults during the prequels and are middle-aged now for the new trilogy. Likewise, fans who grew up with the prequel trilogy are young adults now, encountering the new trilogy. Star Wars' long history also means that its fans tend to be older, including large numbers of folks who are in their thirties, forties, or fifties.

The staggered release of three different trilogies has also led to a number of rifts or schisms within the fan community. With the release of each new trilogy comes the possibility of extending the Star Wars universe that fans so deeply love while also carrying the risk that the new trilogy might go terribly wrong and might not live up to their expectations. When media and cultural studies scholar Will Brooker interviewed fans after the release of *The Phantom Menace*, he found a schism in the fan community between the bashers and the gushers. For the bashers, *The Phantom Menace* was a total disappointment or even a betrayal. Fans criticized the film for depending too heavily on "CGI spectacle over emotion and relationships" and "slapstick over wit."[8] On the other hand, gushers looked to the film to rehabilitate what they could. Brooker explains that some fans tried to "rehabilitate the saga, visiting it over and over again in an attempt to see it in a new light, to celebrate the positive elements and forgive the ones that jarred."[9]

Today, the fandom continues to be divided, though more fans seem to be turning a kinder eye toward the prequel trilogy.[10] For example, one participant explains in my online, open-ended survey, "A lot of people think its [sic] 'cool' to complain about the prequels but I don't think they deserve as much hate as they do."[11] Today, the fans who saw the prequel trilogy as kids are now young adults. These fans may be more likely to be forgiving of Jar Jar Binks and the new trilogy as a whole since they didn't experience the same betrayal or disappointment Generation X fans felt. Some fans find these divides or schisms in the fandom damaging to the community. One fan explains that their least favorite part of Star Wars fandom is the frequent refrain, "The prequels suck!"[12] This fan explains: "Everyone has a different Star Wars experience. I was first introduced to the universe with the prequels. I love Jar Jar while others hate him. I love Hayden Christensen while others can't stand him. That's fine but I can't stand having other people put down others' experiences in the universe."[13] Schisms like the one between fans who love and hate the prequels produce a sense of elite gatekeeping in the Star Wars fandom. One fan explained, "I've never seen a fandom where to like one thing and hate another leads to screams of 'fake fan' more than Star Wars."[14] These schisms and gatekeeping practices build "unnecessary rivalries"[15] and a sense of elitism.

Even across these schisms, Star Wars fans enact their fandom through common fan practices. First, news watching is important within the Star Wars fan community. With each new film, fans track and analyze press releases, interviews, and trailers to figure out what might be coming next.[16] Second, making and wearing costumes (a practice known in fan communities as "cosplay") is a common Star Wars fan practice. Fans make costumes ranging from Stormtrooper armor to Mandalorian helmets to Rebel Alliance uniforms.[17] Indeed, such costumes are so popular that artisan lightsaber makers have emerged to build film-accurate or personalized lightsabers for fans.[18] Third, Star Wars fans are also often collectors. Star Wars trading cards and merchandise like action figures and toys have become collector's items, difficult and expensive to acquire.[19] Beyond tracking news, cosplaying, and collecting, fans also post on discussion boards like TheForce.net, play Star Wars games (RPGs, board games, and video games), attend conventions like Star Wars Celebration Orlando, watch movies and television shows, make edited versions of the Star Wars movies, write fanfiction, make fan art, and record and listen to podcasts.[20]

Who Are Star Wars Fans?

So who are Star Wars fans? The majority of my participants were white middle-aged folks living in the US or the UK. More than 80 percent of my participants live in the US, while 17 percent live in Europe in countries like France, Germany, and Denmark. Most of my participants were young adults or middle-aged adults. The average age was thirty-five years old, and the oldest participant was sixty-three years old. More than 90 percent of my participants identified themselves as white, with only 2 percent identifying as Native American, and another 2 percent identifying as Asian. The 2 percent of participants who chose to write in their racial category and listed "human" may point to some of the problematic white privilege and blindness present in the Star Wars fandom. As both activists and academic theorists of race point out, refusing to see race and to instead identify as a member of the "human race" strengthens a color-blind ideology that fails to recognize structural racism.[21]

GENDER IN THE STAR WARS FANDOM

The majority of Star Wars fans seem to be men—though to what degree is unclear.[22] In fan studies scholar William Proctor's 2013 study of Star Wars fans before the release of the first movie in Disney's new trilogy, 94 percent of participants were men.[23] In my survey of Star Wars fans, only 72 percent of participants were men, while 23 percent identified as women and 3 percent identified as genderqueer. This difference might be attributed to differences in our nonrandom samples. Two factors might be relevant here. First, my own positionality as a woman seeking participants might have invited or encouraged more women to respond. Second, Proctor and I might have found different samples of the Star Wars fan community because of the different locations we used to circulate our calls for participants. While Proctor and Brooker both solicited participants from discussion boards on TheForce.net exclusively, I circulated a request for participants through Twitter, the Star Wars subreddit, the 501st discussion boards, and a men-tion by a well-known Star Wars podcast, in addition to TheForce.net and my own contacts in the fandom. These differences in sampling procedures might explain a difference in the demographics of the participants, not the Star Wars fandom.

However, the differences in our results might also signal changes in the Star Wars fan community between 2002 and 2013. It is possible that in the five years since Proctor conducted his study and the sixteen years since Brooker conducted his, the Star Wars fandom has changed. In 2002, Brooker argued that Star Wars was largely viewed as a "boys' film," established by alleged quotes from George Lucas himself, the gendered nature of the science fiction genre, and the relegation of women in the story to roles of queens, princesses, and mothers.[24] Brooker is careful to point out that even though the film was often treated as appropriate for boys but not girls, girls and women were nonetheless Star Wars fans. Women Star Wars fans made room for themselves in the Star Wars fan community through the creation of fan sites like Star Wars Chicks and Always Luke. The establishment of these spaces in the 1990s and 2000s may have helped shift community attitudes and demographics by 2017.

Disney, too, might be seen as contributing to this shift. Disney's story for *Episode VII: The Force Awakens* places a woman, Rey, as the main character, hero, and ultimately, heir to the Jedi way of life.[25] However, while Disney recognized the need for a woman main character in the story, it had a hard time recognizing the need for corresponding merchandise for that character. The #wheresrey hashtag pointed out Rey's absence from many of the Star Wars toy sets, which seemed to feature all the characters in the movie but her.[26] Fans and activists pointed out the incorrect assumption that men wouldn't want to buy Rey merchandise and that boys wouldn't want to play with Rey toys. Businesses like Her Universe have emerged as remedies to problems related to women and Star Wars merchandising.[27] Disney's *Star Wars Rebels* (2014–18) animated television show also made room for new women characters in the Star Wars universe, while Disney's *Star Wars Forces of Destiny* dives deeper into the stories of the women characters already part of the Star Wars universe, like Rey, Leia, and Jyn Erso.[28]

These shifting dynamics are felt keenly by fans on the ground, particularly by those who grew up with the original trilogy and now have kids of their own. While Star Wars may have been a boys' movie in the 1980s, today, it seems, there is room for girls and women too. One Star Wars fan named Brad, writing for the blog *Future of the Force*, explains how these dynamics unfold for his own family: "It is because of characters like Ahsoka, Jyn, Sabine, and Hera that my daughters—ages 13 and 10—have no inhibitions about jumping right into 'Jedi versus Sith' in the backyard and not feel weird about it, or not go to school wearing their 'I Rebel' t-shirt and be ashamed of it. It allows my son to feel comfortable opting for the female character [Jyn Erso] in the toy aisle."[29] While Brad may be representative of a growing section of the Star Wars fan community, his attitudes are by no means universal. Brad points to the antifeminist backlash that occurred after the announcement of Disney's *Forces of Destiny Project*. He says, "It looks like we still '*have a long ride ahead of us.*'"[30] One fan in the online, open-ended survey captures this sentiment: "As a female, of course there are always men who think they know more, but for the most part, most Star Wars fans are open to new people."[31] Another fan compares Star Wars fandom to video game fandoms, saying, "It [Star Wars fandom] seems less toxic than most video game fandoms, but I do think it has a very high level of adolescent masculinity associated with the fandom (at least, in the pre-Internet days) and, as a result, has many issues that one would expect from that audience."[32] Another fan identifies "the chauvinistic attitude of some of the male fans, as well as art, comics, and designs that support it" as their least favorite aspect of Star Wars fandom.[33] The role of women in the Star Wars fan community and the Star Wars story remains a contested issue.

DIVERSITY AS BACKGROUND AND FAN INTERESTS

Despite these demographic characteristics and boundaries, Star Wars fans responding to my survey repeatedly affirmed that the Star Wars fan community is welcoming and diverse. Consistently, across the board, Star Wars fans responded to the question, "What are some of the most important things newcomers should know about the Star Wars fan community?" with both "welcoming" and "diverse." What do fans mean by diverse? Who is welcomed?

Some fans seemed to emphasize diversity of life experience and background rather than diversity of social identities like race, gender, or sexuality. One fan explained: "It [the Star Wars fan community] is a very welcoming community. Star Wars fans can be found in all walks of life and every part of the globe."[34] Another says, "I know blue-collar, white-collar, frumpy, sexy, buff, slim, introvert, extrovert, brilliant, less-than-brilliant, asocial, and super-social fans. All kinds, all races, all nationalities. The only trope you can use with us is a general obsession with a 1970s sci-fi series."[35] Star Wars fans envision themselves as being welcoming to people with a wide array of life experiences. Other fans seemed to envision diversity as describing the range of fan interests and practices in the Star Wars fandom. One fan said, "The ways Star Wars fans engage with the saga are diverse (from podcasting to cosplaying to fanfiction writing to R2-building, etc.), but all very creative and community-oriented."[36] Another fan explains that this range of fan practices is one of the most important things newcomers should know: "We all have different areas of Star Wars that we love. Some love to build Lego Star Wars, some love Cosplay, some love the original movies only, some are Clone Wars fanatics but no matter what we all have the same foundation between us."[37] For some, the large size of the Star Wars fan community means that it also permits a wide range of fan practices and interests, creating what they see as diversity in the fandom.

Even as fans overwhelmingly described the Star Wars fandom as welcoming, other fans pointed out that gatekeeping, boundary policing, whiteness, and masculinity are often centered in the Star Wars fandom. First, Star Wars fans point out that newcomers to the fandom should know that gatekeepers exist, but they can be ignored or bypassed. One fan said, "There's a percentage of fans who act as gatekeepers and have a definition of fandom tied to knowledge and actions, like all fandoms" and recommended newcomers "not to let them sour their experience."[38] Another recommended "avoid[ing] those people."[39] Another suggested newcomers should "ignore those fans who are gatekeepers, bullies, and otherwise not inclusive."[40] Still another fan recognized the ways in which the community is simultaneously welcoming and exclusionary:

> Some parts of it [Star Wars fandom] are very welcoming! . . . [S]ome parts of it are not. Take advantage of the welcoming bits, but don't let the unwelcoming bits get you down—mostly they're made up of people you wouldn't want to hang out with anyways. Older fans especially can

be a bit elitist, but no matter which bit of Star Wars brought you in, or which bits are keeping you here, you're valid and you're welcome.[41]

The problem of gatekeepers emerged across questions on the open-ended online survey. Fans listed it as one of the important things newcomers should know and also often listed it as their least favorite part of Star Wars fandom.

While elitist gatekeepers may discourage some fans from joining the Star Wars fan community, racist and misogynist behaviors also serve to police boundaries in the fandom. One fan asserted that their least favorite part of Star Wars fandom is "the internet troll types who are racist and misogynistic. There seems to be too much of that lately in the fandom."[42] Another fan asserted that their least favorite part of Star Wars fandom is "the geek male entitled part of it, to be honest! People who think they own the franchise while sticking to an over-simplistic reading of it, hate on finn and almost every single female lead, and get off on vader's badass charisma (while overlooking the complexity of the character) and leia's slave outfit."[43] Another fan added, "I mean, if I could go the rest of my life without some dude sneering at me that I'm 'not a real fan' that would be great."[44] One fan pointed out how racism and misogyny and Star Wars' welcoming nature exist together: "I've found a lot of welcoming individuals in SW fandom. On the other hand, I have seen appalling bullying, screams of racism on all sides, fights over canon, fights over whether you like Lucas or detest him, whether you like the prequels or you hate them."[45] Indeed, both things seem to be true. Much like many other fandoms, Star Wars fandom as a whole may be welcoming, providing a unique place where discussion of the details of the Star Wars universe is highly valued, but it also contains strains of racism and misogyny at the same time that may serve to create boundaries around its community. While all kinds of people love Star Wars, the Star Wars fan community is largely male and white.

The Presence of a Star Wars Ethical Framework

Questions of values and ethics are at the very heart of fans' beloved Star Wars. George Lucas envisioned Star Wars as a modern myth, capable of providing moral lessons and powerful values to a new generation. In an interview with Bill Moyers in 1999, Moyers asked about author Joseph Campbell's assertion that "all the great myths, the primitive myths, the great stories, have to be regenerated if they're going to have any impact."[46] Moyers asks, "Are you saying, 'I am trying to recreate the myths of old?'" Lucas said, "Well, when I did *Star Wars*, I consciously set about to recreate myths and the classic mythological motifs. And I wanted to use those motifs to deal with issues that existed today."[47] One of Lucas's primary influences was Joseph Campbell, most famous for writing *The Hero with a Thousand Faces*, a book that examines mythology and the heroes within those myths.[48] While contemporary folklore scholars generally dismiss Campbell's writing as simplistic and specious, it gave Lucas what he was looking for: an understanding of the most essential characteristics of the hero and the hero's myth, common across all mythology.[49] Lucas's focus on myth is reflected even in his writing process. While Lucas was writing the script for the first Star Wars film, he would divide his days into two parts: he would write in the morning and would research mythology and fairy tales in the afternoons.[50] In his biography of George Lucas, Dale Pollock quotes Lucas as saying: "I wanted to make a kids' film that would strengthen contemporary mythology and introduce a kind of basic morality. Nobody's saying the very basic things; they're dealing in the abstract. Everybody's forgetting to tell the kids, 'Hey this is right and this is wrong.'"[51] Jen Gunnels argues that this was especially important for Generation X kids growing up in the late 1970s and early 1980s, when the Star Wars movies were coming out. For kids growing up in a time of "rapid values shifts, the breakdown of the nuclear family, and economic upheaval," Star Wars provided a core set of values that kids could use for "navigating a path to adulthood."[52]

For many Star Wars fans, the films have served as the kind of mythology Lucas had hoped they might. Across studies of Star Wars fandom, Star Wars fans describe the ways in which they abstract moral lessons from Star Wars to apply in their own everyday lives. Brooker quotes one fan as saying, "For many, including myself, what occurs in those movies is a personification of what we are all struggling through: forces of good and evil tugging at our mind."[53] Another participant in Brooker's study explains, "Sure, we may not be able to lift droids, rocks or X-Wings, but we could 'use the Force' in other ways such as helping, loving, caring and supporting, and be our own personal Jedi."[54] One participant asserts that Yoda is one of the central sources of those lessons: "Yoda's teachings can easily be spread into your everyday life." Another participant notes how Star Wars taught her "how the 'inner' person matters more than the 'outer' appearance."[55] Still another Star Wars fan explained how Star Wars provided her with a more compelling moral compass than Catholicism: "I think because of my Catholic education, the Force made more sense than this patriarchal deity in heaven. It didn't coalesce into a specific being; it was all around us, as opposed to God, a single entity. I was pig sick of religion and having it rammed down my throat."[56] Even in a study of cosplay, questions of the lessons of Star Wars applied in everyday living came up in interviews. One fan who cosplayed as Obi-Wan explained what aspects of Obi-Wan he brings into his everyday life: "I'd like to think there's a lot, but I could certainly be more noble. I could certainly be a better leader in my own life. But when it comes right down to it . . . I could be a better person in my own life. Probably when I step into costume, into the role, I think I become a better person than I am in real life and could certainly aspire to be as good as Kenobi."[57] For many fans, this is what Star Wars means to them. In a study of Star Wars fans before the release of *Episode VII: The Force Awakens,* one of Proctor's participants asserted that Star Wars "is a universe that has provided a metaphor to teach many important life lessons, such as patience, determination, focus, humility, and compassion."[58] Even Simon Pegg, actor and Star Wars fan, says that Star Wars "informed my notion of morality."[59] Gunnels argues that for some cosplayers with children, Star Wars cosplay may even be a way to "pass on the same myth that enabled them to negotiate their own growth within our culture."[60] Scholars of Star Wars fans make it clear that fans apply, adapt, and integrate Star Wars' ethical lessons into their everyday lives.[61] Star Wars is a text that is both rich enough for ethical frameworks to be extracted and useful enough for those ethical frameworks to be applied to ethical decisions in everyday life.

Components of the Star Wars Ethical Framework

If mythology, ethics, and moral lessons are at the heart of Star Wars, both in terms of the creator's original intentions and in terms of fans' use of Star Wars in their everyday actions, what kind of ethical frameworks does Star Wars offer? In my survey of Star Wars fans, there was less agreement on the central values of the fan-object than I saw in other fan communities like the Huskers or the VlogBrothers. Star Wars fans listed key values like justice, equality, adventure, dignity, balance, teamwork, perseverance, and charity, among many others. Indeed, in response to the question, "What values are most important to Star Wars fans?" one fan noted, "I must admit that question would be easier if you were asking about Star Trek, lol!"[62] Another fan responded: "I honestly don't know. For every fan who believes in the hopeful message of Star Wars, I'll find you another who excuses the crimes of the First Order (mainly Kylo Ren)."[63] Indeed, Brooker argues that "Star Wars has always lent itself to diverse political readings." The Star Wars films, he says, are about "a lot of things and thus nothing specific."[64] Similarly, Henry Jenkins frames Star Wars as "ideologically up for grabs." He says, "For every fan who is outraged by the colonialist fantasies driving Jar Jar Binks, there may be other fans for whom this is a perfect realization of their own reactionary conception of contemporary society."[65]

We might explain this wide variety of possible ethical frameworks in a number of ways. First, there has been little rhetorical work in Star Wars fandom to identify preferred readings and dominant interpretations. As was demonstrated in chapter 1, it takes significant rhetorical work to establish a preferred reading that can be used to extract an ethical framework. In Star Wars fandom, that hasn't been done yet, and so many possible ethical frameworks circulate in the fan community. Second, across three trilogies, offshoot films, television shows, comics, and novels, the Star Wars universe is vast, and that vastness is reflected in the wide range of ethical frameworks available. In an interview with Star Wars fan Jeffrey Cagle, author of the *Imperial Talker* blog, Cagle said that the lessons and themes are "layered a little bit. With Star Wars, I think you can even break it down by different trilogies or different series, or the book series."[66] Third, George Lucas pulled from many of the world's religions to create the Jedi and the Jedi's philosophy of the Force.[67] Lucas explains, "I see *Star Wars* as taking all of the issues that religion represents and trying to distill them down into a more modern and more easily accessible construct that people can grab onto to accept the fact that there is a greater mystery out there."[68] There are entire books about Star Wars and Christianity or Buddhism—titles like *Christian Wisdom of the Jedi* and *The Dharma of Star Wars*.[69] For example, one Star Wars fan points out in a blog post that the Jedi reflect beliefs from the Stoics, the Epicureans, and St. John: that there is a kind of oneness to the Force, that Jedi ought to embrace moderation, and that Jedi must have faith in the Force.[70] Ultimately, Star Wars fans find both a rich text to draw ethical frameworks from and an ethical framework that is complex and flexible, lending itself to a wide range of values, lessons, and tenets.

GOOD VERSUS EVIL

Even among the large number of responses from Star Wars fans, two broad themes emerged: good versus evil and loyalty toward family and friends. At the heart of the Star Wars story is a battle between good and evil. Fans asserted that Star Wars is about "Good over evil,"[71] "Basic good vs. evil,"[72] and "the triumph of good vs. evil."[73] Fans explained that Star Wars is a story of a "big struggle between the oppression of the bad guys" and the attempt by the "good guys to stand up for what is just."[74] We see the good vs. evil theme emerge across the huge timeline in the Star Wars stories: in the rebels' fight against Palpatine and Vader's Empire, the Jedi's fight against the Sith in the Old Republic, and Rey's fight against the First Order. George Lucas speaks to the central role the conflict between good and evil plays in the films: "What these films deal with is the fact that we all have good and evil inside of us and that we can choose which way we want the balance to go."[75]

George Lucas's quote above also speaks to the complexity of the Star Wars story—that the lines between good and evil are both clearly drawn and fuzzy at the same time, that good both triumphs over evil and seeks balance with evil. For example, Darth Vader is clearly evil in the original trilogy, but his movement from good to evil is filled with many little steps, and in the end, he finds some redemption for himself by dying while protecting his son, Luke. Brooker finds this tension between the triumph of good and evil and the balance between the two in his analysis of the first Star Wars film, *A New Hope*.[76] Brooker argues that Lucas draws the lines between good and evil clearly, signaled through a carefully crafted aesthetic established through color, shots, and film styles: the Rebels and their ships are dirty and often rely on improvisation at the last minute whereas the Empire is orderly, black, white, clean, and shiny. Brooker explains, "Already, then, we can see that the fable of Star Wars allows for considerable ambiguity and movement between its polar oppositions, as signified through the relationship between the two aesthetics."[77] Brooker asserts that in this "supposedly clear-cut conflict between good and evil, Lucas is rooting for both sides."[78] The Star Wars story dives deep into both sides of the good and evil conflict. In Star Wars Legends, there are entire books about the rise of the Sith and Imperial military leaders, such as Admiral Thrawn and Darth Vader. Star Wars fans parse out what makes these characters bad, how they got there, and what choices they made along the way. For Star Wars fans, much of the fun is in finding the gray areas in what appear as either good or bad actions and good or bad characters. Ultimately, Star Wars presents a compelling story about right versus wrong and complexity within gray areas.

Loyalty toward family and friends is a second possible tenet of a Star Wars ethical framework. Fans explained this tenet by pointing to the importance of "camaraderie,"[79] "love for others,"[80] "friendship, loyalty, trust,"[81] and "togetherness."[82] In his interview with Bill Moyers, George Lucas identifies friendship as a key part of the Star Wars myth: "The importance of, say, friendship and loyalty. Most people look at that and say, 'How corny.' But the issues of friendship and loyalty are very, very important to the way we live our lives. But it's not common knowledge among young people. They're still learning. They're still picking up ideas. They're still using these ideas to shape the way they're gonna conduct their life."[83] Loyalty in family and friendship is at the heart of the Star Wars story for both George Lucas and fans.

An emphasis on loyalty in family and friendship occurs throughout the films, television shows, and novels. *A New Hope* is a story of Luke finding family and friends in Leia, Han, Obi-Wan Kenobi, and R2D2 after the Empire kills the aunt and uncle who raised him. In *The Empire Strikes Back,* Han risks his life to go looking for Luke, who went missing while on patrol on the ice planet, Hoth. Both Han and Luke nearly freeze to death. Even in the numerous Star Wars Legends novels that tell the story of Luke, Leia, and Han after the Rebels defeat the Empire, loyalty to each other is central to their stories. Han, Leia, and Luke support and rescue each other and their Rebel friends time and time again. In *Fate of the Jedi: Outcast,* Han and Leia head to Kessel to help Lando with earthquakes that are threatening his business and the entire planet, even though they had promised each other they would retire and stop trying to rescue the rest of the galaxy.[84] Ultimately, loyalty to a friend in need guides their actions.

The new characters in Disney's animated television show *Rebels* follow the same logic, building family and friends and prioritizing loyalty to those friends and family. In *Rebels,* Kanan Jarrus and Herra Syndulla gather a group of misfits who have all lost their own families: Ezra Bridger's parents were killed by the Empire, Sabine Wren was disowned by her own family, and Zeb Orrelios lost his family to genocide committed by the Empire. In the third season, Sabine is faced with a choice of becoming the leader of her home world, which would mean leaving Kanan, Herra, Ezra, and Zeb. Kanan reminds Sabine that the crew of the *Ghost* is her family: "You've come a long way in a very short time. Where you go from here is up to you. But know: this family will stand by you no matter what you choose."[85] Ezra's character is largely defined by his transition from someone who "felt no loyalty to others"[86] (as he spent his time stealing to survive) to a key member of the budding Rebels, committed to the Force and opposed to the Empire.

This emphasis on loyalty is reflected in the workings of the Force as well. One fan explained the difference between the light and dark side of the Force by saying, "Light is about others, dark is about yourself."[87] The emotions that lead to the dark side—fear, hate, and anger—all point to a lack of community, family, and safety in those relationships. Indeed, Anakin turns to the dark side because of his fear of losing Padme. In his 1999 interview with Bill Moyers, George Lucas identifies friendship and "your obligation to your fellow man and to other people that are around you" as one of the themes he was trying to include into his Star Wars myth.[88]

Loyalty in family and friendship and the triumph of good over evil are two of the most agreed-upon Star Wars ethical framework tenets, but others are certainly available to rhetors. Rhetors could certainly invoke ethical frameworks about teamwork, tyranny, and guerrilla tactics, among many others. Yet, as the next section will show, Omaze, UNICEF, and Disney chose not to use any Star Wars ethical framework in the Force for Change campaign at all. Rather, the Force for Change campaign utilized an absent pairing: a civic ethical modality and a Star Wars ethical framework that were never paired.

An Absent Pairing: The 2014–2015 Star Wars Force for Change

Omaze was founded in 2012 explicitly for the purpose of serving major celebrities and brands in their charity fund-raising efforts. At the core of Omaze is a commitment to the once-in-a-lifetime fan experience—whether that's a picnic with Jennifer Lawrence or dodgeball with Ben Stiller. But Omaze's fund-raisers don't auction off these once-in-a-lifetime chances; rather, they utilize a raffle system. Fans can earn a higher probability of winning with more donations, but the chance to win is available to almost any fan (ten dollars is often the required donation for one entry into the raffle). On their website, Omaze pitches their approach to celebrity fund-raising this way: "You get the chance to live your dream experience, influencers support the causes they're passionate about, and charities can spend less time fundraising, and more time making an impact."[89]

The Star Wars Force for Change campaign emerged out of relationships Ryan Cummins, cofounder of Omaze, had with philanthropic firms, philanthropists, and charities, including Rebecca Rottenberg Goldman, executive director of the Katie McGrath & J. J. Abrams Family Foundation. Goldman had been talking with J. J. Abrams and his wife, Katie McGrath, about how the Foundation might leverage some of Abrams's most famous projects through Omaze. When Abrams got word that he was selected to direct the first Disney Star Wars film, they knew this would be the perfect fit. McGrath reportedly told her husband, "If you are going to be the shepherd for the biggest sci-fi franchise of all time, you need to do something good with it."[90] J. J. Abrams and his team brokered the partnership with Disney and Lucasfilm, while Omaze created all the content and ran the public relations for the campaign.

During the first Star Wars Force for Change campaign in 2014–15, fans were given the chance to win a role in *Star Wars Episode VII: The Force Awakens*. For every ten-dollar donation, a fan was entered once into the raffle. The Force for Change campaign also offered a number of rewards fans could earn by making donations at particular levels. The rewards ranged from a Force for Change T-shirt for a donation of one hundred dollars to a personal screening of the *Star Wars Episode VII* movie ahead of the premiere date for fifty thousand dollars. These prizes helped the Force for Change campaign earn wide coverage in the Star Wars fan community.

More than 87 percent of the fans who participated in my online survey said that they had heard of and seen the Force for Change campaign. Nearly 60 percent of participants saw it featured on a Star Wars fan website. A few others saw it on the news, found out through a friend, or saw it somewhere online. Almost half of my participants reported that they participated in the Force for Change campaign by either donating money or sharing the link to the campaign with other people. One fan explained that the Force for Change campaign "made me donate money to a cause I wouldn't have otherwise."[91] By the end of the campaign, the Force for Change campaign raised more than $4.26 million for UNICEF. While the Force for Change campaign raised a remarkable amount of money, the effort had little connection to public culture.

LACKING A PAIRING STRATEGY

The 2014–15 Force for Change campaign did little to pair the Star Wars ethical framework to the ethical modality of donating to UNICEF. The online videos the campaign created did nothing more than announce the campaign's prizes. Even in videos made by J. J. Abrams, the director of *Episode VII: The Force Awakens*, there are no connections between UNICEF and Star Wars. While the website offers a few connections, I argue that even these are only brief, surface-level connections that fail to pair a Star Wars ethical framework to a UNICEF ethical modality, ensuring that the Force for Change had little bearing on supporting UNICEF or the public problems UNICEF works to solve. The first paragraph of text on the website reads:

> Star Wars continues to inspire generations of dreamers and doers to use their creativity to do great things. Between what is now and what can be lies innovation—the triumph of human ingenuity combined with advances in science and technology. Star Wars and Lucasfilm were built on a belief in this tenet, by combining creativity with innovation you can make the impossible now possible.[92]

The campaign seems to be trying to point out that Star Wars was the result of George Lucas's innovation and creativity in special effects. The fact that UNICEF labs try to be innovative and creative too comes across as mere coincidence. Simply identifying a commonality is not enough to pair a Star Wars ethical framework with a civic ethical modality. Indeed, many things may be innovative, but that does not necessarily mean that they are relevant to Star Wars fans just because Star Wars was innovative too. This paragraph of text fails to tell us anything about what Star Wars fans should do, why they should do it, or who they should support.

The second paragraph on the website tries to point to our connectedness across the globe as a reason to participate in the Force for Change campaign:

> As Jedi Master Obi-Wan Kenobi once said, "The Force is an energy field created by all living things. It surrounds us. It penetrates us. It binds the galaxy together." Dedicated to finding creative solutions to some of the world's biggest problems, Force for Change captures the power of innovation to make a positive impact in our global community.[93]

The campaign's mixed metaphors fail to make clear the connection between the Star Wars story and UNICEF's civic issue. Does the Force bind us together like our global community binds us together? Or is the Force the power we use to solve global problems? Is the Force the power of innovation? And who wields the Force? Is UNICEF taking on the role of the Jedi using the Force for good? Or are we Jedi as we donate money? Or is the power of our donations like the power of the Force? The campaign seems to be forcing a tie-in, suggesting two commonalities without fully drawing out their connections for fans and without any clear calls to action based on those commonalities.

The Force for Change ends these two paragraphs on their website with this sentence: "Join us and together we can harness the power of the Force to make a difference around the world."[94] This is a reference to Darth Vader's famous line in *Star Wars Episode V: The Empire Strikes Back* in which Vader tries to draw his son, Luke, to the dark side of the Force. He says, "Join me, and together, we can rule the galaxy as father and son!" The campaign's replacement of Vader's "Join me" with UNICEF's "Join us" invites fans to see UNICEF as Vader and to resist the temptation to agree to "make a difference in the world." The Force for Change's reference fails to properly align the ethical framework of Star Wars with the ethical modality of charity giving, offering only parallels that are counterintuitive and metaphors that contradict one another across the campaign. This reference indicates that the Force for Change sought surface-level tie-ins, using Star Wars as a theme, rather than carefully and deliberately pairing the ethical framework of Star Wars with the ethical modality of UNICEF with any consistency.

The bottom section of the Force for Change website shows an image of Princess Leia picking up an Ewok with the words, "Join us in creating a brighter tomorrow for kids and families around the world" overlaid across the image.[95] The image and its text have little relation to each other—indeed, the image is unrelated to kids or families. The Ewok that Leia is picking up is not a child at all. In *Episode VI: The Return of the Jedi*, Han Solo, Princess Leia, and Luke Skywalker land on Endor in an attempt to take out the shield generator that is protecting the nearby Death Star that the Empire is rebuilding. While trekking through the forest, Luke, Leia, and Han meet the Ewoks, an alien race who look like three-foot-tall teddy bears. The Ewoks initiate Luke, Leia, and Han into their tribe and then save the three rebels when Stormtroopers discover them trying to destroy the shield generator. The Ewoks are anything but helpless children; rather they are capable adult fighters working alongside the Rebels. If the Ewoks are not the children referenced in the text, they may represent distant or foreign peoples around the world. But that metaphor may be more troubling than compelling. The Ewoks appear to have a tribal culture without much advanced technology: they wear feathers and use only spears for defense. If we are invited to imagine the Ewoks as representing the kids and families that UNICEF helps, then we are imagining UNICEF's beneficiaries as primitive peoples in undeveloped worlds. Across each aspect of its campaign website, the Force for Change ends up drawing connections with little consistency or drawing connections with problematic implications.

Fan-Based Appeals in the Force for Change Campaign

The Force for Change campaign's failure to pair a Star Wars ethical framework to a civic modality isn't easily attributable to the nature of the Star Wars text or fandom. Rather, it might be more accurate to say that the campaign organizers of the Force for Change failed to take advantage of the richness of the Star Wars text. While Star Wars has many potential ethical frameworks that could be usefully applied to UNICEF actions, the Force for Change campaign chooses not to anchor its appeals in those frameworks. This is an important rhetorical choice. Without pairing the Star Wars ethical framework to a charity ethical modality, the Star Wars Force for Change campaign fails to make a civic appeal. Instead, the Force for Change campaign relies solely on fan appeals—that is, the campaign invites fans to participate in order to be good fans.

Through participation, fans can demonstrate their status as good fans by demonstrating their knowledge of the Star Wars content world and being good collectors by acquiring new items. The Force for Change offers fans a chance to acquire merchandise, collectibles, and fan experiences they can't get anywhere else. Anna Silverman, a staff member at Omaze, explains in an interview: "We're offering fans a chance to engage with their heroes. And for a lot of people that feels priceless."[96] The only way for a fan to get a chance to experience the making of Star Wars Episode VII is by winning the Force for Change contest. Even the Force for Change Star Wars T-shirts are exclusive to the campaign—one-time offers. Thus, the Force for Change campaign invites fans to participate in the campaign in order to be good fans by being good collectors. Good fans maintain their collections, slowly adding on and taking advantage of one-time offers. If Star Wars fans want to be a part of this particular moment in Star Wars history, they'd better buy the T-shirt. For fans who want to own as many Star Wars items as their budgets will allow, this campaign provides them new items to purchase.

The campaign also invited fans to participate in order to be good, knowledgeable fans. The videos J. J. Abrams shot for the campaign were shot on the set for Star Wars Episode VII, and as such, gave fans a much-desired glimpse into the making of the film. Prior to Abrams's videos for the Force for Change campaign, information about the upcoming movies had been severely limited. As a result, fans discussed and dissected at great length the small glimpses of the movie set, costumes, and story lines Abrams's videos gave them. This is an important practice within fan communities. Brooker argues that fan communities have an impressive ability to "detect, speculate, and piece together rumors from whatever scraps they can get their hands on," even months before a trailer might be released.[97] The Star Wars fandom has a tradition of speculation about upcoming movie releases: Fans gather evidence from scraps of paper, scanned storyboards, and rumors, and they cross-reference such information across their large community.[98] For Star Wars fans, speculation about the next movie is serious business, and indeed, fans have demonstrated that they are quite skilled in this task. In the case of the Force for Change, speculation about the upcoming movie overshadowed the civic aspects of the campaign. By providing highly desired bits of information about the upcoming movie, the Force for Change campaign videos prompt discussion of the fan-object, not of public issues. Indeed, Anna Silverman explained in an interview that "the videos with J. J. Abrams were far and away the biggest drivers."[99]

In Abrams's first video announcing the Force for Change,[100] fans speculated that the set he was speaking from would most likely be the set for the planet Tatooine, giving fans some broad sense of where the movie might take place.[101] In the middle of the campaign, Abrams released a second video announcing a surprise reward, a chance to win an advance private screening of the movie.[102] In the video, Abrams is again speaking on the Star Wars film set, though this time he is standing in front of an X-Wing, a spaceship used in earlier Star Wars films. Fans compared this version of an X-Wing with the version from earlier Star Wars movies, noting that the plane now had a "uni-engine design."[103] The Force for Change campaign announced the winner through a tweet put out by the production company Bad Robot. The tweet was an image of a handwritten note from Abrams that said thank you to all who participated, but in the image, a robotic hand held the note. Fans speculated, "Is this Abrams' way of confirming the rumored plot involving Luke Skywalker's severed hand?"[104] Each video gave fans new information about the movie, and, as a result, the Force for Change videos garnered significant circulation with 2.1 million and 3.1 million views on YouTube, respectively. Thus, while the Force for Change generated significant discussion of Star Wars, it generated little discussion of UNICEF. Without a pairing between the Star Wars ethical framework and the UNICEF ethical modality, there was little incentive for fans to pay attention to UNICEF at all.

This emphasis on increasing fan knowledge of the Star Wars universe and the upcoming movies was further strengthened by Stephen Colbert and Jon Stewart's video for the campaign.[105] In classic Stewart and Colbert style, the two-and-a-half-minute video is packed with joke after joke and garnered nearly two million views on YouTube. The video begins with Stephen Colbert discovering the Force for Change campaign through an email and then calling Jon Stewart to share the exciting news about the possibility of winning the chance to be in the next Star Wars movie. Jon Stewart is excited because, as he says to Stephen Colbert, "I'm the biggest Star Wars fan in the world!" Colbert asserts that actually *he* is the biggest fan in the world, and the two decide to settle their disagreement with a trivia contest. The rest of the video is spent with the two trying to one-up each other on trivia questions, fighting each other with lightsabers, and making references to the Star Wars movies. While the video is entertaining and rather funny, it does nothing to make a civic appeal and instead reinforces the Force for Change campaign's appeal to audience members to be good fans by being knowledgeable about the Star Wars universe.

THE 2015–2017 FORCE FOR CHANGE CAMPAIGNS

Since the initial 2014–15 Force for Change campaign, Disney and Lucasfilm have launched another three campaigns, offering fans opportunities to visit Lucas's own Skywalker Ranch, attend the Star Wars Celebration in London with Mark Hamill, or attend the red-carpet premiere of *Episode VIII: The Last Jedi*. The rest of these campaigns have continued to find the success the first campaign did. In total, the Force for Change has raised more than $10 million for a wide range of charities, doing work internationally and in the US. Across the subsequent Force for Change campaigns, Disney and Lucasfilm have doubled down on their strategy of fan-based appeals. The Force for Change website doesn't present statistics, a fact sheet, or even images of the charity work being done. It presents only a background picture of a lightsaber being handed off, with three graphics: "pledge," "share your story," and "donate." The public issues are literally left off and obscured. Since 2015, the structure of the Force for Change campaign has continued to offer very few opportunities to engage with charities and the public issues they work on. For example, on the 2017 version of the Force for Change website, the "Take Action" page includes only a short, generic pledge: "Our mission is to improve the lives of children around the world. To do that, we want to empower everyone to be forces for change in their own communities. Your mission starts here. To pledge, select your location and watch the power of change illuminate the world!"[106]

At every turn, the Force for Change campaign materials invite fans to dive deeper into Star Wars rather than public issues. For example, at the end of each Force for Change video, there are links to and previews of other related Star Wars videos, including a button to subscribe to the Star Wars YouTube channel, links to get the Star Wars app, and previews of three other YouTube videos, all about the Force for Change or Star Wars more generally. On one video, the three related videos that are linked at the end include the announcement of a new Star Wars Force for Change campaign, the Rogue One teaser trailer, and a video about filmmakers judging fan films— not a single video about the public issue at hand.[107] Disney and Lucasfilm revealed this logic even more clearly in the 2017 Force for Change fundraising campaign that corresponded with the fortieth anniversary of Star Wars. In the video launch for the campaign, Mark Hamill says: "For forty years, you've been the best fans in the world, bringing the franchise to life in ways we never could have imagined. And now it's our chance to celebrate you."[108] Disney and Lucasfilm framed this 2017 Force for Change campaign as a way to say thank you to fans rather than as any kind of civic engagement. Of course, thank-yous and once-in-a-lifetime-chances to interact with fan-objects are desirable in their own right. But Disney and Lucasfilm made the choice to prioritize fan engagement with Star Wars over any kind of political mobilization or public issue education.

FAN REACTIONS TO THE FORCE FOR CHANGE CAMPAIGNS

Fan reactions to the Force for Change reflect this focus on fan experiences rather than any kind of pairing of Star Wars and public issues. Fans generally recognized that UNICEF was a good cause, but none of the fan comments in my survey spoke to the public issues in which UNICEF sought to intervene. Most of my survey participants called the campaign a "great idea",[109] "awesome,"[110] "brilliant,"[111] and "a good cause."[112] Fans' comments reflected the Force for Change campaign's focus on interaction with the Star Wars fan-object. One fan said, "I am interested in having a real chance of winning,"[113] while another noted that the "rewards are awesome."[114] Another fan praised this aspect of the campaign specifically: "[I] love the idea that a kind donation can get you an opportunity that every SW [Star Wars] fan has dreamed of."[115] Indeed, the rewards were motivating for fans.

One fan explained, "The involvement of actors made it seem more human rather than just a brand associating itself with a charity name, and I imagine the unique collectables would be a big incentive for some."[116] Another fan said, "It also makes people feel good watching people like Mark Hamill or John Boyega surprise random fans during the current campaign."[117] For these fans, the Force for Change was an incredible opportunity to interact with their fan-object, reflecting the fan-based appeals the Force for Change campaign made.

Even while the Force for Change campaign offered fans highly valued opportunities to interact with their fan-object, that didn't stop fans from recognizing the advantages the campaign accrued for Disney. A few fans were cautious about the motives or impacts a major corporation like Disney might have. One participant said, "When a multibillion dollar company starts asking for money I wonder what they do with their own to begin with,"[118] while another pointed out that the Force for Change campaign means "Disney gets a tax break."[119] Another asserted that the campaign felt "very corporate" and felt like a "marketing grab hiding behind the mask of a charitable foundation."[120] Yet for many fans, this was not a deterrent. Recognizing that Disney is launching the campaign in the hope of garnering good press does not negate the fact that the Force for Change campaign is the only way fans have a chance to be in the next Star Wars movie.

While the Force for Change may not have successfully paired a Star Wars ethical framework with a UNICEF charity civic modality, some fans may have done that rhetorical work for Disney and Lucasfilm. One fan explains, "I participated because SW [Star Wars] gives people a real sense of hope and optimism, especially with the recent political climate, so I wanted to be able to involve myself with a positive cause."[121] While the Force for Change hardly mentioned hope at all, this fan saw a commitment to hope in the Star Wars story and in UNICEF's mission, pairing a Star Wars ethical framework with a UNICEF charity ethical modality.

OMAZE, DISNEY, AND LUCASFILM AS CIVIC ACTORS

One reason Omaze can get away with a lack of connection between the fan-object and the public issue is their close ties to industry creators. Because Omaze is partnering with Lucasfilm and J. J. Abrams, they have a remarkable number of prizes and merchandise to give away: visits to the set, inside information, and merchandise with official Star Wars licensing. These prizes make the "ultimate fan experience" frame easy for Lucasfilm, Disney, and Abrams to invoke. Grassroots fan campaigns don't have those same resources—the Harry Potter Alliance can't give away a chance to visit the set of *Fantastic Beasts and Where to Find Them*. Thus, the "ultimate fan experience" frame is not available in the same way to these grassroots fan groups. Without access to exclusive prizes and once-in-a-lifetime fan experiences, grassroots fan groups have to find other ways to persuade fans to participate in civic activities. Most often, this is a pairing between fan-based ethical frameworks and civic ethical modalities.

Silverman points out that Omaze isn't opposed to stronger connections between their celebrities and their public issues—in fact, Omaze is looking for ways to strengthen those connections in future campaigns. Silverman explains, "I think that we see a huge opportunity to create a more seamless integration between the cause and the celebrity; sometimes they are very disjointed."[122] The research in this book demonstrates that Omaze's goal is certainly possible. Cases like the Harry Potter Alliance, the Project for Awesome, and the Husker Coaches Challenge show that fan-objects can be connected to public issues in powerful ways when fan-based ethical frameworks are paired with civic ethical modalities.

Conclusion: Absent Pairing and Disengagement from Public Culture

The Force for Change campaign as a whole does little to engage public culture, offering neither discussion of civic issues nor engagement between citizens. Without pairing the Star Wars ethical framework to a civic ethical modality (donations to UNICEF), there is no connection to public culture at all. There is little difference between buying a Star Wars T-shirt from Disney and buying a Star Wars T-shirt from the Force for Change online campaign store. Fans are invited to buy the T-shirt for the same reasons. Knowing that the money is going to charity does not change the reason for the purchase: acquiring Star Wars items.

By providing fans with desired information about the upcoming Star Wars movie through the Force for Change videos and by providing fans with collectible merchandise and a chance to be part of the story they love so much, the Force for Change might be said to enrich fan culture. However, it does little to enrich public culture, instead relying on appeals to fans' desire to be knowledgeable about their fan-object and to be good collectors. While the Force for Change raised a remarkable amount of money, the political role it played for citizens and the public discussion of problems UNICEF tries to solve was minimal. The Force for Change may have been fun for fans, but without pairing a popular culture ethical framework with a civic ethical modality, it did little to enrich public culture or the civic lives of fans. As a case of civic failure, the Force for Change campaign highlights how fan-based citizenship performances may or may not impact public culture: the crux is the pairing of the fan-based ethical framework and the civic ethical modality.

CONCLUSION

FAN-BASED CITIZENSHIP PERFORMANCES AND THE FUTURE OF PUBLIC ENGAGEMENT

When Anny Rusk woke up to the news that Donald Trump had won the 2016 presidential election, she was crushed. She had been a staunch Hillary Clinton supporter and had long dreamed of electing a woman president who might prioritize women's rights. Anny gave herself the next day to mourn—to be sad before turning her attention to what actions she could take to create social change during Trump's term.[1] Like many Americans, Anny said that the results of the 2016 presidential election functioned as a call to action for her: "Having this man in office is galvanizing me, and I hope the rest of us, who have become complacent in certain areas."[2] Within a week, Anny had joined the Order of 1460, a Facebook group whose mission was to do one positive thing every day during Trump's presidency. It was there that Anny learned about the Harry Potter Alliance (HPA).

Anny was immediately hooked by the HPA's combination of fantasy and activism. But with the nearest chapter an hour south of the North Side of Chicago where she lived, Anny decided to start her own chapter. She quickly tapped into her network of writers, librarians, and teachers and soon gathered seven other people who also felt crushed by Trump's win and were looking for ways to create positive change. One collaborator, Christina, felt devastated after the election and wanted to take action to leave a better world for the next generation.[3] Another collaborator was looking for a counterbalance to her pro-Trump, conservative work environment.[4] Most of the chapter members were "not thrilled with the election," and as librarians and children's literature writers, they saw great power in stories to create social change.[5] With all of this in mind, they named their Harry Potter Alliance community chapter the Patronuses after the charm in the Harry Potter stories that is cast to drive away the Dementors. Leanne, another member of the Patronuses, explains that the Patronus is "this beautiful thing from your best self. The Patronus is created from love and your most wonderful memory and it's protective. It's to fight off the darkness."[6] Within the first six months, the chapter had already run two campaigns. For fan-citizens like Anny, Leanne, and Christina, fan-based citizenship functioned as an important way to enact activism and civic engagement in the Trump era. Anny put it this way: "If there were no Trump, there would be no Patronuses."[7]

That Anny, Leanne, and Christina turned to fan-based citizenship as a way to counterbalance Trump's policies should not be surprising. The research in this book demonstrates that fan-based citizenship performances can be remarkably meaningful and powerful in a digital and fluid world. Fan-based citizenship performances like those of the Patronuses are made possible by a fluid world that enables individuals to easily choose among institutions for membership, identity, and values. This fluidity of institutional choice requires new theoretical terms: ethical framework and ethical modality. I defined *ethical framework* as a worldview or a frame of understanding based on an ethic that is theoretical and all-encompassing. I defined an *ethical modality* as a way of meeting an ethical obligation to the ethical framework. Institutions typically *pair* preferred ethical modalities with ethical frameworks. But with a fluid world's increased choice among institutions, such pairings can become unpaired. In cases of fan-based citizenship performances, fans unpair typical political ethical frameworks from modalities (like Democratic Party ideology from fair trade) and re-pair noncivic ethical frameworks (like Harry Potter) with civic ethical modalities (like fair trade petitions and alternative products).

The cases of the TeamMates' Coaches Challenge, the Nerdfighters' Project for Awesome, and Greenpeace's #SavetheArctic #BlockShell campaign demonstrate how unpairing ethical frameworks from modalities opens up new possibilities for citizenship performances, even across vastly different fan communities. In their Coaches Challenge campaign, TeamMates invited local community members to volunteer to mentor youth in schools by *connecting*, drawing parallels, links, and metaphors between the Huskers and volunteering to mentor. Drawing on an ethical framework of being neighborly, working hard, and staying down-to-earth, TeamMates called upon Nebraskans to join the Husker team and beat their rivals. While TeamMates used *connecting* as a strategy to pair a popular culture ethical framework with a civic ethical modality, the VlogBrothers used *expanding* as their central rhetorical strategy. In the Project for Awesome, John and Hank expanded the Nerdfighteria ethical framework to include not only noncivic modalities like fan activities but also civic modalities like donating money, deliberating about public issues, and discussing the efficacy of charities to solve global and local problems. In addition to *connecting* and *expanding*, the case of the Greenpeace LEGO campaign illustrated a third rhetorical strategy to pair fan-based ethical frameworks with civic ethical modalities: *retelling*. In their video, Shell's oil literally drowned the LEGO world, destroying the creativity and imagination at the center of the LEGO toys and community. By retelling the story of *The LEGO Movie*, Greenpeace showed the threat Shell posed to the LEGO ethical framework. Nerdfighteria, TeamMates, and Greenpeace illustrate three different rhetorical strategies that pair fan-based ethical frameworks with civic ethical modalities: *connecting, expanding,* and *retelling*. These rhetorical strategies tie fandom (Huskers, the VlogBrothers, and LEGO) to civic actions, making fandom relevant and applicable to public issues.

The LEGO and Star Wars case studies point to threats that have the potential to nullify the connection between fandom and public culture, even when civic actions emerge. In the LEGO case study, we saw how an effective pairing of a LEGO ethical framework with a Greenpeace ethical modality can come undone when that ethical modality contradicts fans' commitments to their fan-object, LEGO. Fan-based civic appeals must be undergirded by a love of the fan-object. The case of Greenpeace's LEGO campaign demonstrates that for fans, love of the fan-object comes first. The case of the Star Wars Force for Change campaign illustrates a second barrier to fan-based citizenship performances: absent or weak pairings. The Star Wars Force for Change campaign featured absent pairings that failed to strengthen public culture. While the Star Wars Force for Change campaign raised a significant amount of money, it did so through noncivic appeals and fan ties rather than any connection to public culture. Both the Greenpeace LEGO case and the Star Wars UNICEF case demonstrate ways in which fan-based citizenship performances may appear to be quite successful but in the end fail to engage either fans (like LEGO) or public culture (like Star Wars). Ultimately, all of the cases in this book are important not only because of the way they help us envision fans as political actors but also for what they tell us about public culture. In the rest of the conclusion, I point out four major implications this book offers for research on fandom, citizenship, and the internet.

The Shape of Public Culture Today

One of the central implications of this book is that fan-based citizenship is an important part of public culture today—to ignore fan-based citizenship would be to ignore a central part of contemporary public culture. Indeed, scholars across political science, communication, journalism, and rhetoric have noted that citizenship is changing. As our world has become networked, digital, and fluid, citizens have developed new civic practices suited to shifting methods of circulation, identification, and public formation. Fan-based citizenship performances have emerged as one of those new civic practices. By connecting popular culture ethical frameworks with civic ethical modalities, fan-based civic appeals invite fans to see themselves as citizens and public subjects, as public beings with a stake in public life. Indeed, political subjectivity is a process, and fandom offers a particular path through which individuals can come to see themselves as connected to citizenship, civic engagement, and social movement activism.[8] Cases like the Harry Potter Alliance, TeamMates, and the Project for Awesome all demonstrate that fandom can open up additional entries to public culture.

The integration of fan-based citizenship in public culture is part of a broader shift toward what Henry Jenkins, Joseph Kahne, Ellen Middaugh, and Danielle Allen call participatory politics, the political version of participatory cultures.[9] If participatory cultures are communities of folks, often online, in which there are relatively low barriers to entry, an emphasis on creation and production and "some type of informal mentorship" that unfolds in horizontal, nonhierarchical ways, then participatory politics occurs when those groups of people turn their attention to political goals, applying the practices built up in their participatory cultures toward political ends.[10] Participatory politics is ultimately social and interactive, peer-based and cooperative, and nonhierarchical and separate from elite institutions and actors.[11] Henry Jenkins, Sangita Shresthova, Liana Gamber-Thompson, Neta Kligler-Vilenchik, and Arley Zimmerman point to charities like Invisible Children, movements like the DREAMers, and organizations like the Harry Potter Alliance as cases of participatory politics.[12] Fan-based citizenship is part of the bigger shift in young people's political lives, away from elite institutions with passive audiences and toward participatory cultures with active audiences.

Across sports, YouTube, movies, books, and toys, fans can be powerful political actors when fan-based civic appeals are made. Whether fan communities are predominantly teenagers, young men, middle-aged women, or local families, fan-based civic appeals can carry immense persuasive power, grounded in fan identifications and the ethical obligations those carry. The four cases selected for this project are not unique in their ability to connect popular culture with civic action in powerful ways. Harry Potter, the Huskers, the VlogBrothers, LEGO, and Star Wars are not exceptional. Rather, many fan groups cultivate the deep, affective fan identifications and the complex ethical frameworks from popular culture fan-objects necessary for fan-based citizenship performances. This book demonstrates that fan-based citizenship performances are increasingly emerging as an important part of our public culture.

Online Communities Ground Citizenship Performances

Another implication emerging from the research in this book is that online communities are increasingly serving as a source of community, public values, and ultimately, citizenship performances. For example, we saw how fair-trade activism emerged out of the online Harry Potter fan community while charity donations and public issue deliberation emerged out of the VlogBrothers online community. These online communities are rich and robust sources of social interaction for fans—rich and robust enough to give rise to civic community to such a degree that we might say that fan communities take on the function of Jürgen Habermas's coffeehouses and John Dewey's local communities that are essential for the emergence of publics.[13] Simply put, fan communities provide the grounding, anchoring, and strong ties essential for public action.[14]

The cases in this book demonstrate that online communities are important not just for the affiliations or the organizational structures they offer but also for the ways in which public values (through the form of ethical frameworks) emerge. As citizens disengage from traditional sources of civic belonging, scholars might be apt to wonder where citizens are getting their political values from, if not from these traditional sources. Part of the answer might be online communities. Online communities are increasingly grounding public action—that is, they increasingly serve as the source of public values, warrants, and social truths used and invoked in rhetorical exchanges and artifacts. Ultimately, online fan communities function as an important part of public culture, serving as sources of values, identity, and a sense of public self.

Racism, Belonging, and Implications for Civic Action

The third implication coming out of the research in this book concerns the limits of the civic activities of predominantly white fandoms. Indeed, many of the fan communities discussed in this book are predominantly white, and some even struggle to create a welcoming environment for people of color. Nerdfighteria, Star Wars fandom, LEGO fandom, and the Huskers are predominantly white.[15] This has two major implications: it affects who can be a fan and thus who can be a citizen, and it affects the kinds of civic actions a fan community deems worthy or important.

Fan studies scholar Rukmini Pande argues that while fandom is often "theorized as inclusive and liberating," fan communities "are not immune to hierarchies structured by privilege accruing to income, class, racial, ethnic, and cultural identity, disability, etc."[16] In predominantly white fan communities, fans of color (FOC) experience microaggressions from other fans, the burden of educating white fans about fanworks that are racist, and boundary policing that makes it difficult to find belonging in these fan communities. The result is that predominantly white fan communities can easily replicate already existing power structures, making fans of color "feel unwelcome" as Henry Jenkins argues,[17] creating a community space that is "inaccessible or inhospitable" for members of marginalized groups as Suzanne Scott argues,[18] and positioning "an investment in whiteness" as "foundational to some groups of fans" as Rebecca Wanzo argues.[19] This affects who gets to be a fan, and, in the case of fan-based citizenship, who gets to be a citizen. Fan-based citizenship has the opportunity to offer new pathways to citizenship. For folks who aren't invited into the local Elks club, who don't fit into the Republican Party, or who don't see themselves reflected in the Catholic Church, fan-based citizenship offers an additional pathway into politics: fandom. The productive potential of that pathway can be minimized if the same hierarchies that structure our political parties, churches, and civic organizations structure our fan communities too. Fan-based citizenship has the potential to connect people to politics in powerful ways, but we ought to make sure we're not just offering new pathways for the same people.

The racial demographics of predominantly white fandoms affect not only who gets to be a fan and citizen but also the kinds of civic actions a fan community deems important and thus which public issues are worthy of action. For example, the nerdfighters' Project for Awesome features a wide range of public issues each year, including humane societies, clean water projects, foodbanks, libraries, and many more. But there are few racial justice nonprofits or activist organizations featured during the Project for Awesome. This betrays the bias of a predominantly white fan community: fans choose to focus on issues like clean water and foodbanks rather than racial justice. While the Project for Awesome is certainly not a case of "either/or" (indeed, these are all worthy causes), the lack of racial justice organizations featured on the Project for Awesome page as individual video submissions, much less as winning charities, shows the civic priorities of a predominantly white fan community.

The predominantly white demographics affect not only the civic priorities of a fan community but also what goes unsaid about these civic priorities. In the case studies investigated in this book, discussions of structures of racism, sexism, and homophobia often go unspoken. For example, the TeamMates mentoring organization argues that the community need for mentors is a worthy public issue—worthy of citizens' volunteer time and donations. Mentors help kids and teenagers feel like they matter and help give them hope. Yet, TeamMates largely avoids discussing any social and institutional structures that would create the need for mentors, particularly among some groups more than others. TeamMates doesn't reference the racist structures that limit opportunity for people of color or create the conditions for single-parent families in Nebraska, nor does it reference the lasting legacy of a racist history that continues to disadvantage predominantly black North Omaha and predominantly Mexican South Omaha today. There is a tendency for predominantly white fandoms to avoid centering discussions of racist institutions and structures—to position these discussions as unnecessary or tangential to their political and civic work. Fandom offers the potential for new kinds of civic action and new lines of connection between citizens—but that possibility can be realized only if our fan communities do a better job of being inclusive than our existing political communities have.

Possible Futures for Fan-Based Citizenship

Last, this book points to important implications for two possible futures of fan-based citizenship performances: one in which fan-based citizenship has a fuller role in electoral politics and one in which media corporations co-opt fan-based citizenship performances. First, fan-based citizenship may be poised to be more fully integrated into electoral politics. The cases highlighted in this book represent the state of fan-based citizenship during 2010–15, in which most cases of fan-based citizenship were taken up by fans, charities, or media companies rather than by elected officials or official political actors like PACs. Yet, these cases have garnered increasing media attention and often have been wildly successful, making the fan-based citizenship approach attractive to officials working in campaigns and electoral politics. Cases like the Harry Potter Alliance, the Project for Awesome, and TeamMates have enabled this shift. Fans' grassroots organizing, community building, and civic experimentation have provided the foundation for politicians' use of fan-based civic appeals. With this precedent set, we might be able to imagine a future in which Barack Obama doesn't just tacitly allow Nerds for Obama (chapter 1) to continue to sell its "Wizards for Obama" T-shirts but rather actively promotes Nerds for Obama and integrates it into his campaign. This may point to one possible future of fan-based citizenship: a fuller role for fan-based civic appeals in electoral politics. Whether politicians will use fan-based civic appeals to their fullest potential or reduce them to one-off, inauthentic gimmicks remains to be seen. But with fandom continuing to grow and increasingly finding mainstream traction and cultural cachet, fan-based citizenship performances are well positioned to become an increasingly important part of electoral politics in the future.

A second possible future for fan-based citizenship is corporate appropriation. I opened this book with the story of the Harry Potter Alliance, an organization made up of fans who connected the ethical framework of Harry Potter with civic ethical modalities like fair trade, and opened this conclusion with the story of an HPA chapter. Many of the HPA's campaigns point toward a productive future for fan-based citizenship performances. However, the HPA's Hunger Games campaign offers a cautionary tale about corporate appropriation. On March 1, 2012, the Harry Potter Alliance launched their Hunger Is Not a Game campaign, the first campaign for their Imagine Better Project.[20] In partnership with Oxfam's GROW campaign, the Harry Potter Alliance called fans of *The Hunger Games* to help end hunger.[21] At movie theaters during the premier of *The Hunger Games* film, fans gathered signatures for Oxfam's petition to reform US policies on international food aid and collected food for local food banks.[22] But by March 23, Lionsgate, the company that produced *The Hunger Games*, had issued Oxfam a cease and desist notice.[23] Lionsgate had started its own charity project tied to the release of *The Hunger Games* film: collecting donations for the United Nations World Food Program and Feeding America. Liat Cohen, Lionsgate's lawyer, asked Oxfam to remove any reference to the Hunger Is Not a Game campaign. The letter claimed that the Hunger Is Not a Game campaign infringed on Lionsgate's intellectual property, that the campaign distorted the title of the movie, and that the campaign was "causing damage to Lionsgate and our marketing efforts."[24]

The Harry Potter Alliance and Oxfam decided not to acquiesce to any of the requests in the cease and desist letter. Soon after, a Hunger Games fan created a petition that stated support for the Hunger Is Not a Game campaign. The petition quickly gained momentum, gathering more than eighteen thousand signatures.[25] Soon after, the campaign received support from Eli Pariser, board president of MoveOn.org and cofounder of Upworthy, and from Judd Apatow, a well-known Hollywood director. In the end, Lionsgate backed down. But the story of the Hunger Is Not a Game campaign illustrates the dangers of corporate appropriation of fan-based citizenship performances.[26] As fan-based citizenship performances continue to find success and impact major policies and discourses, it is inevitable that they will gain the attention of media companies like Lionsgate. Fan communities have traditionally found protection from corporate cease and desist letters by moving underground. But for fan-based citizenship performances, moving underground is not an option. The very success of these citizenship performances depends on publicity. Lionsgate's corporate appropriation of the HPA's Hunger Is Not a Game campaign represents one possible future for fan-based citizenship performances, albeit a grim future. Hopefully, media companies will choose to support and partner with fan groups doing innovative civic projects rather than appropriating projects and suing fans.

The fluidity of modern society opens up many possibilities for new forms of civic engagement and social change. As citizens continue to reimagine social movements and civic engagement, scholars will have to engage shifting citizen ideals, inconsistent logics of publicity, and unusual public sphere structures. I hope that the concepts of ethical frameworks and ethical modalities provide scholars with a much-needed theoretical base to move beyond dismissing fan-based citizenship performances and instead engage in rigorous theorizing and analysis of the ways in which popular culture and civic action are tied together in a fluid and digital world. I hope the case studies here provide a detailed and rigorous grounding from which to explore other strategies of fan-based citizenship performances. Indeed, much remains to be done, and I hope scholars continue to take up some of the many questions associated with fan performances of citizenship. As a scholar and as a fan, I know that I am excited about the future of fan-based citizenship because one thing is clear: politics for the love of fandom is powerful.

CODA

TAKEAWAYS FOR PRACTITIONERS

The cases of fan-based citizenship performances examined in this book offer lessons for new ways to encourage, invite, and support participation in public engagement anchored in fan ties. These lessons are important not only to scholars but also practitioners doing this work on the ground. Discussion of public issues, the framing of our obligations to others, and understanding what's at stake in various policy proposals are relevant to politicians, activists, nonprofit directors, and citizens. I hope that the research in this book not only helps scholars understand the ways in which citizenship is changing but also helps folks on the ground see public culture, activism, and citizenship in new ways.

I believe this is important, in part, based on my own experience doing public work. In 2012, I spoke at the National Conference of State Legislatures about what fan activism means at the state level. For many of these state legislators and their staff members, the concept of fan activism was new. But they listened with interest, asked questions, and wanted to know more. While I can't talk to every politician and staff member personally, I hope this book can serve as a kind of surrogate. Academic research like this book can provide politicians with an understanding of their constituents' shifting political affiliations. Citizens are no longer restricted to party identities, agendas, and organizations. Rather, citizens exert pressure on their governments as part of their fan identities as well. Politicians at every level of government—local, state, and federal—will need to understand this shift to understand their constituents. I believe this book is important not only for practitioners working in the government but also for fan activists working within fan communities. While fan activists know fandom and their particular communities well, I hope that the case studies in this book provide examples of new communication strategies that activists might use in their own communities. I identify some of the lessons the case studies examined here offer for practitioners creating, inventing, audiencing, and participating in fan-based citizenship performances, whether as a fan, a staff member at a charity, a chief of staff on a political campaign, or a major media corporation.

1. Take fans seriously. One of the central premises of this book has been that fandom matters. It's fun, of course, but it's also powerful and important and as such deserves to be taken seriously. Fan studies scholars, and fans themselves, have worked hard to shed the stereotype of fans as losers in their parents' basements or as head-over-heels devotees incapable of rational thought.[1] Indeed, this book has pushed against those stereotypes, showing fans to be thoughtful, creative, insightful, and diverse. If you're a fan, you already know this. But if you're a communications staff person on a political campaign or a nonprofit executive director who has been approached by a fan group, this may be your first time working with the kinds of superfans who often get scoffed at and mocked. Don't laugh when fans get excited about their fan-objects. Don't make fun of their extensive amounts of knowledge. Ask questions, engage, and ultimately, take fans and their fandom seriously.

2. Remember that the love of the fan-object always comes first. This, too, might be obvious to fans, and less obvious to other folks. Fan-based civic appeals work because of the commitment to the fan-object. Without that love of the fan-object, fan-based civic appeals become much less powerful, much less motivating, and much less important to the audience member. Therefore, fan-based civic appeals must draw on and harness that love of the fan-object rather than contradict it. Indeed, the LEGO case study demonstrates how important this is. While Greenpeace successfully paired a LEGO ethical framework with a civic ethical modality, Greenpeace's argument was ultimately rejected by LEGO fans because the argument asked fans to boycott LEGO. A commitment to a fan-object is almost always a fan's top priority.

3. Know what ethical framework you're invoking. Popular culture always has many interpretations. Whether Harry Potter is a story about youth engagement, resistance against tyranny, or a group of kids with a white savior complex depends on each reader's interpretation of the text. Rhetors must coordinate these interpretations in order to invoke them as part of a coherent ethical framework. For practitioners on the ground, that means being aware of the already established interpretations circulating and knowing which interpretations are popular and which ones aren't. Practitioners must invite fan-citizens to see one ethical framework over all the other possible choices. This requires persuasion, argument, and invitation. Thinking through the specific ethical framework that is being invoked also serves as a check to make sure popular culture isn't being invoked simply as a gimmick. When Harry Potter is used as a theme at a charity gala, it's not being used to make fan-based civic appeals. Just because Harry Potter and a water charity exist in the same room at the same event doesn't mean fan-based citizenship is occurring. If your goal is to reach fans and invite productive public engagement, make sure you know what ethical framework you're invoking. Fans increasingly expect companies to use popular culture as more than a gimmick. Doing so requires a careful understanding of ethical frameworks offered by the popular culture object. Today, not knowing the ethical frameworks at play is a risky move for any media company. Fans see deep ethical implications in their fan-objects. If the company doesn't see the ethical framework, fans certainly will.

4. Pair the popular culture ethical framework with an ethical modality. Folks planning campaigns that utilize fan-based civic appeals might adopt one of the strategies used by the cases in this book—connecting, expanding, or retelling—applying that strategy to a different popular culture object and political issue. I found this useful in my own work with students at a local alternative high school. In 2012, I spent a semester working with students at lunchtime, helping them build a fan activist campaign.[2] Students chose the fan-object *Doctor Who* and the political issue of global warming. I showed students the ways in which the Harry Potter Alliance utilized a strategy of connecting to pair Harry Potter's values with intervention in Sudan. Students took that as a model—looking for their own metaphors, links, and parallels between *Doctor Who* and global warming. I hope that a book focused on communication strategies proves particularly helpful for practitioners who are tasked with designing communication campaigns that invite and persuade fans to take civic action. While I hope that practitioners adopt some of the communication strategies outlined in this book, I also hope that practitioners continue to develop new communication strategies we haven't yet seen. Maybe the case studies in this book will help practitioners see their work in new ways, learning from case studies they had never heard of before. Ultimately, I hope practitioners continue to invent new rhetorical strategies that pair ethical frameworks and ethical modalities.

Whether practitioners adopt communication strategies outlined in this book or develop new ones, it is crucial for practitioners to utilize a strong pairing of an ethical framework and civic modality. Without a strong communication strategy to pair those, practitioners run the risk of encountering the same problem Omaze and Disney experienced in the Force for Change. While Star Wars was a rich text with many ethical frameworks, Omaze and Disney did not connect any of those to their Force for Change campaign that raised money for UNICEF. Omaze and Disney raised a significant amount of money, but their campaign was removed almost entirely from public culture. Fans' donations and purchases were disconnected from the public issues UNICEF hoped to impact. The Force for Change case demonstrates that it is not enough to have a powerful ethical framework and an important public issue—rather, the two must be paired together. Indeed, this takes communicative work. It is not automatic. Fans do not automatically read Harry Potter and become activists. It takes rhetorical invitations, persuasion, and community organizing. If your goal is to impact public issues in a meaningful way, make sure the pairing between the popular culture ethical framework and the civic ethical modality is strong.

5. Do good activist and civic work. Fan-based civic appeals, like any other communication strategy or persuasive tactic, need to be grounded in theories and best practices that guide good activist and civic work. Fan-based citizenship performances, campaigns, and appeals are not automatically productive, progressive, or emancipatory. Practitioners who utilize fan-based civic appeals must still work hard to make sure their civic modalities are ethical. DC Entertainment's We Can Be Heroes campaign demonstrates what problematic fan-based civic appeals look like and the ways in which they limit the civic potential of the campaign. In 2012, DC Entertainment launched the We Can Be Heroes campaign, which tied the Justice League to work to end hunger in the Horn of Africa. The campaign raised more than $2 million for Save the Children, International Rescue Committee, and Mercy Corps.[3] The We Can Be Heroes campaign effectively paired a Justice League ethical framework with a charity ethical modality through a strategy of connecting but in the process reinforced problematic modes of public engagement.

The campaign reinforced neoliberal logics that prevent a solution to the underlying causes of starvation in the Horn of Africa. Lillie Chouliaraki argues that contemporary humanitarianism, like the work done by DC Entertainment's partner charities Save the Children, International Rescue Committee, and Mercy Corps, relies on a "neoliberal logic of micro-economic explanations that ignores the systemic causes of global poverty."[4] The DC Entertainment campaign supported charities that provide water, peanut paste, and other food to prevent people from starving—but the campaign did not tackle the cause of the Horn of Africa's famine or the poverty or lack of development that debilitates the nations within the Horn of Africa. By doing so, DC Entertainment ignored the economic and political structures put in place by the West that make regions in Africa vulnerable to famines and discourage rapid and sustainable development.[5] Thus, even as the campaign succeeded in garnering donations, the campaign reinforced the neoliberal logics that undergird the very system that leaves people in the Horn of Africa starving. DC Entertainment's We Can Be Heroes campaign demonstrates that fan-based citizenship campaigns are not always desirable, emancipatory, and progressive. Rather, the theories and best practices that guide ethical activist and civic work must be applied just as carefully to fan-based citizenship campaigns as to any other civic project.

Ultimately, I hope this book is useful not only for academics but also for practitioners building and participating in fan-based citizenship performances. By tracing five case studies in this book, I hope practitioners can learn from others' experiences in a number of ways. These cases offer models for successful fan-based citizenship performances—models that could be applied to other issues and other fan communities. But these cases also tell the stories of mistakes or drawbacks organizations have made in trying to enact fan-based citizenship. Further, I hope these cases offer inspiration—that is, sparks for new ideas unimagined by the actors in each case or by me. Citizenship is a creative process—it involves invention, imagination, and iteration. I hope these cases studies offer fodder for that creative process.

NOTES

Introduction

1. "Success Stories; "About the HPA"; "HPA 5 Year Anniversary BLOWOUT"; all from The Harry Potter Alliance webpage.

2. "Fan Power—BBC Radio 4."

3. "Find a Chapter, " The Harry Potter Alliance webpage; Flock, "Alohomora"; Martin, "From Young Adult Book Fans to Wizards of Change."

4. Maloney, "The Marketing Tactics for Hunger Games"; Baker-Whitelaw, "Harry Potter Alliance Battles Income Inequality with #MyHungerGames"; A. Bennett, "#MyHungerGames"; Jilani, "Activists Launch #MyHungerGames to Tell Real Story of American Inequality"; Sniderman, "How Non-Profits Are Tapping Internet Memes & Pop Culture"; Cashin, "Harry Potter Fans Scored an Awesome Victory in the Fight against Child Slavery."

5. Wiedeman, "The Harry Potter Alliance Stages a Fast-Food Protest"; Rosenberg, "How 'Harry Potter' Fans Won a Four-Year Fight against Child Slavery"; L. Bury, "Hunger Games Fans Campaign against Real Inequality"; Martin, "From Young Adult Book Fans to Wizards of Change"; Bonzio, "Power of Transmedia Unveiled in Italy"; Davidson, "How Harry Potter Struck a Blow Against Slavery"; Heigl, "Harry Potter Chocolate Goes 100% Fair Trade, Thanks to Fans."

6. "Success Stories," The Harry Potter Alliance webpage, 1.

7. Jenkins, "Cultural Acupuncture" (2012); Jenkins et al., *By Any Media Necessary;* Jenkins and Shresthova, "Up, up, and Away!"

8. *Oxford English Dictionary Online,* Oxford University Press, March 2015, s.v. "Citizenship, N," www.oed.com/view/Entry/33521?redirectedFrom=citizenship.

9. Coleman and Blumler, *The Internet and Democratic Citizenship,* 4–5.

10. Coleman and Blumler, *The Internet and Democratic Citizenship,* 4–5.

11. Coleman and Blumler, *The Internet and Democratic Citizenship,* 4–5.

12. Coleman and Blumler, *The Internet and Democratic Citizenship,* 4–5.

13. Coleman and Blumler, *The Internet and Democratic Citizenship,* 4–5.

14. See, for example, Skocpol, *Diminished Democracy*; Zukin et al., *A New Engagement?*; Xenos and Moy, "Direct and Differential Effects of the Internet on Political and Civic Engagement"; Gierzynski, *Harry Potter and the Millennials*; and Carmines, Ensley, and Wagner, "Who Fits the Left-Right Divide?"

15. Asen, "A Discourse Theory of Citizenship," 194.

16. Asen, "A Discourse Theory of Citizenship."

17. Asen, "A Discourse Theory of Citizenship," 194.

18. R. Bauman, *Verbal Art as Performance*, 37–38.

19. Ray, "The Rhetorical Ritual of Citizenship," 7.

20. Ray, "The Rhetorical Ritual of Citizenship," 18.

21. Ray, "The Rhetorical Ritual of Citizenship," 18.

22. Ray, "The Rhetorical Ritual of Citizenship," 18.

23. Asen, "A Discourse Theory of Citizenship," 205.

24. Hariman and Lucaites, *No Caption Needed*, 26; Hariman and Lucaites, "Performing Civic Identity"; Hariman and Lucaites, "Public Identity and Collective Memory in U.S. Iconic Photography"; Hariman, "Political Parody and Public Culture."

25. McGuigan, "The Cultural Public Sphere," 435.

26. Dahlgren, "The Internet, Public Spheres, and Political Communication"; Dahlgren, *Media and Political Engagement*.

27. Dahlgren, *Media and Political Engagement*, 103.

28. Dahlgren, *Media and Political Engagement*.

29. Part of recognizing the cultural, social, and historical situatedness of citizenship is recognizing the ways in which particular bodies are disciplined, excluded, and normalized by discourses of citizenship and the state. Amy Brandzel argues that citizenship is "the central structure for reifying the norms of whiteness, heterosexuality, consumerism, and settler colonialism within the US" and that these norms "are brutally enforced against nonnormative bodies, practices, behaviors, and forms of affiliation" (*Against Citizenship*, 4). For example, citizens and law enforcement may interact with legal citizens like sex workers as noncitizens, and discourses like those around jobs or immigration pit citizens against noncitizens framed as dangerous and threatening. When individuals refuse to read particular bodies as citizens, discourses of citizenship can justify bias, deportation, and bodily harm. In this book, I recognize that some fans may not be read as citizens, and thus may not have particular civic practices available to them. I recognize that fans who are not read as citizens may experience exclusion from the polity and may face bodily and psychological threats. This may mean that some fans don't participate in activities like the Harry Potter Alliance's, may participate differently, or may participate because they have been excluded from other more traditional forms of citizenship (Brandzel, *Against Citizenship*).

30. Earl and Kimport, "Movement Societies and Digital Protest"; Bethan, "Being of Service."

31. Chávez, *Queer Migration Politics*, 156.

32. Earl and Kimport, "Movement Societies and Digital Protest."

33. Menon, "A Participation Observation Analysis of the Once & Again Internet Message Bulletin Boards"; Jenkins, "Cultural Acupuncture" (2012); Scardaville, "Accidental Activists";

Adams, "Hell Hath No Fury Like a Scorned Soap Fan"; Harris, "A Sociology of Television Fandom."

34. Lopez, "Fan-Activists and the Politics of Race in *The Last Airbender*"; Tabron, "Girl on Girl Politics."

35. Dimitrov, "Gender Violence, Fan Activism and Public Relations in Sport"; Spaaij, "Football Hooliganism in the Netherlands"; Greenberg, "Tossing the Red Flag"; Rowe, "Cultures of Complaint."

36. Jenkins, "'Cultural Acupuncture" (2012), 2.1.

37. Jenkins et al. also identify this issue in their study of participatory politics (Jenkins et al., *By Any Media Necessary*).

38. Zuckerman, "New Media, New Civics?," 54.

39. Jenkins and Shresthova, "Up, up, and Away!," 1.9.

40. Ibid.

41. Bennett, "Changing Citizenship in the Digital Age"; Bennett, "1998 Ithiel De Sola Pool Lecture"; Dahlgren, *Media and Political Engagement*; Williams and Delli Carpini, *After Broadcast News*.

42. Livingstone, *Audiences and Publics*.

43. Livingstone, *Audiences and Publics*, 9.

44. Jones, *Entertaining Politics*; Xenos and Becker, "Moments of Zen"; Baym and Jones, *News Parody and Political Satire across the Globe*.

45. Morales, "Harry Potter Alliance Kicks off Equality FTW Fundraiser," 8.

46. Cartter, "Activist Alumnus Inspires Students," 1.

47. Abercrombie and Longhurst, *Audiences*; Busse and Gray, "Fan Cultures and Fan Communities"; Booth, *Playing Fans*.

48. Busse and Gray, "Fan Cultures and Fan Communities," 425.

49. Abercrombie and Longhurst, *Audiences*; Fiske, "The Cultural Economy."

50. Busse and Gray, "Fan Cultures and Fan Communities," 425; Abercrombie and Longhurst, *Audiences*, 130.

51. John Fiske calls this "textual productivity," which he describes as occurring when "fans produce and circulate among themselves texts which are often crafted with production values as high as any in the official culture" (Fiske, "The Cultural Economy," 39).

52. Hellekson and Busse, *The Fan Fiction Studies Reader*.

53. Abercrombie and Longhurst, *Audiences*, 130; Jenkins, *Textual Poachers*.

54. See fan discussions like, obsession_inc, "Affirmational Fandom vs. Transformational Fandom."

55. Stein and Busse, *Sherlock and Transmedia Fandom*, 16.

56. Booth, *Playing Fans*, 13.

57. Broadnax, "Racialized Nerdiness."

58. Osborne and Coombs, "Performative Sport Fandom."

59. Osborne and Coombs, "Performative Sport Fandom."

60. *Blerds Online*; BlerdNationTM.

61. Lopez, "Fan-Activists and the Politics of Race in *The Last Airbender*."

62. Booth, *Playing Fans*; deBoer, "Geeks, You Are No Longer Victims. Get over It."

63. Busse, "Fan Labor and Feminism," 111; Booth, *Playing Fans*; Jenkins, "When Fandom Goes Mainstream"; deBoer, "Geeks, You Are No Longer Victims. Get over It."

64. "MtvU Fandom Awards."

65. Busse, "Fan Labor and Feminism"; Booth, *Playing Fans*.

66. Gray, Sandvoss, and Harrington, *Fandom*.

67. Hellekson and Busse, *Fan Fiction and Fan Communities*; Booth, *Playing Fans*; Baym, *Tune in, Log On*.

68. Song, *Virtual Communities*; R. Howard, *Digital Jesus*.

69. *Rheingold, The Virtual Community*.

70. Rheingold, *The Virtual Community*.

71. Baym, *Personal Connections in the Digital Age*, 74.

72. R. Howard, "Electronic Hybridity," 202.

73. Jenkins, *Textual Poachers*.

74. Penley, *Close Encounters*; Jenkins, *Textual Poachers*.

75. Jenkins, Itō, and boyd, *Participatory Culture in a Networked Era*, 3.

76. Baym, *Tune in, Log On*.

77. Hellekson and Busse, *Fan Fiction and Fan Communities*.

78. For research on the Harry Potter Alliance, see Hinck, "Theorizing a Public Engagement Keystone"; Jenkins, "'Cultural Acupuncture" (2012); Jenkins, "Fan Activism as Participatory Politics"; Kligler-Vilenchik, "Case Study: The Harry Potter Alliance"; Jenkins, "How 'Dumbledore's Army' Is Transforming Our World"; Jenkins, "Cultural Acupuncture" (2015); McCaughey, "The Harry Potter Alliance"; J. Phillips, "The Harry Potter Alliance"; Jenkins and Shresthova, "Up, up, and Away!"; Jenkins et al., *By Any Media Necessary*; Kligler-Vilenchik and Shresthova, "Learning through Practice"; and Kligler-Vilenchik et al., "Experiencing Fan Activism."

79. Van Zoonen, *Entertaining the Citizen*, 60–67.

80. Van Zoonen, *Entertaining the Citizen*, 60–67.

81. J. Gray, "Of Snowspeeders and Imperial Walkers."

82. J. Gray, "Of Snowspeeders and Imperial Walkers."

83. Leavitt and Horbinski, "Even a Monkey Can Understand Fan Activism."

84. Leavitt and Horbinski, "Even a Monkey Can Understand Fan Activism."

85. Jenkins, *Convergence Culture*, 257.

86. Jenkins, "Cultural Acupuncture" (2012).

87. Li, "The Absence of Fan Activism in the Queer Fandom of Ho Denise Wan See (HOCC) in Hong Kong."

88. Duncombe, *Dream*; Duncombe, "Imagining No-Place"; Yockey, "Wonder Woman for a Day."

89. Cochran, "Past the Brink of Tacit Support"; Jones, "Being of Service."

90. Cochran, "'Past the Brink of Tacit Support."

91. Yockey, "Wonder Woman for a Day"; L. Bennett, "If We Stick Together We Can Do Anything."

92. Jones, "Being of Service," 4.11.

93. Hinck, "Ethical Frameworks and Ethical Modalities."

94. Aden, *Huskerville*.

95. While these fan communities vary across age, gender, sexuality, and geographic location, they are all predominantly white fandoms. In the conclusion of this book, I consider the implications of the predominantly white demographics of these fandom communities for civic action.

96. Fans sometimes take action on behalf of the character and sometimes on behalf of the the book series or fan-object. For fans, the characters, actors, and the fan-object itself are often wrapped up together.

97. Jenkins and Shresthova, "Up, up, and Away!"; Jenkins, "Cultural Acupuncture" (2012); Kligler-Vilenchik, "Case Study: The Harry Potter Alliance"; Kligler-Vilenchik and Shresthova, "Learning through Practice"; Jenkins, "Fan Activism as Participatory Politics."

Chapter One

1. Wizard wrock is music written about Harry Potter.

2. DeGeorge, Skype interview by the author.

3. "Nerds for Obama."

4. DeGeorge, Skype interview by the author.

5. Hinck, "Ethical Frameworks and Ethical Modalities."

6. Henry Jenkins suggests that fans discussed the political aspects and implications of their fan-objects, even well before the development of the World Wide Web. Jenkins argues that fans discuss, speculate, and deliberate about questions like, "Why has Uhura been unable to achieve promotion within Star Fleet while Chekov and Sulu now command their own ships?" or "Could Starsky and Hutch be gay lovers?" (*Textual Poachers*, 83). Fans utilize fan-objects as cultural resources with which to understand the political issues in their own lives. Historian Nan Enstad offers an additional historical example of what we might call fan-based citizenship performances. In a study of early twentieth-century women factory workers, she found that dime novels, fashion, and film helped them imagine themselves as ladies, workers, and Americans. Through popular culture, these women established a radical politics and went on strike in large numbers, despite being excluded from typical labor discourses supporting the male worker (Enstad, *Ladies of Labor*).

7. Delli Carpini, "Political Communication Research in the Digital Media Environment."

8. Chávez, "Counter-Public Enclaves and Understanding the Function of Rhetoric in Social Movement Coalition-Building"; Lucas, "Coming to Terms"; Skocpol, *Diminished Democracy*; Verba, Schlozman, and Brady, *Voice and Equality*.

9. Verba, Schlozman, and Brady, *Voice and Equality*, 18.

10. Bennett and Segerberg, *The Logic of Connective Action*; Skocpol, *Diminished Democracy*.

11. Abbate, *Inventing the Internet*; Bennett and Segerberg, *The Logic of Connective Action*; L. Bennett, "Political Life in Late Modern Society"; Couldry, *Why Voice Matters*.

12. Asen, "A Discourse Theory of Citizenship"; L. Bennett, "Political Life in Late Modern Society"; P. Howard, *New Media Campaigns and the Managed Citizen*.

13. What Giddens calls late modernity, Bauman calls postmodernity.

14. Z. Bauman, *Liquid Times*, 1.

15. Bauman argues that a liquid society has problematic disadvantages: it produces situations in which identities are fleeting and empty, where individuals flit from identity to identity, group to group, searching for long-term social connection and finding only precarity. Indeed, this can be the result of a liquid society. But it is not the only result. The presence of liquid identities based on fluid institutional membership has opened up opportunities for fan-based citizenship, cases which can be characterized by social connection rather than emptiness. Indeed, scholars like Rebecca Williams and Gary Crawford have argued that fandom provides ontological security. Ultimately, cases like the Harry Potter Alliance demonstrate that identities enabled by a fluid world can be quite meaningful and powerful (see Elliott, *The Contemporary Bauman;* Z. Bauman, *Liquid Modernity;* Z. Bauman, *Liquid Times;* Williams, "In Focus"; Crawford, *Consuming Sport;* and Lawrence, "We Are the Boys from the Black Country!").

16. Giddens, *Modernity and Self-Identity,* 20.

17. Giddens, *Modernity and Self-Identity,* 29.

18. L. Bennett, "Changing Citizenship in the Digital Age," 13.

19. Beck, *Risk Society,* 135.

20. Giddens, *Modernity and Self-Identity,* 14.

21. Beck, *Risk Society.*

22. Hinck, "Fluidity in a Digital World."

23. Z. Bauman, *Liquid Times,* 24.

24. Peck, *Constructions of Neoliberal Reason;* Beck, *Risk Society.*

25. Z. Bauman, *Liquid Times,* 24–25.

26. Papacharissi, *A Private Sphere.*

27. Bennett and Segerberg, *The Logic of Connective Action.*

28. Giddens, *Modernity and Self-Identity,* 214.

29. Mukherjee and Banet-Weiser, *Commodity Activism.*

30. Portwood-Stacer, *Lifestyle Politics and Radical Activism.*

31. Bennett and Segerberg, *The Logic of Connective Action,* 23.

32. Bennett and Segerberg, *The Logic of Connective Action.*

33. Bennett and Segerberg, *The Logic of Connective Action,* 13.

34. Fry, "Millennials Overtake Baby Boomers as America's Largest Generation"; Twenge, Campbell, and Freeman, "Generational Differences in Young Adults' Life Goals, Concern for Others, and Civic Orientation, 1966–2009."

35. Coleman, "Doing IT for Themselves"; L. Bennett, "Changing Citizenship in the Digital Age."

36. Here, my use of the term "worldview" is anchored in Geertz's conceptualization of "worldview" and its relationship to ethics, reality, and lived experience (Clifford Geertz, "Ethos, World-View and the Analysis of Sacred Symbols," *Antioch Review* 17, no. 4 [1957]: 421–37, https://doi.org/10.2307/4609997).

37. See Abercrombie and Longhurst, *Audiences;* Busse and Gray, "Fan Cultures and Fan Communities"; Gray, Sandvoss, and Harrington, *Fandom;* Hellekson and Busse, *The Fan Fiction Studies Reader;* Hills, *Fan Cultures;* Jenkins, *Textual Poachers;* and Sandvoss, *Fans.*

38. Critical-cultural scholars recognize that seemingly nonpolitical cultural objects or

communication artifacts are often very political. Of course, Harry Potter is political in the sense that the story has implications for gender or race imaginaries. But my point here is that Harry Potter is not civic in the sense that it is not supposed to be used to justify public policy decisions or positions on political issues. However, this does not mean that media institutions never invite fans to view media objects as political. Indeed, during negotiations with Universal Studios, J. K. Rowling stipulated that Coca-Cola could not be sold within the Wizarding World of Harry Potter, staking a clear position on the relationship between the Harry Potter franchise and public health (Nicholson, "Florida").

39. Aristotle, *Nicomachean Ethics*; Mill, *Utilitarianism*; Kant, *Grounding for the Metaphysics of Morals*.

40. Varela, *Ethical Know-How*.

41. Brouwer and Asen, *Public Modalities*.

42. Brouwer and Asen, *Public Modalities*, 16.

43. Brouwer and Asen, *Public Modalities*, 21.

44. This type of theoretical position is common in rhetorical studies but differs from fan studies in some ways. In rhetoric, the critic assumes rhetoric is powerful but not necessarily good—ethically, practically, or politically. It is the job of the critic to make such a determination. In some ways, this contrasts with the role of the scholar as conceptualized in early fan studies. There, the role of the scholar was to save or rescue fans, fan practices, and fan cultures because fans were so often framed by popular discourses and academic research as irrational, emotional, and undeserving of academic study. Gray, Sandvoss, and Harrington argue that fan studies was founded on the claim that "fandom is beautiful" (*Fandom*, 1). Recently, however, fan studies scholars have also begun to turn their attention to problematic aspects of fandom. For example, in 2017, *Participations,* a journal for audience studies research, including fan studies, invited submissions for a themed section on toxic fan practices. In this book, I blend both rhetoric and fan studies' interpretations of the role of the critic: I assume that fans are worthy of study and that fan practices don't warrant characterization as infantile or irrational, but I don't necessarily assume that all fan practices, communities, and cases are good—ethically, practically, or politically (see Gray, Sandvoss, and Harrington, *Fandom;* and "CFP: Themed Section of Participations Journal on Toxic Fan Practices").

45. "About the HPA," The Harry Potter Alliance webpage.

46. "Not in Harry's Name," The Harry Potter Alliance webpage.

47. Brown, *Is Harry Potter Chocolate Made by Child Slaves?*

48. "Show Us the Report" (italics in original).

49. See, for example, Hall, "Encoding/Decoding."

50. Hunting and Hains, "Discriminating Taste."

51. While this point may seem obvious to media scholars who may be accustomed to viewing media texts as polysemic and examining the dominant and resistant readings audiences may have, the point is an important one for rhetoricians unaccustomed to examining popular culture objects. This is particularly important because agreeing on a preferred interpretation of a media text is a necessary precursor to fan-based civic appeals.

52. Busse and Gray, "Fan Cultures and Fan Communities"; Bennett and Segerberg, *The Logic of Connective Action;* R. Howard, "The Vernacular Web of Participatory Media."

53. Busse and Gray, "Fan Cultures and Fan Communities."

54. Hills, *Fan Cultures;* MacDonald, "Uncertain Utopia"; Thornton, *Club Cultures;* Tulloch and Jenkins, *Science Fiction Audiences.*

55. Enstad, *Ladies of Labor,* 13.

56. Chávez, "Border (In)Securities"; Gray, "Queer Nation Is Dead/Long Live Queer Nation"; Zaeske, "Signatures of Citizenship."

57. Busker, "Fandom and Male Privilege."

58. Hinck, "Why Rhetoricians Need to Pay Attention to Fan Culture"; Thomas and Ellis, *Chicks Dig Comics.*

59. Wichelns, "The Literary Criticism of Oratory"; Medhurst, "The Academic Study of Public Address"; Gehrke, *The Ethics and Politics of Speech.*

60. boyd, *It's Complicated.*

61. LaFrance, "Raiders of the Lost Web"; "Internet History Is Fragile"; Barone, Zeitlyn, and Mayer-Schönberger, "Learning from Failure."

62. Krogh, *The DAM Book.*

63. McKinnon et al., *Text + Field,* 4.

64. Middleton et al., *Participatory Critical Rhetoric;* McKinnon et al., *Text + Field;* Middleton, Senda-Cook, and Endres, "Articulating Rhetorical Field Methods."

65. For more on rhetorical methods, see Middleton et al., *Participatory Critical Rhetoric;* McKinnon et al., *Text + Field;* Middleton, Senda-Cook, and Endres, "Articulating Rhetorical Field Methods"; McHendry et al., "Rhetorical Critic(Ism)'s Body"; Pezzullo, *Toxic Tourism;* R. Howard, *Digital Jesus;* Asen, *Democracy, Deliberation, and Education;* Middleton, "'SafeGround Sacramento' and Rhetorics of Substantive Citizenship"; Chávez, *Queer Migration Politics;* Pezzullo, "Resisting 'National Breast Cancer Awareness Month'"; Hess, "Critical-Rhetorical Ethnography"; and Senda-Cook, "Rugged Practices."

66. Silvestri, "Context Drives Method," 165.

67. Mathieu et al., "Methodological Challenges in the Transition towards Online Audience Research"; Evans and Stasi, "Desperately Seeking Methodology"; Hills, *Fan Cultures.*

68. Lawrence, "We Are the Boys from the Black Country!," 5–6.

69. Lawrence, "We Are the Boys from the Black Country!," 5–6.

70. Jenkins, *Textual Poachers;* "Who the &%&# Is Henry Jenkins?"

71. For research on aca-fans and the various ways aca-fandom has been taken up, see Gunnels and Klink, "We Are All Together"; Tchouaffe, "Revisiting Fandom in Africa"; T. Phillips, "Embracing the 'Overly Confessional'"; Booth, "Fandom in/as the Academy"; Dwyer, "The Gathering of the Juggalos and the Peculiar Sanctity of Fandom"; Coker and Benefiel, "We Have Met the Fans, and They Are Us"; Jenemann, "Stop Being an Elitist, and Start Being an Elitist"; Ng, "Telling Tastes"; Mittell, "On Disliking Mad Men"; Jenkins, "On Mad Men, Aca-Fandom, and the Goals of Cultural Criticism"; J. Gray, "SCMS 2011 Workshop"; Busse, "SCMS 2011 Workshop"; Click, "SCMS 2011 Workshop"; Brooker, "SCMS 2011 Workshop"; Stein and Busse, "SCMS 2011 Workshop"; Bogost, "Against Aca-Fandom"; R. Bury, "Aca-Fandom and Beyond: Rhianon Bury and Matt Yockey (Part Two)"; Yockey, "Aca-Fandom and Beyond: Rhianon Bury and Matt Yockey (Part Two)"; Perren, "Aca-Fandom and Beyond: Jonathan Gray, Matt Hills, and Alisa Perren (Part One)"; Hills, "Aca-Fandom and Beyond:

Jonathan Gray, Matt Hills, and Alisa Perren (Part One)"; J. Gray, "Aca-Fandom and Beyond: Jonathan Gray, Matt Hills, and Alisa Perren (Part One)"; Hills, *Fan Cultures;* Jenkins, *Textual Poachers;* Evans and Stasi, "Desperately Seeking Methodology"; Stein, "On (Not) Hosting the Session That Killed the Term 'Acafan'—Antenna"; and Freund and Fielding, "Research Ethics in Fan Studies."

72. Zubernis and Larsen, *Fandom at the Crossroads;* Zubernis and Larsen, *Fandom at the Crossroads.*

73. Stein, "On (Not) Hosting the Session That Killed the Term 'Acafan'—Antenna."

74. McHendry et al., "Rhetorical Critic(Ism)'s Body."

75. Black, "On Objectivity and Politics in Criticism."

76. Black, "A Note on Theory and Practice in Rhetorical Criticism," 334.

77. Black, "A Note on Theory and Practice in Rhetorical Criticism."

78. Black, "On Objectivity and Politics in Criticism."

79. Jonathan Gray argues that the reflexivity in media studies research demanded by aca-fan, must also occur in scholarship in which researchers are antifans or protofans (Gray, "Aca-Fandom and Beyond: Jonathan Gray, Matt Hills, and Alisa Perren [Part One]").

80. Hills, *Fan Cultures.*

81. M. Gray, *Out in the Country,* 195.

82. M. Gray, *Out in the Country,* 195.

Chapter Two

1. Irwin and Quealy, "The Places in America Where College Football Means the Most."

2. Aden, *Huskerville,* 10.

3. Aden, *Huskerville,* 10.

4. Aden, *Huskerville.*

5. Kruse, "Apologia in Team Sport," 270.

6. "Americans to Rest of World"; Quinn, *Sports and Their Fans.*

7. Plunkett, *Plunkett's Sports Industry Almanac 2011,* 31.

8. Plunkett, *Plunkett's Sports Industry Almanac 2011,* 30.

9. "The Sports Market."

10. "Americans to Rest of World."

11. NCAA, "2013 National College Football Attendance"; "2013 NFL Football Attendance—National Football League–ESPN."

12. Butterworth, "The Athlete as Citizen," 1.

13. Butterworth, "The Athlete as Citizen."

14. Bairner, *Sport, Nationalism, and Globalization,* 22; E. Smith, *Race, Sport, and the American Dream,* 11.

15. Branch, "The Awakening of Colin Kaepernick"; Reid, "Opinion | Eric Reid"; "NFL Fans Are Divided over How Players Express Themselves Politically"; Belson, "Kaepernick vs. the N.F.L."; Snider, "Are NFL Player Protests 'massively, Massively' Hurting TV Ratings?"

16. Butterworth, "The Athlete as Citizen," 2.

17. Dunning, *Sport Matters*, 6.

18. Aden, *Huskerville*, 178.

19. Crawford, *Consuming Sport*, 61.

20. Only three schools in Nebraska play Division I sports: University of Nebraska–Lincoln (UNL), University of Nebraska–Omaha (UNO), and Creighton University (CU). Both UNO and CU are Division I schools, but neither has a football team. "Mavs Enjoy Highlights of First D-I Campaign"; "University of Nebraska"; "League Bio."

21. Hince, phone interview by the author, September 20, 2013; Aden, *Huskerville*.

22. "Nebraska's Five National Titles."

23. "Nebraska's Five National Titles."

24. "Bob Devaney."

25. "History of Nebraska Football."

26. "Tom Osborne"; Associated Press, "Nebraska Governor Is Victor in G.O.P. Primary."

27. Aden, *Huskerville*, 24.

28. Aden, *Huskerville*, 42.

29. Aden, *Huskerville*, 27.

30. Leung, "I Have a Dream: College Tuition"; Husker Participant A, interview; Northrop, personal interview by the author, November 1, 2013.

31. "TeamMates Mentoring Program, Nebraska (NE)."

32. "FAQ."

33. "FAQ."

34. "Data."

35. "Who We Are"; TeamMates, "TeamMates Annual Report: 2016."

36. "Who We Are."

37. "TeamMates Gala"; "City-Wide Mentor Meet-Up."

38. Hince, phone interview by the author, September 20, 2013.

39. Erickson, "Press Release: TeamMates Mentoring Program Kicks off 2013 Coaches Challenge."

40. Hince, phone interview by the author, September 20, 2013.

41. "Big 10 School Profile: Nebraska"; "Football—2010 Schedule/Results"; "Football—2011 Schedule/Results."

42. Erickson et al., "Press Release: Iowa, Kansas, & Nebraska Kick off Coaches Challenge with Addition of Michigan and Minnesota."

43. "Take the Coaches Mentoring Challenge in Iowa!"

44. Aden, *Huskerville*.

45. Aden, *Huskerville*, 82.

46. "Nebraska Agriculture Fact Card."

47. Aden, *Huskerville*, 80.

48. Aden, *Huskerville*, 77.

49. Osborne, *More Than Winning*, 138.

50. "The Top 10 Schools in Total Academic All-America® Honorees (as of July 2013)."

51. Interview by the author with a former Husker track athlete, November 13, 2013.

52. NCAA, "Graduation Success Rate Report: University of Nebraska, Lincoln."

53. Smith, *Race, Sport, and the American Dream*, 17.

54. "Outside the Lines."

55. "List: Huskers Land 18 Preferred Walk-Ons."

56. Qtd. in Aden, *Huskerville*, 88.

57. Aden, *Huskerville*.

58. McDonald, "Mapping Whiteness and Sport," 246.

59. York, "Nebraska Fans Never Tire of Storybook Scripts Written by Walk-Ons."

60. Aden, *Huskerville*, 118.

61. Aden, *Huskerville*, 122.

62. Pillen, personal interview by the author, November 1, 2013.

63. Aden, *Huskerville*, 123.

64. "Memorial Stadium."

65. *Big Red Anthem—Brown (Official Video)*.

66. Hince, phone interview by the author, September 20, 2013.

67. Osborne, *More Than Winning*, 144.

68. Osborne, *More Than Winning*, 144.

69. Murray, "Nebraska Ought to Be Ashamed."

70. Reuters, "Ex-NFL Player's Cellmate Was Strangled to Death in Cell"; Breech, "Coroner's Report Reveals Contents of Lawrence Phillips' Suicide Note."

71. Lopresti, "No Coach Ever Solved Lawrence Phillips."

72. Chatelain, "The Mystery of Lawrence Phillips."

73. Sherman, "Lawrence Phillips Continues to Cast Shadow over Nebraska, Tom Osborne."

74. Aden, *Huskerville*, 101.

75. Aden, *Huskerville*, 107.

76. *Osborne, More Than Winning*.

77. "Memorial Stadium."

78. "Huskers Rank in Top 10 in Attendance."

79. Qtd. in Aden, *Huskerville*, 107.

80. Pillen, personal interview by the author, November 1, 2013.

81. Aden, *Huskerville*, 109.

82. "Football—2011 Schedule/Results."

83. thruthesegates, *Morty Schapiro Interview*.

84. *This Is Nebraska (Big Red Anthem 2)*.

85. *Nebraska Football 2014—Be Ready*.

86. It is perhaps unsurprising that the marginalization of women in sport fandom parallels the marginalization of women in media fandom. Indeed, sexism and misogyny are systemic (Busse, "Geek Hierarchies, Boundary Policing, and the Gendering of the Good Fan"; Bacon-Smith, *Enterprising Women*).

87. Osborne and Coombs, "Performative Sport Fandom."

88. Grossfeld, "A Voice for the Victims."

89. Rampell, "Football Upsets Increase Domestic Violence, Study Finds."

90. Bruce, "Reflections on Communication and Sport"; Messner, "Reflections on Communication and Sport"; Lenskyj, "Reflections on Communication and Sport"; Smith, Choueiti,

and Pieper, "Race/Ethnicity in 600 Popular Films"; Hunt, Ramon, and Price, "2014 Hollywood Diversity Report."

91. Brooks and Althouse, "African American Head Coaches and Administrators"; Shropshire and Winslow, foreword to *In Black and White;* Braddock, Smith, and Dawkins, "Race and Pathways to Power in the National Football League"; Bozeman and Fay, "Minority Football Coaches' Diminished Careers."

92. Northrop, personal interview by the author, November 1, 2013.

93. Northrop, personal interview by the author, November 1, 2013.

94. HN Staff, "'And I'm . . .' by Ramon Brown | Album Premier."

95. Diaz De Leon, email interview by the author, October 15, 2013.

96. *Big Red Anthem—Brown (Official Video).*

97. *This Is Nebraska (Big Red Anthem 2).*

98. *This Is Nebraska (Big Red Anthem 2).*

99. Jenkins, "'Cultural Acupuncture" (2012).

100. Jenkins, "Cultural Acupuncture (2012); Kligler-Vilenchik et al., "Experiencing Fan Activism"; Jones, "Being of Service"; Jenkins, *Textual Poachers;* Jenkins, *Convergence Culture;* Hinck, "Theorizing a Public Engagement Keystone."

101. Qtd. in West, "Analogizing Interracial and Same-Sex Marriage," 561; Levin, "Aristotle's Theory of Metaphor."

102. Lakoff and Johnson, "Conceptual Metaphor in Everyday Language."

103. Richards, *The Philosophy of Rhetoric.*

104. Burke's terministic screens serve a similar function. Burke argues that sets of terminology can function as filters, directing our attention toward some places and directing our attention away from others (Burke, *Language as Symbolic Action*).

105. See, for example, Ivie, "Cold War Motives and the Rhetorical Metaphor"; Ivie, "The Metaphor of Force in Prowar Discourse"; Ivie, "Metaphor and the Rhetorical Invention of Cold War 'Idealists'"; Osborn, "Archetypal Metaphor in Rhetoric"; Osborn, "The Trajectory of My Work with Metaphor"; Cisneros, "Contaminated Communities"; Black, "The Second Persona"; Condit, "Pathos in Criticism"; and Farrell and Goodnight, "Accidental Rhetoric."

106. Qtd. in Copeland and Struck, *The Cambridge Companion to Allegory,* 2.

107. Abrams and Harpham, *A Glossary of Literary Terms,* 5.

108. Fletcher, *Allegory,* 2.

109. Copeland and Struck, *The Cambridge Companion to Allegory.*

110. Edward T. L. C., "J. K. Rowling at Carnegie Hall Reveals Dumbledore Is Gay."

111. Edward T. L. C., "J. K. Rowling at Carnegie Hall Reveals Dumbledore Is Gay."

112. West, "Analogizing Interracial and Same-Sex Marriage," 571.

113. West, "Analogizing Interracial and Same-Sex Marriage."

114. Erickson et al., "Press Release: Iowa, Kansas, & Nebraska Kick Off Coaches Challenge with Addition of Michigan and Minnesota."

115. "The 4-1-1 with Chad Kelsay."

116. Interview by the author with a former Husker track athlete, November 13, 2013.

117. Pillen, personal interview by the author, November 1, 2013.

118. Erickson et al., "Press Release: Iowa, Kansas, & Nebraska Kick Off Coaches Challenge with Addition of Michigan and Minnesota."

119. Erickson et al., "Press Release: Iowa, Kansas, & Nebraska Kick Off Coaches Challenge with Addition of Michigan and Minnesota."

120. "1996 Tostitos Fiesta Bowl."

121. *Nebraska Football 2014—Be Ready.*

122. Olson, "Most to Prove in the Big 12."

123. Walker, personal interview by the author, October 31, 2013.

124. Walker, personal interview by the author, October 31, 2013.

125. Aden, *Huskerville*, 102.

126. Unfortunately, in 2017, TeamMates moved away from the Husker framing and renamed the Coaches Challenge as the Back to School Challenge because, in 2016, TeamMates expanded to include chapters just over the state border in Kansas and Wyoming. For these chapters, the Nebraska Husker framing didn't make sense. So TeamMates transformed the Coaches Challenge into a Back to School Challenge. While the Nebraska Husker football coach may no longer be central to the campaign, TeamMates encourages chapters to reach out to their local coaches as part of the Back to School campaign. While the Back to School Challenge emphasizes the role mentors play in the education and lives of school-aged children and teenagers, it completely leaves behind the fan-based ethical framework that was at the center of the Coaches Challenge campaign.

127. Pillen, personal interview by the author, November 1, 2013.

128. Hince, phone interview by the author, September 20, 2013.

Chapter Three

1. H. Green and J. Green, "Vlogbrothers (YouTube)."

2. J. Green, "John Green."

3. H. Green, "About EcoGeek."

4. Green and Green, "The Vlogbrothers."

5. As with most fan communities, there is also an element of celebrity. Nerdfighter fans' fandom of the vlog as a media text blurs with their fandom of John and Hank as celebrities, though fans sometimes try to manage the tension between those two types of fandoms. One participant explored this tension in the survey: "I am concerned that too much of the focus of nerdfighteria is on John and Hank as idols/celebrities, which they don't want to be, but they have become because of the size of the community and the way that most other YouTube fandoms/fandoms in general function. It seems often like people are creating things in the hopes that they will get "noticed" by John and Hank—which is a valid desire because they are super cool, but misses the great opportunity for other nerdfighters to see it and engage—much more likely and more fun. This ends up extending to the sort of screaming mob-like behavior at events because the whole focus is on the CENTER where John/Hank are, when what we need to be a strong community is to turn to those next to us and engage in every direction. /

I think we need to reemphasize participation and that the goal is this bigger conversation not being "knighted" by idols" (Nerdfighter Participant AX, online, open-ended survey).

6. Kiva, "Kiva- Kiva Lending Team: Nerdfighters."

7. H. Green, *Thoughts on the Project for Awesome.*

8. "Project for Awesome 2017."

9. Griffith and Papacharissi, "Looking for You."

10. Burgess and Greene, *YouTube*, 6.

11. Molyneaux et al., "Exploring the Gender Divide on YouTube"; Christian, "Real Vlogs."

12. Griffith and Papacharissi, "Looking for You"; Molyneaux et al., "Exploring the Gender Divide on YouTube."

13. Molyneaux et al., "Exploring the Gender Divide on YouTube"; Anarbaeva, "YouTubing Difference"; Kennedy, "Exploring YouTube as a Transformative Tool in the 'The Power of MAKEUP!' Movement"; Kurpiel, "The Stylistics of Selected American, Italian and Polish Challenge Vlogs"; Snelson, "Vlogging about School on YouTube"; Oh and Oh, "Vlogging White Privilege Abroad."

14. See, for example, Jenkins, *Convergence Culture*; Gray, Sandvoss, and Harrington, *Fandom*; For a notable exception, see Christian, "Fandom as Industrial Response: Producing Identity in an Independent Web Series."

15. Scholars have also examined the VlogBrothers in relation to young adult literature and ritual communication. (Garcia, *Critical Foundations in Young Adult Literature*; Anderson, "Siblings in Cyberspace").

16. J. Green, *Brotherhood 2.0, February 1, 2007.*

17. Jackie A., "The 'Nerdfighter' Arcade Game?—Nerdfighters."

18. Jackie A., "The 'Nerdfighter' Arcade Game?—Nerdfighters."

19. Jackie A., "The 'Nerdfighter' Arcade Game?—Nerdfighters."

20. J. Green, *Harry Potter Nerds Win at Life.*

21. Quantitative scholars point out the ways in which these kinds of narratives function to build culture in online communities like Nerdfighteria. For a quantitative analysis of the nerdfighter online community, see Leyton Escobar, Kommers, and Beldad, "Using Narratives as Tools for Channeling Participation in Online Communities."

22. Understanding the general demographic information of the nerdfighter fandom can be difficult because of a necessary reliance on snowball sampling. But we can triangulate data between a number of sources to begin to get what is likely a somewhat accurate picture of who participates in the Nerdfighteria fandom. The demographic questions from my survey of fifty nerdfighters may not be representative, but they offer a good orientation to some general characteristics of nerdfighters. Second, Hank Green, conducted a survey of the Nerdfighteria fandom in 2014, asking questions about demographic information as well as fan experiences and what nerdfighters would like to see more of from John and Hank. This survey has many more respondents than mine (nearly 100,000 respondents), but Hank's survey is still not necessarily representative, and it is limited in the questions he chose to ask. Last, we can triangulate these data points with nerdfighters' general perceptions and discourses about who is in their fandom. By triangulating all three sources of demographic, we can gain a picture of the nerdfighter fandom that is likely at least somewhat accurate.

23. Nerdfighter Participant Z, online, open-ended survey.

24. Nerdfighter Participant AP, online, open-ended survey.

25. Nerdfighter Participant AI, online, open-ended survey.

26. Nerdfighter Participant AF, online, open-ended survey.

27. Kligler-Vilenchik argues that the VlogBrothers videos comprise the nerdfighters' content world while also taking part in a wider taste community, focused around *Doctor Who*, Harry Potter, literature, and science. In this chapter, I follow Kligler-Vilenchik's later analysis, agreeing that the nerdfighters have a shared content world comprised of John and Hank's vlogs (see Kligler-Vilenchik, "Decreasing World Suck"; Kligler-Vilenchik, "Mechanisms of Translation").

28. Abbott, *An Introduction to Narrative*, 25.

29. J. Green, *Oct. 26: Discussing Nepal While Eating Toilet Paper.*

30. Gray, *Watching with the Simpsons*, 4.

31. H. Green, *Nerdfighteria Island.*

32. Wilkinson points out the way in which John Green's book *Paper Towns* emphasizes values that Nerdfighteria takes up as a community. But Wilkinson's analysis is limited to just one of John's books and thus cannot be extrapolated to the values articulated by John and Hank in their vlogs and the values enacted by nerdfighters (Wilkinson, "Nerdfighters, 'Paper Towns,' and Heterotopia").

33. J. *Green, Harry Potter Nerds Win at Life.*

34. Nerdfighter Participant AH, interview.

35. H. Green, *Hank vs. Hank*; J. Green, *Oct. 26: Discussing Nepal While Eating Toilet Paper*; J. Green, *Health Care Overhaul Summarized Via Massive Pig.*

36. Nerdfighter Participant S, online, open-ended survey.

37. Nerdfighter Participant I, online, open-ended survey.

38. Nerdfighter Participant H, online, open-ended survey.

39. Nerdfighter Participant AS, online, open-ended survey.

40. Nerdfighter Participant Q, online, open-ended survey.

41. For an intricate unpacking of the VlogBrothers' notion of "imagining others complexly," see D. Smith, "Imagining Others More Complexly."

42. Nerdfighter Participant AO, online, open-ended survey.

43. Nerdfighter Participant AG, online, open-ended survey.

44. Nerdfighter Participant BE, online, open-ended survey.

45. Nerdfighter Participant P, online, open-ended survey.

46. H. Green, *$40,000 of Red Balloons.*

47. Nerdfighter Participant Z, online, open-ended survey.

48. Nerdfighter Participant BB, online, open-ended survey.

49. Nerdfighter Participant U, online, open-ended survey.

50. Nerdfighter Participant M, online, open-ended survey.

51. H. Green, "SciShow."

52. H. Green, *The Science of Lying*; H. Green, *What You Need to Know about Ebola.*

53. *CrashCourse.*

54. *CrashCourse*; H. Green, "SciShow."

55. J. Green, *Influence, Airports, and the Nerdfighter Book Club*; J. Green, *Our Old Friend Complexity*.

56. H. *Green, March 20th*.

57. J. Green, *Brotherhood 2.0*.

58. Nerdfighter Participant S, online, open-ended survey.

59. Nerdfighter Participant AJ, online, open-ended survey.

60. Nerdfighter Participant AO, online, open-ended survey.

61. Nerdfighter Participant AU, online, open-ended survey.

62. Nerdfighter Participant Q, online, open-ended survey.

63. "About," VidCon.

64. Hinck, "Shifting Patterns of Football Fandom, Team Ownership, and Digital Media Cultures."

65. Nerdfighter Participant AS, online, open-ended survey.

66. Nerdfighter Participant AX, online, open-ended survey.

67. In some ways, my notion of an expanding rhetorical strategy resonates with Neta Kligler-Vilenchik's notion of mechanisms of translation, which she defines as "ways that groups can leverage the same spaces, practices, and language that are honed in the context of online participatory cultures and are employed by participants for sociability and enjoyment to extend participatory politics." However, Kligler-Vilenchik's mechanisms of translation emphasize structure and fan practices rather than rhetorical strategies. In her analysis of the nerdfighters, she identifies the establishment of a community and public, fan practices, and social norms around civil speech as mechanisms of translation that connect the VlogBrothers participatory culture with civic engagement. In this chapter, I turn my attention to the communication that enables, invites, and persuades nerdfighters to make that connection between the VlogBrothers and civic engagement (see Kligler-Vilenchik, "Mechanisms of Translation"; Kligler-Vilenchik, "Decreasing World Suck").

68. J. Green, *Giving Away over $700,000*.

69. J. Green, *The Bank of Nerdfighteria*.

70. J. Green, *Economics and Dentistry*.

71. J. Green, *The Bank of Nerdfighteria*.

72. Green and Green, *P4a, Space Pasta, and Giant Squids of Anger*.

73. Nerdfighter Participant AL, interview.

74. Nerdfighter Participant AN, interview.

75. J. Green, *The Bank of Nerdfighteria*.

76. J. Green, *Giving Away over $700,000*.

77. Nerdfighter Participant Q, online, open-ended survey.

78. Nerdfighter Participant Z, online, open-ended survey.

79. Nerdfighter Participant AB, online, open-ended survey.

80. Nerdfighter Participant U, online, open-ended survey.

81. Nerdfighter Participant AB, online, open-ended survey.

82. Nerdfighter Participant AJ, online, open-ended survey.

83. Nerdfighter Participant AR, online, open-ended survey.

84. Nerdfighter Participant AW, online, open-ended survey.

85. Nerdfighter Participant BF, online, open-ended survey.

86. H. Green, *I Got Nothin . . .*

87. J. Green, *Dec. 28th: John's Last Brotherhood 2.0 Video.*

88. H. Green, *Project for Awesome: Explanation and Humane Societies.*

89. H. Green, *Thoughts on the Project for Awesome.*

90. Nerdfighter Participant AZ, online, open-ended survey.

91. H. Green, *One More Day until the P4A!!!*

92. H. Green., *One More Day until the P4A!!!*

93. H. Green, *Announcing the 2009 Project for Awesome!!!*

94. H. Green, *Project for Awesome Time!! What Does It Mean?*

95. Nerdfighter Participant L, online, open-ended survey.

96. Nerdfighter Participant AE, online, open-ended survey.

97. Hathaway, "What Is Gamergate, and Why?"; Massanari, "# Gamergate and the Fappening."

98. Mantilla, *Gendertrolling;* Hess, "The Next Civil Rights Issue"; Jane, "Back to the Kitchen, Cunt."

99. Hess, "The Next Civil Rights Issue."

100. Hess, "The Next Civil Rights Issue."

101. Jane, "'Back to the Kitchen, Cunt."

102. Bennett, "Changing Citizenship in the Digital Age"; Schudson, *The Good Citizen.*

Chapter Four

1. Neate, "Lego Builds Yet Another Record Profit to Become World's Top Toymaker."

2. Neate, "Lego Builds Yet Another Record Profit to Become World's Top Toymaker."

3. Ringen, "How Lego Became the Apple of Toys."

4. Hills, "LEGO Dimensions Meets Doctor Who"; Nørgard and Toft-Nielsen, "Gandalf on the Death Star"; Aldred, "(Un)Blocking the Transmedial Character."

5. Zakarin, "LEGO's $116 Million Deal with Shell Oil Draws Protests, Ironic LEGO Art (Photos)."

6. Zakarin, "LEGO's $116 Million Deal with Shell Oil Draws Protests, Ironic LEGO Art (Photos)"; "Shell."

7. *LEGO: Everything Is NOT Awesome.* The GreenpeaceVideo YouTube channel, 2014, www.youtube.com/watch?v=qhbliUqo_r4.

8. "Lego Is Keeping Bad Company," 12.

9. Zakarin, "LEGO's $116 Million Deal with Shell Oil Draws Protests, Ironic LEGO Art (Photos)"; "New"; "LEGO Is Keeping Bad Company."

10. Flynn, "Everything Is Not Awesome with LEGO and Shell, Says Greenpeace"; D. Green, "Greenpeace Tells Lego to Ditch Shell [+ video]"; Petroff, "Lego Ditches Shell after Arctic Oil Protests"; Boehrer, "Greenpeace to Shell"; Gass, "How Did Greenpeace Get LEGO to Ditch Shell Play Sets?"; O'Reilly, "Here's the Chilling Greenpeace Video That Ended Lego's $116 Million Deal with Shell"; Duff, "How LEGO Got Awesome to #SaveTheArctic."

11. Duff, "How LEGO Got Awesome to #SaveTheArctic."

12. Baichtal and Meno, *The Cult of LEGO*.

13. Baichtal and Meno, *The Cult of LEGO*.

14. *BIONICLE*, Internet Movie Database; Baker, *Lego*.

15. Lord and Miller, *The Lego Movie*; Baldo, *Lego Atlantis*; Baker, *Lego*.

16. "All Time Box Office"; "The LEGO Movie."

17. Sorokanich, "Two More Summer Lego Movies Are Coming!"

18. Baichtal and Meno, *The Cult of LEGO*, 20.

19. Geraghty, *Cult Collectors*, 167.

20. Geraghty, *Cult Collectors*, 167–68.

21. Baichtal and Meno, *The Cult of LEGO*, 7.

22. This isn't to say that AFOLs don't buy LEGO sets. Rather, the main draw for AFOLs is the unusual pieces in a particular set.

23. pbegin, "LUG Statistics in the World—General LEGO Discussion."

24. Although I conducted fieldwork with my local Cincinnati LUG, OKI LUG (Ohio-Kentucky-Indiana LUG), LUGs are international. Fan studies scholars Sophie Gwendolyn Einwachter and Felix M. Simon investigated a German LUG called Schwabenstein 2×4, which, like so many other LUGs, sought to provide AFOLs with a place to build and talk together (Einwachter and Simon, "How Digital Remix and Fan Culure Helped the Lego Comeack").

25. pbegin, "LUG Statistics in the World—General LEGO Discussion."

26. Garlen, "Block Party: A Look at Adult Fans of LEGO," 121.

27. Johnson, "Chicks with Bricks."

28. Pickett, "Part I"; Pickett and Wade, "Part II"; Pickett and Wade, "Part III"; Pickett, "Part IV."

29. Pickett and Wade, "Part III."

30. Johnson, "Chicks with Bricks."

31. Davidson and Junge, *A LEGO Brickumentary*.

32. Davidson and Junge, *A LEGO Brickumentary*.

33. Johnson, "Figuring Identity," 322.

34. Education, "LEGO Education."

35. Education, "Elementary Competitions—LEGO Education."

36. "Preschool—LEGO Education."

37. Mervis, "NSF Makes a New Bid to Boost Diversity."

38. Mervis, "NSF Makes a New Bid to Boost Diversity," 1017.

39. Quiñones-Hinojosa and Colón Ramos, "Racism in the Research Lab."

40. Kaiser, "NIH Uncovers Racial Disparity in Grant Awards."

41. Mervis, "NIH Program Fails to Launch Blacks in Biotech."

42. Corbett and Hill, "Solving the Equation."

43. Corbett and Hill, "Solving the Equation."

44. Massinger and Massinger, "How Women Are Harassed Out of Science"; Williams, Phillips, and Hall, "Double Jeopardy?"

45. Schmidt, "I'm Not a Sexist."

46. Wootson Jr., "A Google Engineer Wrote That Women May Be Unsuited for Tech Jobs. Women Wrote Back."

47. LEGO Participant BQ, online, open-ended survey.

48. LEGO Participant AU, online, open-ended survey.

49. LEGO Participant BM, online, open-ended survey.

50. LEGO Participant P, online, open-ended survey.

51. LEGO Participant BC, online, open-ended survey.

52. LEGO Participant S, online, open-ended survey.

53. Of course, narrative media about LEGO, like its television shows and films, contain many meanings with many possible corresponding readings, including some readings that might be seen as contradictory with the LEGO Group's business practices. For example, *The LEGO Movie* celebrates creativity apart from directions, yet LEGO's sets emphasize directions and particular builds. Fans largely manage these multiple meanings and contradictions by emphasizing some meanings over others. In this chapter, I focus on the ways in which the narrative media offers discourses that line up with and support the AFOL ethical framework. These are certainly not the only meanings inherent in the films or television shows, but they demonstrate one way in which LEGO discourses line up with the AFOL ethical framework.

54. Gibson, *AFOL: A Blockumentary.*

55. LEGO Participant BT, online, open-ended survey.

56. LEGO Participant CL, online, open-ended survey.

57. LEGO Participant W, online, open-ended survey.

58. LEGO Participant W, online, open-ended survey.

59. Baichtal and Meno, *The Cult of LEGO,* 32.

60. LEGO Participant CG, online, open-ended survey.

61. LEGO Participant BQ, online, open-ended survey.

62. LEGO Participant Y, online, open-ended survey.

63. LEGO Participant BZ, online, open-ended survey.

64. LEGO Participant AE, online, open-ended survey.

65. Barnes, "The Lego Movie Writer/Directors."

66. Sampson, "Block Party."

67. Lord and Miller, "Writers Built 'The LEGO Movie,' Block by Block, on Belief."

68. "About Us—About Us LEGO.Com."

69. Johnson, "Figuring Identity," 320.

70. Johnson, "Figuring Identity," 308.

71. Johnson, "Chicks with Bricks" 309.

72. LEGO Participant BP, online, open-ended survey.

73. LEGO Participant CK, online, open-ended survey.

74. LEGO Participant S, online, open-ended survey.

75. LEGO Participant AC, online, open-ended survey.

76. LEGO Participant Y, online, open-ended survey.

77. LEGO Participant BZ, online, open-ended survey.

78. LEGO Participant BZ, online, open-ended survey.

79. LEGO Participant BZ, online, open-ended survey.

80. LEGO Participant BH, online, open-ended survey.

81. LEGO Participant BC, online, open-ended survey.

82. LEGO Participant BC, online, open-ended survey.

83. LEGO Participant BD, online, open-ended survey.

84. Lord and Miller, *The Lego Movie.*

85. LEGO Participant AI, online, open-ended survey.

86. LEGO Participant BE, online, open-ended survey.

87. LEGO Participant BF, online, open-ended survey.

88. LEGO Participant BX, online, open-ended survey.

89. LEGO Participant BR, online, open-ended survey.

90. LEGO Participant CK, online, open-ended survey.

91. LEGO Participant CG, online, open-ended survey.

92. LEGO Participant BE, online, open-ended survey.

93. LEGO Participant CK, online, open-ended survey.

94. LEGO Participant Y, online, open-ended survey.

95. LEGO Participant AS, online, open-ended survey.

96. LEGO Participant AE, online, open-ended survey.

97. LEGO Participant AK, online, open-ended survey.

98. LEGO Participant BP, online, open-ended survey.

99. LEGO Participant CL, online, open-ended survey.

100. LEGO Participant BT, online, open-ended survey.

101. LEGO Participant Z, online, open-ended survey.

102. Lord and Miller, *The LEGO Movie.*

103. Lord and Miller, "Writers Built 'The LEGO Movie,' Block by Block, on Belief."

104. Lord and Miller, "Writers Built 'The LEGO Movie,' Block by Block, on Belief."

105. "History"; "About," Greenpeace USA.

106. Katz-Kimchi and Manosevitch, "Mobilizing Facebook Users against Facebook's Energy Policy," 249.

107. DeLuca, *Image Politics;* Delicath and Deluca, "Image Events, the Public Sphere, and Argumentative Practice," 315; Brunner and DeLuca, "The Argumentative Force of Image Networks."

108. Brunner and DeLuca, "The Argumentative Force of Image Networks: Greenpeace's Panmediated Global Detox Campaign"; DeLuca, *Image Politics.*

109. Gray, *Watching with the Simpsons;* Hutcheon, *A Theory of Parody.*

110. Baym and Jones, *News Parody and Political Satire across the Globe;* Gray, *Watching with the Simpsons;* Jones, *Entertaining Politics.*

111. Hariman, "Political Parody and Public Culture."

112. Jamison, *Fic,* 18.

113. Hellekson and Busse, *The Fan Fiction Studies Reader,* 7.

114. Kuhn, "The Rhetoric of Remix"; McIntosh, "A History of Subversive Remix Video before YouTube"; Russo and Coppa, "Fan/Remix Video (a Remix) [Editorial]."

115. McIntosh, "A History of Subversive Remix Video before YouTube"; Wilkins, *State of the Union . . . Not Good.*

116. McIntosh, "A History of Subversive Remix Video before YouTube"; Killa, *Perhaps, Perhaps, Perhaps.*

117. Tegan and Sara and The Lonely Island, *Everything Is AWESOME!!!*

118. Tegan and Sara and The Lonely Island, *Everything Is AWESOME!!!.*

119. LEGO Participant AM, online, open-ended survey.

120. LEGO Participant AU, online, open-ended survey.

121. LEGO Participant AR, online, open-ended survey.

122. LEGO Participant AD, online, open-ended survey.

123. LEGO Participant BM, online, open-ended survey.

124. LEGO Participant R, online, open-ended survey.

125. Hinck, "Ethical Frameworks and Ethical Modalities."

126. Katz-Kimchi and Manosevitch, "Mobilizing Facebook Users against Facebook's Energy Policy."

Chapter Five

1. Schrodt, "The 10 Biggest Blockbuster Movies of All Time, and How Much They Raked In."

2. "The 50th Academy Awards | 1978."

3. LaSalata, "Celebration Orlando 2017 Sets New Attendance Record at over 70,000 Fans."

4. Jenkins and Hassler-Forest, "Foreword: 'I Have a Bad Feeling about This': A Conversation about Star Wars and the History of Transmedia," 16.

5. "J. J. Abrams Confirms STAR WARS VII Script Is Done"; Leonard, "How Disney Bought Lucasfilm—and Its Plans for 'Star Wars.'"

6. Generation X is defined as people who were born between 1965 and 1980, while the millennial generation is comprised of people born between 1981 and 1998. Generation Z has emerged as a term for the generation born after millennials (see Street et al., "The Generations Defined"; and The Hartman Group, "New Kids On The Block").

7. "Retcon" is short for "retroactive continuity," meaning that a part of a fictional story was revised to suit new or upcoming stories. The term is used frequently within fan communities (see "Star Wars Legends"; and "Retcon").

8. Brooker, *Using the Force*, 84.

9. Brooker, *Using the Force*, 79.

10. Indeed, some fans argue that Jar Jar Binks is criticized too much and that he actually played an important role in the story. Others fan theorize that Jar Jar Binks is secretly a Sith Lord, a powerful and evil user of the Force (Greenring, "This Fan Theory about Jar Jar Binks Will Blow Your Mind").

11. Star Wars Participant R, online, open-ended survey.

12. Star Wars Participant AU, online, open-ended survey.

13. Star Wars Participant AU, online open-ended survey.

14. Star Wars Participant BN, online, open-ended survey.

15. Star Wars Participant B, online, open-ended survey.

16. Brooker, *Using the Force*; Proctor, "'Holy Crap, More Star Wars! More Star Wars?'"

17. Gunnels, "A Jedi like My Father before Me"; Farris, "Fan-Driven Identity Narratives"; Phillips, "The Butcher, the Baker, the Lightsaber Maker [Symposium]"; "The 501st Legion"; "Little Warrior | Mandalorian Mercs Costume Club."

18. F. Phillips, "The Butcher, the Baker, the Lightsaber Maker [Symposium]."

19. Groskopf, "Hoarding and Community in Star Wars Card Trader."

20. F. Phillips, "The Star Wars Franchise, Fan Edits, and Lucasfilm"; Wille, "Fan Edits and the Legacy of The Phantom Edit"; Wille, "Dead Links, Vaporcuts, and Creativity in Fan Edit Replication"; Joly-Corcoran and Ludlow, "Fans, Fics & Films . . . 'Thank the Maker(s)!'"; Scott, "Immersive and Interactive Adaptation and Extensions of Star Wars"; Brooker, *Using the Force*.

21. Ramsey, *Just Stop Talking about Race!!*; Terrill, "Unity and Duality in Barack Obama's 'A More Perfect Union'"; Omi and Winant, *Racial Formation in the United States*.

22. SpotRight Marketing firm found that the average follower of the @StarWars twitter account is a forty-six-year-old man, married with children. During the opening weekend of *The Last Jedi*, 58 percent of the audience were men (Lang, "Box Office"; Valinksy, "Spoiler Alert").

23. Proctor, "'Holy Crap, More Star Wars! More Star Wars?'"

24. Brooker, *Using the Force*.

25. Henry Jenkins argues that "Lucas had a particularly narrow conception of Star Wars' audience that reflected his own white, male worldview, and he drew on a set of genre conventions, largely without reflection, that dated back to the late nineteenth/early twentieth century, and which smacked of the cultural logic of colonialism" (Jenkins and Hassler-Forest, "Foreword: 'I Have a Bad Feeling about This': A Conversation about Star Wars and the History of Transmedia," 26).

26. Jao, "Daisy Ridley Calls Demand for Rey Merchandise 'Amazing,' Expect More in the Future."

27. Johnson, "May the Force Be with Katie."

28. Elderkin, "Women of Star Wars Get Highlighted in New Series of Animated Shorts."

29. Historian, "Star Wars Role Models."

30. Historian, "Star Wars Role Models."

31. Star Wars Participant P, online, open-ended survey.

32. Star Wars Participant AG, online, open-ended survey.

33. Star Wars Participant F, online, open-ended survey.

34. Star Wars Participant BB, online, open-ended survey.

35. Star Wars Participant K, online, open-ended survey.

36. Star Wars Participant AZ, online, open-ended survey.

37. Star Wars Participant BQ, online, open-ended survey.

38. Star Wars Participant G, online, open-ended survey.

39. Star Wars Participant M, online, open-ended survey.

40. Star Wars Participant AP, online, open-ended survey.

41. Star Wars Participant BP, online, open-ended survey.

42. Star Wars Participant P, online, open-ended survey.

43. Star Wars Participant BO, online, open-ended survey.

44. Star Wars Participant BP, online, open-ended survey.

45. Star Wars Participant BN, online, open-ended survey.

46. "The Mythology of 'Star Wars' with George Lucas."

47. "The Mythology of 'Star Wars' with George Lucas."

48. Campbell, *The Hero with a Thousand Faces*.

49. Dundes, "Folkloristics in the Twenty-First Century (AFS Invited Presidential Plenary Address, 2004)"; Jorgensen, "Why Folklorists Hate Joseph Campbell's Work."

50. Pollock, *Skywalking*, 134.

51. Pollock, *Skywalking*, 144.

52. Gunnels, "'A Jedi Like My Father before Me," 4.11.

53. Brooker, *Using the Force*, 5.

54. Brooker, *Using the Force*, 6.

55. Brooker, *Using the Force*, 5.

56. Brooker, *Using the Force*, 212.

57. Gunnels, "A Jedi Like My Father before Me," 4.4.

58. Proctor, "'Holy Crap, More Star Wars! More Star Wars?," 211.

59. Brooker, *Using the Force*, 82.

60. Gunnels, "A Jedi Like My Father before Me," 5.2.

61. Of course, not every fan wants to apply Star Wars to their everyday lives or to civic engagement. There are some fans who look to Star Wars to provide a sense of escape. This section of fandom is big enough that the Star Wars politics podcast, *Beltway Banthas*, took the issue head-on in their very first episode: "There is a line that we are going to walk with this show between those who want to study every aspect of Star Wars, even the politics of Star Wars and those that really just want to be immersed in the fantasy and lore of Star Wars in a way that is detached from your daily existence. Because there's definitely an angle to my fandom that I retreat into Star Wars because I don't want to think about the crap that I see on TV anymore. I don't want to see it. I just want to be in that X-Wing and fly away. And it is really, really important for Star Wars fans to have that. However, there are other Star Wars fans who are much more analytical." For the hosts of *Beltway Banthas*, it was important to recognize those different sections of the Star Wars fan community and to recognize those needs even arising in the same fan (both escapism and an analytical view of the politics of Star Wars). (Kent and Salih, *Pilot*).

62. Star Wars Participant F, online, open-ended survey.

63. Star Wars Participant BN, online, open-ended survey.

64. Brooker and Hassler-Forest, "Afterword: 'You'll Find I'm Full of Surprises': The Future of Star Wars," 293.

65. Jenkins and Hassler-Forest, "Foreword: 'I Have a Bad Feeling about This': A Conversation about Star Wars and the History of Transmedia," 30.

66. Cagle, Skype interview by the author, June 2, 2017.

67. "The Mythology of 'Star Wars' with George Lucas."

68. "The Mythology of 'Star Wars' with George Lucas."

69. Bortolin, *The Dharma of Star Wars*; Staub, *Christian Wisdom of the Jedi Masters*; McDowell, *The Gospel According to Star Wars*.

70. Belfast, "Star Wars."

71. Star Wars Participant C, online, open-ended survey.

72. Star Wars Participant O, online, open-ended survey.

73. Star Wars Participant S, online, open-ended survey.

74. Star Wars Participant BG, online, open-ended survey.

75. "The Mythology of 'Star Wars' with George Lucas."

76. Brooker, *Star Wars*.

77. Brooker, *Star Wars*, 26.

78. Brooker, *Star Wars*, 22.

79. Star Wars Participant E, online, open-ended survey.

80. Star Wars Participant I, online, open-ended survey.

81. Star Wars Participant AD, online, open-ended survey.

82. Star Wars Participant AC, online, open-ended survey.

83. "The Mythology of 'Star Wars' with George Lucas."

84. Allston, *Fate of the Jedi: Outcast*.

85. "Kanan Jarrus (Character)."

86. "Ezra Bridger."

87. @PattyBones2, "Light Is about Others, Dark Is about Yourself."

88. "The Mythology of 'Star Wars' with George Lucas."

89. "Enter to Win Your Dream Experience."

90. Silverman, phone interview by the author, August 15, 2014.

91. Star Wars Participant BJ, online, open-ended survey.

92. "Star Wars."

93. "Star Wars."

94. "Star Wars."

95. "Star Wars."

96. Silverman, phone interview by the author, August 15, 2014.

97. Brooker, *Using the Force*, 116.

98. Brooker, *Using the Force*.

99. Silverman, phone interview by the author, August 15, 2014.

100. Abrams, *Star Wars: Force for Change—A Message from J. J. Abrams*.

101. "Let's Take a Closer Look at the New Alien in STAR WARS."

102. Abrams, *Star Wars: Force for Change—An Update from J. J. Abrams*.

103. *Sweet Star Wars 7 Surprises! Crazier than We Thought! (Nerdist News w/ Jessica Chobot)*.

104. "STAR WARS."

105. *Jon Stewart and Stephen Colbert Battle for Title of World's Biggest Star Wars Fan!*

106. "Star Wars."

107. Star Wars, *Star Wars: Force for Change—Your Chance to Win an Autographed Rogue One Stormtrooper Helmet*, 2016, www.youtube.com/watch?v=9O7dxSVbMHA.

108. Star Wars, *Mark Hamill & Daisy Ridley's Epic Star Wars*.

109. Star Wars Participant J, online, open-ended survey.

110. Star Wars Participant L, online, open-ended survey.

111. Star Wars Participant AB, online, open-ended survey.

112. Star Wars Participant O, online, open-ended survey.

113. Star Wars Participant BH, online, open-ended survey.

114. Star Wars Participant BK, online, open-ended survey.

115. Star Wars Participant AU, online, open-ended survey.

116. Star Wars Participant E, online, open-ended survey.

117. Star Wars Participant BQ, online, open-ended survey.

118. Star Wars Participant BG, online, open-ended survey.

119. Star Wars Participant BN, online, open-ended survey.

120. Star Wars Participant BP, online, open-ended survey.

121. Star Wars Participant E, online, open-ended survey.

122. Silverman, phone interview by the author, August 15, 2014.

Conclusion

1. Rusk, online interview by the author, May 24, 2017.

2. Rusk, online interview by the author, May 24, 2017.

3. Moorehead et al., Facetime interview by the author, June 10, 2017.

4. Moorehead et al., Facetime interview by the author, June 10, 2017.

5. Moorehead et al., Facetime interview by the author, June 10, 2017.

6. Moorehead et al., Facetime interview by the author, June 10, 2017.

7. Rusk, online interview by the author, May 24, 2017.

8. For analysis of the process of subjectivity, see Zaeske, "Signatures of Citizenship," 148.

9. Kahne, Middaugh, and Allen, "Youth, New Media, and the Rise of Participatory Politics"; Cohen and Kahne, "Participatory Politics"; Jenkins et al., *By Any Media Necessary*; Jenkins, *Convergence Culture.*

10. Jenkins, *Confronting the Challenges of Participatory Culture.*

11. Kahne, Middaugh, and Allen, "Youth, New Media, and the Rise of Participatory Politics."

12. Jenkins et al., *By Any Media Necessary.*

13. Dewey, *The Public and Its Problems;* Habermas, *The Structural Transformation of the Public Sphere.*

14. Hinck, "Theorizing a Public Engagement Keystone."

15. Some of these fan communities skew more heavily white than others. About 90 percent of my Star Wars survey respondents and 93 percent of my LEGO respondents identified as white. However, 74 percent of nerdfighters in Hank's Nerdfighteria Census identified as white.

16. Pande, "Squee from the Margins," 210.

17. Jenkins, "Fandom Studies as I See It," 97.

18. Scott, "Fangirls in Refrigerators," 3.4.

19. Wanzo, 1.4. See also Carrington, *Speculative Blackness.*

20. Vaughn, "Hunger Is NOT a Game."

21. Grossman-Cohen, "The Hunger Games Fans Join Oxfam America, Harry Potter Alliance to say: 'Hunger Is Not a Game.'"

22. "How 'Hunger Games' Actually Fights Hunger."

23. Martin, "Fan Power."

24. Rosenberg, "EXCLUSIVE."

25. McCready, "Don't Stop Hunger Games Fans From Fighting Hunger!"

26. Martin, "Fan Power."

Coda

1. Jenkins, *Textual Poachers; Bennett and Booth, Seeing Fans.*

2. Hinck, "Companions Against Global Warming."

3. DC Entertainment, "Press Release: DC Entertainment announces 'We Can Be Heroes,' an Unprecedented Giving Campaign to Fight the Hunger Crisis in the Horn of Africa."

4. Chouliaraki, *The Ironic Spectator,* 9.

5. Tabb, *Economic Governance in the Age of Globalization.*

BIBLIOGRAPHY

Abbate, Janet. *Inventing the Internet.* Cambridge: MIT Press, 1999.

Abbott, H. Porter. *An Introduction to Narrative.* New York: Cambridge University Press, 2001.

Abercrombie, Nick, and Brian Longhurst. *Audiences: A Sociological Theory of Performance and Imagination.* London: Sage, 1998.

"About." Greenpeace USA. Accessed August 29, 2016. www.greenpeace.org/usa /about/.

"About." VidCon. Accessed June 11, 2017. http://vidcon.com/about/.

"About Us—About Us LEGO.Com." LEGO. 2016. www.lego.com/en-us/aboutus.

Abrams, J. J. *Star Wars: Force for Change—A Message from J. J. Abrams.* Video. Star Wars YouTube Channel, 2014. www.youtube.com/watch?v=XfNiC9iKM0Q&index =2&list=PL148kCvXk8pALpyZVxIj3KX10IH-Sk7Jc.

———. *Star Wars: Force for Change—An Update from J. J. Abrams.* Video. Star Wars YouTube Channel, 2014. www.youtube.com/watch?v=xWBGrkc360M&index =1&list=PL148kCvXk8pALpyZVxIj3KX10IH-Sk7Jc.

Abrams, M. H., and Geoffrey Galt Harpham. *A Glossary of Literary Terms.* 8th ed. International student ed. Boston: Thomson, Wadsworth, 2005.

Adams, Sarah Jane. "Hell Hath No Fury Like a Scorned Soap Fan: A Case Study of Soap Opera Fan Activism." Master's thesis, North Dakota State University of Agriculture and Applied Science, 2012.

Aden, Roger C. *Huskerville: A Story of Nebraska Football, Fans, and the Power of Place.* Jefferson, NC: McFarland, 2007.

Aldred, Jessica. "(Un)Blocking the Transmedial Character: Digital Abstraction as Franchise Strategy in Travellers' Tales' LEGO Games." In *LEGO Studies: Examining the Building Blocks of a Transmedial Phenomenon,* edited by Mark J. P. Wolf, 105–17. New York: Routledge, Taylor and Francis, 2014.

"All Time Box Office." Box Office Mojo, n.d. www.boxofficemojo.com/alltime/do mestic.htm.

Allston, Aaron. *Fate of the Jedi: Outcast*. New York: Del Rey, 2009.

"Americans to Rest of World: Soccer Not Really Our Thing." *Pew Social & Demographic Trends* (blog), June 14, 2006. www.pewsocialtrends.org/2006/06/14 /americans-to-rest-of-world-soccer-not-really-our-thing/.

Anarbaeva, Samara M. "YouTubing Difference: Performing Identity in Video Communities." *Journal for Virtual Worlds Research* 9, no. 2 (2016). https://journals.tdl .org/jvwr/index.php/jvwr/article/view/7193.

Anderson, H. "Siblings in Cyberspace: Carey's Ritual Model of Communication in the Digital Age." *Intersect: The Stanford Journal of Science, Technology and Society* 4, no. 1 (2011): 92–100.

Aristotle. *Nicomachean Ethics*. Translated by Terence Irwin. 2nd ed. Indianapolis: Hackett, 1999.

Asen, Robert. *Democracy, Deliberation, and Education*. University Park: Pennsylvania State University Press, 2015.

———. "A Discourse Theory of Citizenship." *Quarterly Journal of Speech* 90, no. 2 (2004): 189–211.

Associated Press. "Nebraska Governor Is Victor in G.O.P. Primary." *New York Times*, May 11, 2006, sec. National. www.nytimes.com/2006/05/11/us/11nebraska.html.

Bacon-Smith, Camille. *Enterprising Women: Television Fandom and the Creation of Popular Myth*. Philadelphia: University of Pennsylvania Press, 1992.

Baichtal, John, and Joe Meno. *The Cult of LEGO*. San Francisco: No Starch Press, 2011.

Bairner, Alan. *Sport, Nationalism, and Globalization: European and North American Perspectives*. SUNY Series in National Identities. Albany: State University of New York Press, 2001.

Baker, Howard E., dir. *Lego: The Adventures of Clutch Powers*. Santa Monica, CA: Threshold Animation Studios, 2010.

Baker-Whitelaw, Gavia. "Harry Potter Alliance Battles Income Inequality with #My HungerGames." *The Daily Dot* (blog), November 18, 2014. www.dailydot.com /entertainment/harry-potter-alliance-my-hunger-games/.

Baldo, Mark, dir. *Lego Atlantis*. Threshold Entertainment, 2010.

Barnes, Henry. "*The Lego Movie* Writer/Directors: 'We Wanted to Make an Anti-Totalitarian Movie for Kids.'" *Guardian*, December 12, 2014, Film sec. www.the guardian.com/film/2014/dec/12/lego-movie-writers-phil-lord-christopher-mil ler-interivew.

Barone, Francine, David Zeitlyn, and Viktor Mayer-Schönberger. "Learning from

Failure: The Case of the Disappearing Web Site." *First Monday* 20, no. 5 (April 27, 2015). http://firstmonday.org/ojs/index.php/fm/article/view/5852.

Bauman, Richard. *Verbal Art as Performance.* Prospect Heights, IL: Waveland, 1984.

Bauman, Zygmunt. *Liquid Modernity.* Malden, MA: Polity, 2000.

———. *Liquid Times: Living in an Age of Uncertainty.* Malden, MA: Polity, 2007.

Baym, Geoffrey, and Jeffrey Jones. *News Parody and Political Satire across the Globe.* New York: Routledge, 2013.

Baym, Nancy. *Personal Connections in the Digital Age.* Malden, MA: Polity, 2010.

———. *Tune In, Log On: Soaps, Fandom, and Online Community.* Thousand Oaks, CA: Sage, 2000.

Beck, Ulrich. *Risk Society: Towards a New Modernity.* London: Sage, 2010.

Belfast, Andrew. "Star Wars: The Nature of the Force." *Future of the Force* (blog), April 9, 2017. https://futureoftheforce.com/star-wars-the-nature-of-the-force-98772ab9c68.

Belson, Ken. "Kaepernick vs. the N.F.L.: A Primer on His Collusion Case." *New York Times,* December 8, 2017, Sports sec. www.nytimes.com/2017/12/08/sports/kaepernick-collusion.html.

Bennett, Alanna. "#MyHungerGames: My Story of Poverty, and Why the Hashtag Is So Important." *The Mary Sue* (blog), November 21, 2014. www.themarysue.com/my-hunger-games/.

Bennett, Lance. "Changing Citizenship in the Digital Age." In *Civic Life Online: Learning How Digital Media Can Engage Youth,* edited by Bennett, 1–24. Cambridge: MIT Press, 2008.

———. "1998 Ithiel De Sola Pool Lecture: The UnCivic Culture: Communication, Identity, and the Rise of Lifestyle Politics." *PS: Political Science and Politics* 31, no. 4 (1998): 740–61.

———. "Political Life in Late Modern Society: Communication, Citizenship, and Participation in a Time of Institutional Decline." Paper presented at the conference "Communication, Consumers, and Citizens: Revisiting the Politics of Consumption," University of Wisconsin–Madison, March 4, 2011.

Bennett, Lance, and Alexandra Segerberg. *The Logic of Connective Action: Digital Media and the Personalization of Contentious Politics.* Cambridge: Cambridge University Press, 2013.

Bennett, Lucy. "'If We Stick Together We Can Do Anything': Lady Gaga Fandom, Philanthropy and Activism through Social Media." *Celebrity Studies* 5, no. 1–2 (April 3, 2014): 138–52. https://doi.org/10.1080/19392397.2013.813778.

Bennett, Lucy Kathryn, and Paul Booth, eds. *Seeing Fans: Representations of Fandom in Media and Popular Culture.* New York: Bloomsbury Academic, 2016.

"Big 10 School Profile: Nebraska." Big 10 Football, n.d. www.bigten.org/schools/neb/big10-schools-neb-body.html.

Big Red Anthem—Brown (Official Video), HD, 2011. www.youtube.com/watch?v=hg5vbyqxtPc&feature=youtube_gdata_player.

Black, Edwin. "A Note on Theory and Practice in Rhetorical Criticism." *Western Journal of Speech Communication* 44 (1980): 331–36.

———. "On Objectivity and Politics in Criticism." *American Communication Journal* 4 (2000). http://acjournal.org.

———. "The Second Persona." *Quarterly Journal of Speech* 57, no. 2 (1970): 109–19.

*BlerdNation*TM. Accessed January 3, 2016. www.blerdnation.com/.

Blerds Online. Accessed January 3, 2016. www.blerdsonline.com/.

"Bob Devaney." Huskers.com. Accessed December 12, 2013. www.huskers.com/ViewArticle.dbml?ATCLID=919762&DB_OEM_ID=100.

Boehrer, Katherine. "Greenpeace's Lego Video Aims to End Shell Partnership (Updated)." *Huffington Post*, July 11, 2014. www.huffingtonpost.com/2014/07/08/greenpeace-lego-video-shell_n_5567541.html.

Bogost, Ian. "Against Aca-Fandom," July 29, 2010. http://bogost.com/writing/blog/against_aca-fandom/.

Bonzio, Roberto. "Power of Transmedia Unveiled in Italy." *Forbes*, October 3, 2011. www.forbes.com/sites/robertobonzio/2011/10/03/power-of-transmedia-unveiled-at-tedx-rome-conference/.

Booth, Paul. "Fandom in/as the Academy." *Flow: A Critical Forum on Television and Media Culture* (blog), December 17, 2010. www.flowjournal.org/2010/12/fandom-in-as-the-academy/.

———. *Playing Fans: Negotiating Fandom and Media in the Digital Age*. Iowa City: University of Iowa Press, 2015.

Bortolin, Matthew. *The Dharma of Star Wars*. Boston: Wisdom, 2005.

boyd, danah. *It's Complicated: The Social Lives of Networked Teens*. New Haven: Yale University Press, 2014.

Bozeman, Barry, and Daniel Fay. "Minority Football Coaches' Diminished Careers: Why Is the 'Pipeline' Clogged? Minority Football Coaches' Diminished Careers." *Social Science Quarterly* 94, no. 1 (March 2013): 29–58. https://doi.org/10.1111/j.1540-6237.2012.00931.x.

Braddock, J. H., E. Smith, and M. P. Dawkins. "Race and Pathways to Power in the National Football League." *American Behavioral Scientist* 56, no. 5 (February 9, 2012): 711–27. https://doi.org/10.1177/0002764211433802.

Branch, John. "The Awakening of Colin Kaepernick." *New York Times*, September 7, 2017, Sports sec. www.nytimes.com/2017/09/07/sports/colin-kaepernick-nfl-protests.html.

Brandzel, Amy. *Against Citizenship: The Violence of the Normative.* Champaign: University of Illinois Press, 2016.

Breech, John. "Coroner's Report Reveals Contents of Lawrence Phillips' Suicide Note." CBSSports.Com, June 16, 2016. www.cbssports.com/nfl/news/coroners -report-reveals-contents-of-lawrence-phillips-suicide-note/.

Broadnax, Jamie. "Racialized Nerdiness: Does Race Play a Role in Being Nerdy?" *Black Girl Nerds* (blog), April 15, 2013. http://blackgirlnerds.com/racialized -nerdiness-does-race-play-a-role-in-being-nerdy/.

Brooker, Will. "SCMS 2011 Workshop: Acafandom and the Future of Fan Studies: Will Brooker's Provocation." *Transform* (blog), March 16, 2011. http://lstein.wordpress .com/2011/03/16/scms-2011-workshop-acafandom-and-the-future-of-fan-studies/.

———. *Star Wars.* BFI Film Classics. New York: Palgrave Macmillan on behalf of the British Film Institute, 2009.

———. *Using the Force: Creativity, Community, and Star Wars Fans.* New York: Continuum, 2002.

Brooker, Will, and Dan Hassler-Forest. "Afterword: 'You'll Find I'm Full of Surprises': The Future of Star Wars." In *Star Wars and the History of Transmedia Storytelling,* edited by Sean Guynes and Hassler-Forest. Amsterdam: Amsterdam University Press, 2018.

Brooks, Dana, and Ronald Althouse. "African American Head Coaches and Administrators: Progress But . . . ?" In *Racism in College Athletics: The African American Athlete's Experience,* edited by Brooks and Althouse, 85–117. Morgantown, WV: Fitness Information Technology, 2000.

Brouwer, Daniel C., and Rob Asen. *Public Modalities: Rhetoric, Culture, Media, and the Shape of Public Life.* Tuscaloosa: University of Alabama Press, 2010.

Brown, Dan. *Is Harry Potter Chocolate Made by Child Slaves?* 2013. www.youtube .com/watch?v=cuu7ocrn32s&feature=youtube_gdata_player.

Bruce, T. "Reflections on Communication and Sport: On Women and Femininities." *Communication and Sport* 1, no. 1–2 (January 16, 2013): 125–37. https://doi.org /10.1177/2167479512472883.

Brunner, Elizabeth A., and Kevin Michael DeLuca. "The Argumentative Force of Image Networks: Greenpeace's Panmediated Global Detox Campaign." *Argumentation & Advocacy* 52, no. 4 (2016). http://search.ebscohost.com/login .aspx?direct=true&profile=ehost&scope=site&authtype=crawler&jrnl=10511 431&AN=116275698&h=lX8CjjZLQQniFMYuYaNEW65bxowZRPoXrt%2F dpM3wh9opNGaPbystbOZo2S5mIdNvRcVQD5ZBSev5yUh10%2FHGd Q%3D%3D&crl=c.

Burgess, Jean, and Joshua Greene. *YouTube: Online Video and Participatory Culture.* Malden, MA: Polity, 2009.

Burke, Kenneth. *Language as Symbolic Action*. Berkeley: University of California Press, 1969.

Bury, Liz. "Hunger Games Fans Campaign against Real Inequality." *Guardian*, November 26, 2013. www.theguardian.com/books/2013/nov/26/hunger-games-fans -harry-potter-alliance.

Bury, Rhianon. "Aca-Fandom and Beyond: Rhianon Bury and Matt Yockey (Part Two)." *Confessions of an Aca-Fan: The Official Weblog of Henry Jenkins*, September 26, 2011. http://henryjenkins.org/2011/09/aca-fandom_and_beyond_ rhianon_1.html.

Busker, Rebecca Lucy. "Fandom and Male Privilege: Seven Years Later." *Transformative Works and Cultures* 13 (2013). https://doi.org/10.3983/twc.2013.0473.

Busse, Kristina. "Fan Labor and Feminism: Capitalizing on the Fannish Labor of Love." *Cinema Journal* 54, no. 3 (2015): 110–15.

———. "Geek Hierarchies, Boundary Policing, and the Gendering of the Good Fan." *Participations* 10, no. 1 (2013): 73–91.

———. "SCMS 2011 Workshop: Acafandom and the Future of Fan Studies: Kristina Busse's Provocation." *Transform* (blog), March 16, 2011. http://lstein.wordpress .com/2011/03/16/scms-2011-workshop-acafandom-and-the-future-of-fan-studies/.

Busse, Kristina, and Jonathan Gray. "Fan Cultures and Fan Communities." In *The Handbook of Media Audiences*, edited by Virginia Nightingale, 425–553. Malden, MA: Wiley-Blackwell, 2011.

Butterworth, Michael L. "The Athlete as Citizen: Judgment and Rhetorical Invention in Sport." *Sport in Society*, July 2013, 1–17. https://doi.org/10.1080/174304 37.2013.806033.

Cagle, Jeffrey. Skype interview by the author. June 2, 2017.

Campbell, Joseph. *The Hero with a Thousand Faces*. 3rd ed. Novato, CA: New World Library, 2008.

Carmines, E. G., M. J. Ensley, and M. W. Wagner. "Who Fits the Left-Right Divide? Partisan Polarization in the American Electorate." *American Behavioral Scientist* 56, no. 12 (December 1, 2012): 1631–53. https://doi.org/10.1177/000276421 2463353.

Carrington, André M. *Speculative Blackness: The Future of Race in Science Fiction*. Minneapolis: University of Minnesota Press, 2016.

Cartter, Allyson. "Activist Alumnus Inspires Students." *Justice*. October 15, 2012. www.thejustice.org/activist-alumnus-inspires-students-1.2927958#.Uub74 Pbnb-b.

Cashin, Declan. "Harry Potter Fans Scored an Awesome Victory in the Fight against Child Slavery." *BuzzFeed* (blog), January 19, 2015. www.buzzfeed.com /declancashin/harry-potter-fans-scored-an-awesome-victory-in-the-fight-aga.

"CFP: Themed Section of Participations Journal on Toxic Fan Practices." Fan Studies Network, January 3, 2017. https://fanstudies.org/2017/01/03/cfp-themed
-section-of-participations-journal-on-toxic-fan-practices/.

Chatelain, Dirk. "The Mystery of Lawrence Phillips." *Omaha World Herald*, April 14, 2015, Big Red Today sec. www.omaha.com/huskers/blogs/the-mystery-of
-lawrence-phillips/article_885befd8-e2b2–11e4-b184–3339536b5702.html.

Chávez, Karma. "Border (in)Securities: Normative and Differential Belonging in LGBTQ and Immigrant Rights Discourse." *Communication and Critical/Cultural Studies* 7, no. 2 (June 2010): 136–55. https://doi.org/10.1080/147914210037
63291.

———. "Counter-Public Enclaves and Understanding the Function of Rhetoric in Social Movement Coalition-Building." *Communication Quarterly* 59, no. 1 (2011): 1–18.

———. *Queer Migration Politics: Activist Rhetoric and Coalitional Possibilities*. Feminist Media Studies Series. Urbana: University of Illinois Press, 2013.

Chief SW Historian. "Star Wars Role Models." *Future of the Force* (blog), April 22, 2017. https://futureoftheforce.com/star-wars-role-models-6d372de44c47.

Chouliaraki, Lilie. *The Ironic Spectator: Solidarity in the Age of Post-Humanitarianism*. Cambridge: Polity, 2013.

Christian, Aymar Jean. "Fandom as Industrial Response: Producing Identity in an Independent Web Series." *Transformative Works and Cultures* 8 (2011). https://doi
.org/10.3983/twc.2011.0250.

———. "Real Vlogs: The Rules and Meanings of Online Personal Videos." *First Monday* 14, no. 11 (2009). www.firstmonday.org/htbin/cgiwrap/bin/ojs/index.php
/fm/article/view/2699/2353.

Cisneros, J. David. "Contaminated Communities: The Metaphor of 'Immigrant as Pollutant' in Media Representations of Immigration." *Rhetoric & Public Affairs* 11, no. 4 (2008): 569–601.

"City-Wide Mentor Meet-Up." TeamMates. Accessed December 10, 2013. http://team
mates.org/city-wide-mentor-meet-up-recruitment-drive/.

Click, Melissa. "SCMS 2011 Workshop: Acafandom and the Future of Fan Studies: Melissa Click's Provocation." *Transform* (blog), March 16, 2011. http://lstein
.wordpress.com/2011/03/16/scms-2011-workshop-acafandom-and-the-future
-of-fan-studies/.

Cochran, Tanya R. "'Past the Brink of Tacit Support': Fan Activism and the Whedon-verses." *Transformative Works and Cultures* 10 (2012). http://journal.transforma
tiveworks.com/index.php/twc/article/view/331/295.

Cohen, Cathy, and Joseph Kahne. "Participatory Politics: New Media and Youth Political Action." MacArthur Foundation Youth and Participatory Politics Research

Network, 2012. https://ypp.dmlcentral.net/sites/default/files/publications
/Participatory_Politics_New_Media_and_Youth_Political_Action.2012.pdf.

Coker, Catherine, and Candace Benefiel. "We Have Met the Fans, and They Are
Us: In Defense of Aca-Fans and Scholars." *Flow: A Critical Forum on Television
and Media Culture* (blog), December 17, 2010. www.flowjournal.org/2010/12
/we-have-met-the-fans/.

Coleman, Stephen. "Doing IT for Themselves: Management versus Autonomy in
Youth e-Citizenship." In *Civic Life Online: Learning How Digital Media Can Engage Youth,* edited by Lance Bennett, 189–206. Cambridge: MIT Press, 2008.

Coleman, Stephen, and Jay G. Blumler. *The Internet and Democratic Citizenship:
Theory, Practice and Policy.* New York: Cambridge University Press, 2009.

Condit, Celeste. "Pathos in Criticism: Edwin Black's Communism-As-Cancer Metaphor." *Quarterly Journal of Speech* 99, no. 1 (February 2013): 1–26. https://doi.org
/10.1080/00335630.2012.749417.

Copeland, Rita, and Peter T. Struck, eds. *The Cambridge Companion to Allegory.* New
York: Cambridge University Press, 2010.

Corbett, Christianne, and Catherine Hill. "Solving the Equation: The Variables for
Women's Success in Engineering and Computing." American Association of
University Women, 2015. www.aauw.org/aauw_check/pdf_download/show_pdf
.php?file=solving-the-equation.

Couldry, Nick. *Why Voice Matters: Culture and Politics after Neoliberalism.* Los Angeles: Sage, 2010.

CrashCourse. PBS Digital Studies & YouTube. Accessed February 7, 2018. www.you
tube.com/channel/UCX6b17PVsYBQoip5gyeme-Q.

Crawford, Garry. *Consuming Sport: Fans, Sport and Culture.* New York: Routledge,
2004.

Dahlgren, Peter. "The Internet, Public Spheres, and Political Communication: Dis-
persion and Deliberation." *Political Communication* 22 (2005): 147–62.

———. *Media and Political Engagement: Citizens, Communication, and Democracy.*
Communication, Society and Politics. New York: Cambridge University Press,
2009.

"Data." TeamMates. Accessed December 12, 2013. http://teammates.org/about
-teammates/data/.

Davidson, Danica. "How Harry Potter Struck a Blow against Slavery." *MTV Act*
(blog), January 14, 2015. http://act.mtv.com/posts/harry-potter-slavery/.

Davidson, Kief, and Daniel Junge, dirs. *A LEGO Brickumentary.* Global Emerging
Markets and HeLo, 2015.

DC Entertainment. "Press Release: DC Entertainment Announces 'We Can Be Heroes,' an Unprecedented Giving Campaign to Fight the Hunger Crisis in the Horn

of Africa," January 23, 2012. www.wecanbeheroes.org/wp-downloads/heroes
_launch_release.pdf.

deBoer, Fredrik. "Geeks, You Are No Longer Victims. Get over It." *New York Times: Room for Debate,* September 18, 2014, Opinion sec. www.nytimes.com/room fordebate/2014/09/18/when-geeks-rule/geeks-you-are-no-longer-victims-get -over-it.

DeGeorge, Paul. Skype interview by the author. July 17, 2015.

Delicath, John W., and Kevin Michael Deluca. "Image Events, the Public Sphere, and Argumentative Practice: The Case of Radical Environmental Groups." *Argumentation* 17, no. 3 (2003): 315–33.

Delli Carpini, Michael X. "Political Communication Research in the Digital Media Environment: Challenges and Opportunities." Paper presented at the Ivan Preston Research Colloquium, Madison, WI, October 11, 2013.

DeLuca, Kevin Michael. *Image Politics: The New Rhetoric of Environmental Activism.* New York: Guilford, 1999.

Dewey, John. *The Public and Its Problems.* Chicago: Swallow, 1954.

Diaz De Leon, Ramon. Email interview by the author. October 15, 2013.

Dimitrov, Roumen. "Gender Violence, Fan Activism and Public Relations in Sport: The Case of 'Footy Fans against Sexual Assault.'" *Public Relations Review* 34, no. 2 (2008): 90–98.

Duff, Ian. "How LEGO Got Awesome to #SaveTheArctic." *Greenpeace International* (blog), October 9, 2014. www.greenpeace.org/international/en/news/Blogs /makingwaves/save-the-arctic-lego-dumps-shell/blog/50917/.

Duncombe, Stephen. *Dream: Re-Imagining Progressive Politics in an Age of Fantasy.* New York: New Press, 2007.

———. "Imagining No-Place." *Transformative Works and Cultures* 10 (2012). https://doi .org/10.3983/twc.2012.0350.

Dundes, Alan. "Folkloristics in the Twenty-First Century (AFS Invited Presidential Plenary Address, 2004)." *Journal of American Folklore* 118, no. 470 (2005): 385–408.

Dunning, Eric. *Sport Matters: Sociological Studies of Sport, Violence, and Civilization.* New York: Routledge, 1999.

Dwyer, Michael. "The Gathering of the Juggalos and the Peculiar Sanctity of Fandom." *Flow: A Critical Forum on Television and Media Culture* (blog), December 17, 2010. www.flowjournal.org/2010/12/the-gathering-of-the-juggalos/.

Earl, Jennifer, and Katrina Kimport. "Movement Societies and Digital Protest: Fan Activism and Other Nonpolitical Protest Online." *Sociological Theory* 27, no. 3 (2009): 220–43.

Education, LEGO. "Elementary Competitions—LEGO Education." https://educa-

tion.lego.com. Accessed September 10, 2017. https://education.lego.com/en-us
/elementary/competitions.

———. "LEGO Education." https://education.lego.com. Accessed September 10,
2017. https://education.lego.com/en-us.

Edward T. L. C. "J. K. Rowling at Carnegie Hall Reveals Dumbledore Is Gay; Nev-
ille Marries Hannah Abbott, and Much More." *The-Leaky-Cauldron.Org* (blog),
October 20, 2007. www.the-leaky-cauldron.org/2007/10/20/j-k-rowling-at-car
negie-hall-reveals-dumbledore-is-gay-neville-marries-hannah-abbott-and-scores
-more/.

Einwachter, Sophie Gwendolyn, and Felix M. Simon. "How Digital Remix and Fan
Culture Helped the Lego Comeback." *Transformative Works and Cultures* 17, no.
25 (2017). http://doi.org/10.3983/twc.2017.1047.

Elderkin, Beth. "Women of Star Wars Get Highlighted in New Series of Animated
Shorts." *Io9: Gizmodo* (blog), April 13, 2017. http://io9.gizmodo.com/women-of
-star-wars-get-highlighted-in-new-series-of-ani-1794283158.

Elliott, Anthony, ed. *The Contemporary Bauman.* London: Routledge, 2007.

Enstad, Nan. *Ladies of Labor, Girls of Adventure: Working Women, Popular Culture,
and Labor Politics at the Turn of the Twentieth Century.* New York: Columbia
University Press, 1999.

"Enter to Win Your Dream Experience." Omaze. Accessed September 12, 2017.
www.omaze.com/how-we-think.

Erickson, Callie. "Press Release: TeamMates Mentoring Program Kicks Off 2013
Coaches Challenge." September 1, 2013. http://teammates.org/wp-content/
uploads/2013/08/Coaches-Challenge-Internal-Press-Release.doc.

Erickson, Callie, Adam Lounsbury, Cheri Faunce, Mai-Anh Kapanke, and Amber
Troupe. "Press Release: Iowa, Kansas, & Nebraska Kick Off Coaches Challenge
with Addition of Michigan and Minnesota." August 1, 2013. http://teammates
.org/wp-content/uploads/2013/08/Press-Release-Coaches-Challenge.doc.

Evans, Adrienne, and Mafalda Stasi. "Desperately Seeking Methodology: New Directions in Fan Studies Research." *Participations* 11, no. 1 (2014): 4–23.

"Fan Power—BBC Radio 4." *BBC 4 Radio.* BBC, November 11, 2013. www.bbc.co
.uk/programmes/b03gvd82.

"FAQ." TeamMates. Accessed December 10, 2013. http://teammates.org/about-team
mates/faq/.

Farrell, Thomas B., and G. Thomas Goodnight. "Accidental Rhetoric: The Root Metaphors of Three Mile Island." *Communication Monographs* 48 (1981): 271–300.

Farris, Anelise. "Fan-Driven Identity Narratives: The Performative Culture of Star
Wars Cosplayers." *New Directions in Folklore* 15, no. 1/2 (2018). https://scholar
works.iu.edu/journals/index.php/ndif/article/view/24291/29939.

"The 50th Academy Awards | 1978." Academy of Motion Picture Arts and Scien.ces. Accessed May 12, 2017. www.oscars.org/oscars/ceremonies/1978/S.

Fiske, John. "The Cultural Economy of Fandom." In *The Adoring Audience*, edited by Lisa A. Lewis. 30–49. New York: Routledge, 1992.

Fitzgerald, Isaac, and Tanner Greenring. "This Fan Theory about Jar Jar Binks Will Blow Your Mind." *BuzzFeed* (blog), November 3, 2015. www.buzzfeed.com/isaac fitzgerald/darth-jar-jar.

"The 501st Legion." Accessed May 12, 2017. www.501st.com/.

Fletcher, Angus. *Allegory: The Theory of a Symbolic Mode.* Princeton, NJ: Princeton University Press, 2012.

Flock, Elizabeth. "Alohomora: How a Group of Harry Potter Fans Is Unlocking the Election." *US News and World Report,* September 27, 2012. www.usnews.com /news/blogs/washington-whispers/2012/09/27/alohomora-how-a-group-of -harry-potter-fans-is-unlocking-the-election.

Flynn, Kerry. "Everything Is Not Awesome with LEGO and Shell, Says Greenpeace." *Forbes,* July 8, 2014. www.forbes.com/sites/kerryflynn/2014/07/08/everything-is -not-awesome-with-lego-and-shell-says-greenpeace/.

"Football—2010 Schedule/Results." Huskers, n.d. www.huskers.com/SportSelect .dbml?SPSID=3&SPID=22&DB_OEM_ID=100&Q_SEASON=2010.

"Football—2011 Schedule/Results." Huskers, n.d. www.huskers.com/SportSelect .dbml?SPSID=3&SPID=22&DB_OEM_ID=100&Q_SEASON=2011.

"The 4–1–1 with Chad Kelsay." Huskers.com. Accessed February 1, 2014. http://www .huskers.com/ViewArticle.dbml?ATCLID=1281012&DB_OEM_ID=100.

Freund, Katharina, and Dianna Fielding. "Research Ethics in Fan Studies." *Participations* 10, no. 1 (2013). www.participations.org/Volume%2010/Issue%201 /16%20Freund%20Fielding%2010.1.pdf.

Fry, Richard. "Millennials Overtake Baby Boomers as America's Largest Generation," April 25, 2016. www.pewresearch.org/fact-tank/2016/04/25/millennials -overtake-baby-boomers/.

Garcia, Antero. *Critical Foundations in Young Adult Literature: Challenging Genres.* Rotterdam: Sense, 2013.

Garlen, Jennifer. "Block Party: A Look at Adult Fans of LEGO." In *Fan CULTure: Essays on Participatory Fandom in the 21st Century,* edited by Kristin Barton and Jonathan Lampley, 119–30. Jefferson, NC: McFarland, 2014.

Gass, Henry. "How Did Greenpeace Get LEGO to Ditch Shell Play Sets? (+video)." *Christian Science Monitor,* October 9, 2014. www.csmonitor.com/USA/USA-Up date/2014/1009/How-did-Greenpeace-get-LEGO-to-ditch-Shell-play-sets-video.

Gehrke, Pat J. *The Ethics and Politics of Speech: Communication and Rhetoric in the Twentieth Century.* Carbondale: Southern Illinois University Press, 2009.

Geraghty, Lincoln. *Cult Collectors: Nostalgia, Fandom and Collecting Popular Culture.* New York: Routledge, 2014.

Gibson, Jess, dir. *AFOL: A Blockumentary.* 2010. https://vimeo.com/9581676.

Giddens, Anthony. *Modernity and Self-Identity: Self and Society in the Late Modern Age.* Stanford: Stanford University Press, 1991.

Gierzynski, Anthony. *Harry Potter and the Millennials: Research Methods and the Politics of the Muggle Generation.* Baltimore: Johns Hopkins University Press, 2013.

Gray, Jonathan. "Aca-Fandom and Beyond: Jonathan Gray, Matt Hills, and Alisa Perren (Part One)." *Confessions of an Aca-Fan: The Official Weblog of Henry Jenkins* (blog), August 29, 2011. http://henryjenkins.org/2011/08/aca-fandom_and_beyond_jonathan.html.

———. "Of Snowspeeders and Imperial Walkers: Fannish Play at the Wisconsin Protests." *Transformative Works and Cultures* 10 (2012). https://doi.org/10.3983/twc.2012.0353.

———. "SCMS 2011 Workshop: Acafandom and the Future of Fan Studies: Jonathan Gray's Provocation." *Transform* (blog), March 16, 2011. http://lstein.wordpress.com/2011/03/16/scms-2011-workshop-acafandom-and-the-future-of-fan-studies/.

———. *Watching with the Simpsons: Television, Parody, and Intertextuality.* New York: Routledge, 2006.

Gray, Jonathan, Cornel Sandvoss, and C. Lee Harrington, eds. *Fandom: Identities and Communities in a Mediated World.* New York: New York University Press, 2007.

Gray, Mary L. *Out in the Country: Youth, Media, and Queer Visibility in Rural America.* New York: New York University Press, 2009.

———. "'Queer Nation Is Dead/Long Live Queer Nation': The Politics and Poetics of Social Movement and Media Representation." *Critical Studies in Media Communication* 26, no. 3 (2009): 212–36. https://doi.org/10.1080/15295030903015062.

Green, Dennis. "Greenpeace Tells Lego to Ditch Shell [VIDEO]." *Mashable*, July 10, 2014. http://mashable.com/2014/07/10/greenpeace-lego/.

Green, Hank. "About EcoGeek." EcoGeek. Accessed May 18, 2012. www.ecogeek.org/about.

———. *Announcing the 2009 Project for Awesome!!!* Video. VlogBrothers YouTube channel, 2009. www.youtube.com/watch?v=CZ3R6qw5bMA.

———. *Brotherhood 2.0: March 21st: Put Stuff on Your Head.* VlogBrothers YouTube channel, 2007. www.youtube.com/watch?v=xrJzYoT7s9s&feature=youtube_gdata_player.

———. *$40,000 of Red Balloons.* Video. The VlogBrothers (YouTube), 2009. www.youtube.com/watch?v=CgB8ucWqRUs.

———. *Hank vs. Hank: The Net Neutrality Debate in 3 Minutes.* The VlogBrothers YouTube Channel, 2014. www.youtube.com/watch?v=mc2as06W7jQ&feature =youtube_gdata_player.

———. *I Got Nothin . . .* The VlogBrothers YouTube Channel, 2012. www.youtube. com/watch?v=ZLxcgMxSCUw&feature=youtube_gdata_player.

———. *March 20th: Dancing and the Idiocy of Age.* VlogBrothers YouTube Channel, 2007. www.youtube.com/watch?v=jG9LgibCiow&feature=youtube_gdata _player.

———. *Nerdfighteria Island.* Online video. The VlogBrothers YouTube Channel, 2009. www.youtube.com/watch?v=TyByAkD_onQ.

———. *One More Day until the P4A!!!* The VlogBrothers YouTube Channel, 2008. www.youtube.com/watch?v=_zraqD3ePik.

———. *Project for Awesome: Explanation and Humane Societies.* Video. The Vlog-Brothers YouTube Channel, 2007. www.youtube.com/watch?v=gQQOeT61d3A.

———. *Project for Awesome Time!! What Does It Mean?!* Video. VlogBrothers YouTube Channel, 2013. www.youtube.com/watch?v=d4°w-EZkLjg&feature=youtube _gdata_player.

———. "SciShow." YouTube Channel. Accessed August 17, 2014. www.youtube.com /channel/UCZYTClx2T1°f7BRZ86–8fow.

———. *The Science of Lying.* Video. The SciShow YouTube Channel, 2012. www.you tube.com/watch?v=MX3Hu810XTE&feature=youtube_gdata_player.

———. *Thoughts on the Project for Awesome.* Video. VlogBrothers, 2010. www.you tube.com/watch?v=-6BgPJqAkP0.

———. *What You Need to Know About Ebola.* Video. The SciShow YouTube Channel, 2014. www.youtube.com/watch?v=TGyFhwdtCMk&feature=youtube_gdata _player.

Green, Hank, and John Green. *The Vlogbrothers.* VlogBrothers YouTube Channel. Accessed June 6, 2017. www.youtube.com/user/vlogbrothers#p/u.

———. *Vlogbrothers.* VlogBrothersYouTube Channel, January 19, 2018. www.you tube.com/user/vlogbrothers/about.

Green, John. *Brotherhood 2.0, February 1, 2007.* Video. The VlogBrothers YouTube Channel, 2007. www.youtube.com/watch?v=RPA0aWCMabw.

———. *Dec. 28th: John's Last Brotherhood 2.0 Video.* Video. The VlogBrothers You-Tube Channel, 2007. www.youtube.com/watch?v=XN4sxxYXFb4.

———. *Economics and Dentistry: YOUTUBE'S FAVORITE TOPICS.* Video. The Vlog-Brothers YouTube Channel, 2012. www.youtube.com/watch?v=b2xW6hWnffw& feature=youtube_gdata_player.

———. *Giving Away over $700,000.* Video. The VlogBrothers YouTube Channel, 2014. www.youtube.com/watch?v=8Ym12xJd0oA&feature=youtube_gdata_player.

———. *Harry Potter Nerds Win at Life*. Video. The VlogBrothers YouTube Channel, 2009. www.youtube.com/watch?v=rMweXVWB918.

———. *Health Care Overhaul Summarized Via MASSIVE PIG*. Video. The VlogBrothers YouTube Channel, 2009. www.youtube.com/watch?v=7Z_RVl-ph3s&feature =youtube_gdata_player.

———. *Influence, Airports, and the Nerdfighter Book Club*. Video. The VlogBrothers YouTube Channel, 2014. www.youtube.com/watch?v=rQ_JnlpzM6M&feature =youtube_gdata_player.

———. "John Green," May 18, 2012. http://johngreenbooks.com/.

———. *Oct. 26: Discussing Nepal While Eating Toilet Paper*. Video. The VlogBrothers YouTube Channel, 2007. www.youtube.com/watch?v=DmzaZBAaqJw.

———. *Our Old Friend Complexity: Behind the Beautiful Forevers*. Video. The VlogBrothers YouTube Channel, 2014. www.youtube.com/watch?v=AzanFEBnHhY& feature=youtube_gdata_player.

———. *The Bank of Nerdfighteria*. Video. The VlogBrothers YouTube Channel, 2013. www.youtube.com/watch?v=V15-tBiVzrE&feature=youtube_gdata_player.

Green, John, and Hank Green. *P4a, Space Pasta, and Giant Squids of Anger*. Video. The VlogBrothers YouTube Channel, 2010. www.youtube.com/watch?v=-uTe K3Dv-hs.

Greenberg, Zachary A. "Tossing the Red Flag: Official (Judicial) Review and Shareholder-Fan Activism in the Context of Publicly Traded Sports Teams." *Washington University Law Review* 90 (2012): 1255.

Griffith, Maggie, and Zizi Papacharissi. "Looking for You: An Analysis of Video Blogs." *First Monday* 15, no. 1 (2010). www.firstmonday.org/htbin/cgiwrap/bin /ojs/index.php/fm/article/view/2769/2430.

Groskopf, Jeremy. "Hoarding and Community in Star Wars Card Trader." *Transformative Works and Cultures* 22 (2016). https://doi.org/10.3983/twc.2016.0718.

Grossfeld, Stan. "A Voice for the Victims: Redmond's Coalition Targets 'Rape Culture' in Athletics." *Boston Globe*, June 16, 2004.

Grossman-Cohen, Ben. "The Hunger Games Fans Join Oxfam America, Harry Potter Alliance to Say: 'Hunger Is Not a Game.'" Oxfam America, March 20, 2012. www.oxfamamerica.org/press/the-hunger-games-fans-join-oxfam-america -harry-potter-alliance-to-say-hunger-is-not-a-game/.

Gunnels, Jen. "'A Jedi Like My Father before Me': Social Identity and the New York Comic Con." *Transformative Works and Cultures* 3 (2009). https://doi.org /10.3983/twc.2009.0161.

Gunnels, Jen, and M. Flourish Klink. "'We Are All Together': Fan Studies and Performance." *Flow: A Critical Forum on Television and Media Culture* (blog), December 17, 2010. www.flowjournal.org/2010/12/we-are-all-together/.

Habermas, Jürgen. *The Structural Transformation of the Public Sphere: An Inquiry into a Category of Bourgeois Society.* Cambridge: MIT Press, 1989.

Hall, Stuart. "Encoding/Decoding." In *Media and Cultural Studies: Keyworks,* 2nd ed., edited by Gigi Durham Meenakshi and Douglas M. Kellner, 137–44. Chichester: Wiley-Blackwell, 2012.

Hariman, Robert. "Political Parody and Public Culture." *Quarterly Journal of Speech* 94, no. 3 (August 2008): 247–72. https://doi.org/10.1080/00335630802210369.

Hariman, Robert, and John Louis Lucaites. *No Caption Needed: Iconic Photographs, Public Culture, and Liberal Democracy.* Chicago: University of Chicago Press, 2011.

———. "Performing Civic Identity: The Iconic Photograph of the Flag Raising on Iwo Jima." *Quarterly Journal of Speech* 88, no. 4 (November 2002): 363–92. https://doi.org/10.1080/00335630209384385.

———. "Public Identity and Collective Memory in U.S. Iconic Photography: The Image of 'Accidental Napalm.'" *Critical Studies in Media Communication* 20, no. 1 (January 2003): 35–66. https://doi.org/10.1080/0739318032000067074.

Harris, Cheryl. "A Sociology of Television Fandom." In *Theorizing Fandom: Fans, Subculture, and Identity,* edited by Harris and Alison Alexander, 41–54. Cresskill, NJ: Hampton, 1998.

The Harry Potter Alliance webpage. "About the HPA." PDF. The Harry Potter Alliance. Accessed December 17, 2012. thehpalliance.org/downloads/press/about-the-hpa.pdf.

———. "Find a Chapter." The Harry Potter Alliance, July 7, 2014. http://thehpalliance.org/chapters/find-a-chapter/.

———. "HPA 5 Year Anniversary BLOWOUT." The Harry Potter Alliance, December 18, 2010. http://thehpalliance.org/action/campaigns/hpa5/?nggpage=2.

———. "Not in Harry's Name." The Harry Potter Alliance. Accessed January 13, 2013. http://thehpalliance.org/action/campaigns/nihn/.

———. "Success Stories." The Harry Potter Alliance, December 18, 2010. http://thehpalliance.org/press/success-stories/.

The Hartman Group. "New Kids on the Block: A First Look at Gen Z." *Forbes,* March 31, 2016. www.forbes.com/sites/thehartmangroup/2016/03/31/new-kids-on-the-block-a-first-look-at-gen-z/.

Hathaway, Jay. "What Is Gamergate, and Why? An Explainer for Non-Geeks." *Gawker* (blog), October 10, 2014. http://gawker.com/what-is-gamergate-and-why-an-explainer-for-non-geeks-1642909080.

Heigl, Alex. "Harry Potter Chocolate Goes 100% Fair Trade, Thanks to Fans." PEOPLE .Com, January 14, 2015. www.people.com/article/harry-potter-fans-warner-bros-chocolate-fair-trade.

Hellekson, Karen, and Kristina Busse, eds. *Fan Fiction and Fan Communities in the Age of the Internet: New Essays.* Jefferson, NC: McFarland, 2006.

———, eds. *The Fan Fiction Studies Reader.* Iowa City: University of Iowa Press, 2014.

Hess, Aaron. "Critical-Rhetorical Ethnography: Rethinking the Place and Process of Rhetoric." *Communication Studies* 62, no. 2 (2011): 127–52.

Hess, Amanda. "The Next Civil Rights Issue: Why Women Aren't Welcome on the Internet." *Pacific Standard*, January 6, 2014. www.psmag.com/navigation /health-and-behavior/women-arent-welcome-internet-72170/.

Hills, Matt. "Aca-Fandom and Beyond: Jonathan Gray, Matt Hills, and Alisa Perren (Part One)." *Confessions of an Aca-Fan: The Official Weblog of Henry Jenkins*, August 29, 2011. http://henryjenkins.org/2011/08/aca-fandom_and_beyond_jonathan .html.

———. *Fan Cultures.* New York: Routledge, 2002.

———. "LEGO Dimensions Meets Doctor Who: Transbranding and New Dimensions of Transmedia Storytelling?" *Revista ICONo14. Revista Científica de Comunicación y Tecnologías Emergentes* 14, no. 1 (January 31, 2016): 8. https://doi.org /10.7195/ri14.v14i1.942.

Hince, Suzanne. Phone interview by the author. September 20, 2013.

Hinck, Ashley. "'Companions against Global Warming': A Case of Public Humanities Engagement." In *Time Lords & Tribbles, Winchesters & Muggles: The DePaul Pop Culture Conference*, edited by Paul Booth and Isabella Menichiello, 43–45. Self-published by Booth and Meninchiello, 2017.

———. "Ethical Frameworks and Ethical Modalities: Theorizing Communication and Citizenship in a Fluid World." *Communication Theory* 26, no. 1 (2016): 1–20.

———. "Fluidity in a Digital World: Choice, Communities, and Public Values." In *Theorizing Digital Rhetoric*, edited by Aaron Hess and Amber L. Davisson, 98– 111. New York: Routledge, 2018.

———. "Shifting Patterns of Football Fandom, Team Ownership, and Digital Media Cultures: YouTube, FIFA Videogames, and AFC Wimbledon." In *Digital Football Cultures*, edited by Stefan Lawrence and Garry Crawford. New York: Routledge, Forthcoming.

———. "Theorizing a Public Engagement Keystone: Seeing Fandom's Integral Connection to Civic Engagement through the Case of the Harry Potter Alliance." *Transformative Works and Cultures* 10 (2012). https://doi.org/doi:10.3983 /twc.2012.0311.

———. "Why Rhetoricians Need to Pay Attention to Fan Culture." *Rhetorically Speaking* (blog), May 29, 2014. http://rhetoric.commarts.wisc.edu/?p=150.

"History." Greenpeace Canada. Accessed August 29, 2016. www.greenpeace.org /canada/en/About-us/History/.

"History of Nebraska Football." Huskers.com. Accessed December 12, 2013. www
.huskers.com/ViewArticle.dbml?ATCLID=1060800&DB_OEM_ID=100.

HN Staff. "'And I'm . . .' by Ramon Brown | Album Premier." *Hear Nebraska* (blog),
May 6, 2013. http://hearnebraska.org/content/and-im-ramon-brown-album
-premiere.

"How 'Hunger Games' Actually Fights Hunger: What You Can Do." *Huffington Post,*
March 23, 2012, Impact sec. www.huffingtonpost.com/2012/03/23/hunger
-games-oxfam_n_1375405.html.

Howard, Philip. *New Media Campaigns and the Managed Citizen.* Cambridge: Cambridge University Press, 2006.

Howard, Robert Glenn. *Digital Jesus: The Making of a New Christian Fundamentalist
Community on the Internet.* New York: New York University Press, 2011.

———. "Electronic Hybridity: The Persistent Processes of the Vernacular Web."
Journal of American Folklore 121, no. 480 (2008): 192–218. https://doi.org/10
.1353/jaf.0.0012.

———. "The Vernacular Web of Participatory Media." *Critical Studies in Media Communication* 25, no. 5 (2008): 490–513.

Hunt, Darnell, Ana-Christina Ramon, and Zachary Price. "2014 Hollywood Diversity Report: Making Sense of the Disconnect." Ralph J. Bunche Center for African American Studies, University of California, Los Angeles, February 2014.
www.bunchecenter.ucla.edu/wp-content/uploads/2014/02/2014-Hollywood
-Diversity-Report-2-12-14.pdf.

Hunting, Kyra, and Rebecca Hains. "Discriminating Taste: Maintaining Gendered
Social Hierarchy in a Cross-Demographic Fandom." *Feminist Media Studies,*
Forthcoming.

Husker Participant A. Personal interview by the author, October 31, 2013.

"Huskers Rank in Top 10 in Attendance." Huskers.com. Accessed February 12,
2014. www.huskers.com/ViewArticle.dbml?ATCLID=209403282&DB_OEM
_ID=100.

Hutcheon, Linda. *A Theory of Parody: The Teachings of Twentieth-Century Art Forms.*
Urbana: University of Illinois Press, 2000.

"Internet History Is Fragile. This Archive Is Making Sure It Doesn't Disappear." *PBS
Newshour,* January 2, 2017. www.pbs.org/newshour/bb/internet-history-fragile
-archive-making-sure-doesnt-disappear/.

Irwin, Neil, and Kevin Quealy. "The Places in America Where College Football
Means the Most." *New York Times,* November 2014, Upshot sec. www.nytimes
.com/2014/11/08/upshot/the-places-in-america-where-college-football-means
-the-most.html.

Ivie, Robert. "Cold War Motives and the Rhetorical Metaphor: A Framework of

Criticism." In *Cold War Rhetoric: Strategy, Metaphor, and Ideology*, edited by Martin Medhurst, Ivie, Philip Wander, and Robert Scott, 71–80. Contributions to the Study of Mass Media and Communications, no. 19. New York: Greenwood, 1990.

———. "Metaphor and the Rhetorical Invention of Cold War 'Idealists.'" *Communication Monographs* 54 (1987): 165–82.

———. "The Metaphor of Force in Prowar Discourse: The Case of 1812." *Quarterly Journal of Speech* 68, no. 3 (1982): 240–53.

Jackie A. "The 'Nerdfighter' Arcade Game?—Nerdfighters." *Nerdfighters*, July 7, 2012. http://nerdfighters.ning.com/forum/topics/the-nerdfighter-arcade-game.

Jamison, Anne Elizabeth. *Fic: Why Fanfiction Is Taking over the World*. Dallas: Smart Pop, an imprint of BenBella Books, 2013.

Jane, Emma Alice. "'Back to the Kitchen, Cunt': Speaking the Unspeakable about Online Misogyny." *Continuum: Journal of Media & Cultural Studies* 28, no. 4 (2014): 558–70.

Jao, Charline. "Daisy Ridley Calls Demand for Rey Merchandise 'Amazing,' Expect More in the Future." *The Mary Sue*, October 21, 2016. www.themarysue.com/ridley-rey-reaction-amazing/.

Jenemann, David. "Stop Being an Elitist, and Start Being an Elitist." *Flow: A Critical Forum on Television and Media Culture* (blog). Accessed May 28, 2017. www.flowjournal.org/2010/12/stop-being-an-elitist-and-start-being-an-elitist/.

Jenkins, Henry. *Confronting the Challenges of Participatory Culture: Media Education for the 21st Century*. Cambridge: MIT Press, 2009.

———. *Convergence Culture: Where Old and New Media Collide*. New York: New York University Press, 2006.

———. "'Cultural Acupuncture': Fan Activism and the Harry Potter Alliance." *Transformative Works and Cultures* 10 (2012). https://doi.org/10.3983/twc.2012.0305.

———. "'Cultural Acupuncture': Fan Activism and the Harry Potter Alliance." In *Popular Media Cultures: Fans, Audiences and Paratexts*, edited by Lincoln Geraghty, 206–29. Houndmills, Basingstoke, Hampshire: Palgrave Macmillan, 2015.

———. "Fan Activism as Participatory Politics: The Case of the Harry Potter Alliance." In *DIY Citizenship: Critical Making and Social Media*, edited by Matt Ratto and Megan Boler, 65–73. Cambridge: MIT Press, 2014.

———. "Fandom Studies as I See It." *Journal of Fandom Studies* 2, no. 2 (2014): 89–109.

———. "How 'Dumbledore's Army' Is Transforming Our World: An Interview with the Harry Potter Alliance's Founder, Andrew Slack." *Journal of Media Lit-*

eracy 55, no. 3 (2009). www.journalofmedialiteracy.org/index.php/past-issues
/4-new-media-learning-a-civic-engagement-v55-n3/79-how-dumbledores-army
-is-transforming-our-world-an-interview-with-the-harry-potter-alliances-foun
der-andrew-slack.

———. "On Mad Men, Aca-Fandom, and the Goals of Cultural Criticism." *Confessions of an Aca-Fan: The Official Weblog of Henry Jenkins* (blog), August 11, 2010. http://henryjenkins.org/2010/08/on_mad_men_aca-fan_and_the_nat.html.

———. *Textual Poachers: Television Fans and Participatory Culture.* New York: Routledge, 1992.

———. "When Fandom Goes Mainstream." *Confessions of an Aca-Fan: The Official Weblog of Henry Jenkins* (blog), November 30, 2006. http://henryjenkins
.org/2006/11/when_fandom_goes_mainstream.html.

Jenkins, Henry, and Dan Hassler-Forest. "Foreword: 'I Have a Bad Feeling about This': A Conversation about Star Wars and the History of Transmedia." In *Star Wars and the History of Transmedia Storytelling,* edited by Sean Guynes and Hassler-Forest, 15–34. Amsterdam: Amsterdam University Press, 2018.

Jenkins, Henry, Mizuko ItÐ, and danah boyd. *Participatory Culture in a Networked Era: A Conversation on Youth, Learning, Commerce, and Politics.* Malden, MA: Polity, 2015.

Jenkins, Henry, and Sangita Shresthova. "Up, up, and Away! The Power and Potential of Fan Activism [Editorial]." *Transformative Works and Cultures* 10 (2012). https://doi.org/10.3983/twc.2012.0435.

Jenkins, Henry, Sangita Shresthova, Liana Gamber-Thompson, Neta Kligler-Vilenchik, and Arely Zimmerman. *By Any Media Necessary: The New Youth Activism.* Connected Youth and Digital Futures. New York: New York University Press, 2016.

Jilani, Zaid. "Activists Launch #MyHungerGames to Tell Real Story of American Inequality." *AlterNet* (blog), November 22, 2014. www.alternet.org/activism
/activists-launch-myhungergames-tell-real-story-american-inequality.

"J. J. Abrams Confirms STAR WARS VII Script Is Done." *Nerdist* (blog). Accessed August 17, 2014. www.nerdist.com/2014/01/j-j-abrams-confirms-star-wars-vii
-script-is-done/.

Johnson, Derek. "Chicks with Bricks: Building Creativity across Industrial Design Cultures and Gendered Construction Play." In *LEGO Studies: Examining the Building Blocks of a Transmedial Phenomenon,* edited by Mark J. P. Wolk, 81–104. New York: Routledge, 2014.

———. "Figuring Identity: Media Licensing and the Radicalization of LEGO Bodies." *International Journal of Cultural Studies* 17, no. 4 (2013): 307–25.

———. "'May the Force Be with Katie': Pink Media Franchising and the Postfeminist Politics of HerUniverse." *Feminist Media Studies* 14, no. 6 (November 2, 2014): 895–911. https://doi.org/10.1080/14680777.2014.882856.

Joly-Corcoran, Marc, and Sarah Ludlow. "Fans, Fics & Films . . . 'Thank the Maker(s)!'" In *Star Wars*, edited by Mika Elovaara, 29–37. Chicago: Intellect, 2013.

Jon Stewart and Stephen Colbert Battle for Title of World's Biggest Star Wars Fan! Online video. Omaze YouTube Channel, 2014. www.youtube.com/watch?v=OjgDox fHW4w.

Jones, Bethan. "Being of Service: 'X-Files' Fans and Social Engagement." *Transformative Works and Cultures* 10 (2012). https://doi.org/10.3983/twc.2012.0309.

Jones, Jeffrey. *Entertaining Politics: Satiric Television and Political Engagement.* 2nd ed. Lanham, MD: Rowman and Littlefield, 2010.

Jorgensen, Jeana. "Why Folklorists Hate Joseph Campbell's Work." *Foxy Folklorist: Folklore, Culture, Sex* (blog), May 15, 2017. www.patheos.com/blogs/foxyfolk lorist/why-folklorists-hate-joseph-campbells-work/.

Kahne, Joseph, Ellen Middaugh, and Danielle Allen. "Youth, New Media, and the Rise of Participatory Politics: Working Paper #1." Oakland, CA: Youth and Participatory Politics Research Network, March 19, 2014. http://ypp.dmlcentral. net/sites/default/files/publications/YPP_WorkinPapers_Paper01.pdf.

Kaiser, Jocelyn. "NIH Uncovers Racial Disparity in Grant Awards." *Science*, August 18, 2011.

"Kanan Jarrus (Character)." IMDb. Accessed June 1, 2017. www.imdb.com/ character/ch0414994/quotes.

Kant, Immanuel. *Grounding for the Metaphysics of Morals.* Translated by James W. Ellington. 3rd ed. Indianapolis: Hackett, 1993.

Katz-Kimchi, Merav, and Idit Manosevitch. "Mobilizing Facebook Users against Facebook's Energy Policy: The Case of Greenpeace Unfriend Coal Campaign." *Environmental Communication* 9, no. 2 (April 3, 2015): 248–67. https://doi.org /10.1080/17524032.2014.993413.

Kennedy, Ümit. "Exploring YouTube as a Transformative Tool in the 'The Power of MAKEUP!' Movement." *M/C Journal* 19, no. 4 (2016). http://journal.media-culture.org.au/index.php/mcjournal/article/view/1127.

Kent, Stephen, and Swara Salih. *Pilot.* Beltway Banthas. Accessed May 1, 2016. http://BeltwayBanthas.libsyn.com/rss.

Killa. *Perhaps, Perhaps, Perhaps.* 2005. www.youtube.com/watch?v=awJAnx4Mim8.

Kiva. "Kiva- Kiva Lending Team: Nerdfighters." 2012. www.kiva.org/team/nerd fighters.

Kligler-Vilenchik, Neta. "Case Study: The Harry Potter Alliance." In *Connected Learning: A Research Synthesis Report of the Connected Learning Research Net-*

work, by Mizuko Ito, Kris Gutierrez, Bill Penuel, Katie Salen, Juliet Schor, Julian Sefton-Green, and S. Craig Watkins, 49–53. Irvine, CA: Digital Media and Learning Research Hub, 2013. http://dmlhub.net/sites/default/files/Connected Learning_report.pdf.

———. "'Decreasing World Suck': Fan Communities, Mechanisms of Translation, and Participatory Politics." Case Study Report. University of Southern California's Media Activism, and Participatory Politics Project, June 24, 2013. http://dmlhub.net/sites/default/files/Decreasing%20World%20Suck%20-%20Work ing%20Paper%20-%20MAPP%20-%20June%2025%202013.pdf.

———. "Mechanisms of Translation: From Online Participatory Cultures to Participatory Politics." *Journal of Digital and Media Literacy* 4, no. 1–2 (2016).

Kligler-Vilenchik, Neta, Joshua McVeigh-Schultz, Christine Weitbrecht, and Chris Tokuhama. "Experiencing Fan Activism: Understanding the Power of Fan Activist Organizations through Members' Narratives." *Transformative Works and Cultures* 10 (2012). https://doi.org/doi:10.3983/twc.2012.0322.

Kligler-Vilenchik, Neta, and Sangita Shresthova. "Learning through Practice: Participatory Culture Civics." Case Study Report Working Paper. University of Southern California's Media Activism, and Participatory Politics Project, October 2, 2012. http://dmlhub.net/sites/default/files/Decreasing%20World%20 Suck%20-%20Working%20Paper%20-%20MAPP%20-%20June%2025%20 2013.pdf.

Krogh, Peter. *The DAM Book: Digital Asset Management for Photographers.* 2nd ed. Sebastopol, CA: O'Reilly, 2009.

Kruse, Noreem Wales. "Apologia in Team Sport." *Quarterly Journal of Speech* 67 (1981): 270–83.

Kuhn, Virginia. "The Rhetoric of Remix." *Transformative Works and Cultures* 9 (2012). https://doi.org/10.3983/twc.2012.0358.

Kurpiel, Ryszard. "The Stylistics of Selected American, Italian and Polish Challenge Vlogs." *Styles of Communication* 9, no. 2 (2017).

LaFrance, Adrienne. "Raiders of the Lost Web." *Atlantic,* October 14, 2015. www.the atlantic.com/technology/archive/2015/10/raiders-of-the-lost-web/409210/.

Lakoff, George, and Mark Johnson. "Conceptual Metaphor in Everyday Language." In *Philosophical Perspectives on Metaphor,* 286–325. Minneapolis: University of Minnesota Press, 1981.

Lang, Brent. "Box Office: 'Star Wars: The Force Awakens' Shreds Records with $238 Million Debut." *Variety,* December 20, 2015. http://variety.com/2015/film /box-office/star-wars-force-awakens-box-office-records-1201665753/.

LaSalata, Justin. "Celebration Orlando 2017 Sets New Attendance Record At over 70,000 Fans." *Jedi News—Broadcasting Star Wars News across the Gal-*

axy! (blog), April 18, 2017. www.jedinews.co.uk/conventions-events/articles
/celebration-orlando-2017-sets-new-attendance-record-70000-fans/.

Lawrence, Stefan. "'We Are the Boys from the Black Country'! (Re)Imagining Local,
Regional and Spectator Identities through Fandom at Walsall Football Club."
Social & Cultural Geography 17, no. 2 (February 17, 2016): 282–99. https://doi
.org/10.1080/14649365.2015.1059481.

"League Bio." The BIG EAST Conference, n.d. www.bigeast.com/ot/about.html.

Leavitt, Alex, and Andrea Horbinski. "Even a Monkey Can Understand Fan Activism: Political Speech, Artistic Expression, and a Public of the Japanese Dojin
Community." *Transformative Works and Cultures* 10 (2012). https://doi.org/10
.3983/twc.2012.0321.

LEGO: Everything Is NOT Awesome. The GreenpeaceVideo YouTube channel, 2014.
www.youtube.com/watch?v=qhbliUqo_r4.

"LEGO Is Keeping Bad Company." Greenpeace, July 1, 2014. www.greenpeace.org
/canada/Global/canada/report/2014/06/Lego-Is-Keeping-Bad-Company.pdf.

LEGO Participant AC. Online, open-ended survey, March 3, 2016.

LEGO Participant AD. Online, open-ended survey, March 3, 2016.

LEGO Participant AE. Online, open-ended survey, March 3, 2016.

LEGO Participant AI. Online, open-ended survey, March 3, 2016.

LEGO Participant AK. Online, open-ended survey, March 3, 2016.

LEGO Participant AM. Online, open-ended survey, March 3, 2016.

LEGO Participant AR. Online, open-ended survey, March 3, 2016.

LEGO Participant AS. Online, open-ended survey, March 3, 2016.

LEGO Participant AU. Online, open-ended survey, March 1, 2016.

LEGO Participant BC. Online, open-ended survey, March 3, 2016.

LEGO Participant BD. Online, open-ended survey, March 3, 2016.

LEGO Participant BE. Online, open-ended survey, March 3, 2016.

LEGO Participant BF. Online, open-ended survey, March 3, 2016.

LEGO Participant BH. Online, open-ended survey, March 3, 2016.

LEGO Participant BM. Online, open-ended survey, March 3, 2016.

LEGO Participant BP. Online, open-ended survey, March 3, 2016.

LEGO Participant BQ. Online, open-ended survey, March 3, 2016.

LEGO Participant BR. Online, open-ended survey, March 3, 2016.

LEGO Participant BT. Online, open-ended survey, March 3, 2016.

LEGO Participant BX. Online, open-ended survey, March 3, 2016.

LEGO Participant BZ. Online, open-ended survey, March 3, 2016.

LEGO Participant CG. Online, open-ended survey, March 3, 2016.

LEGO Participant CK. Online, open-ended survey, March 3, 2016.

LEGO Participant CL. Online, open-ended survey, March 3, 2016.

LEGO Participant P. Online, open-ended survey, March 3, 2016.

LEGO Participant R. Online, open-ended survey, March 3, 2016.

LEGO Participant S. Online, open-ended survey, March 3, 2016.

LEGO Participant W. Online, open-ended survey, March 3, 2016.

LEGO Participant Y. Online, open-ended survey, March 3, 2016.

LEGO Participant Z. Online, open-ended survey, March 3, 2016.

"The LEGO Movie." Box Office Mojo, August 21, 2014. www.boxofficemojo.com /movies/?id=lego.htm.

Lenskyj, H. J. "Reflections on Communication and Sport: On Heteronormativity and Gender Identities." *Communication and Sport* 1, no. 1–2 (December 12, 2012): 138–50. https://doi.org/10.1177/2167479512467327.

Leonard, Devin. "How Disney Bought Lucasfilm—and Its Plans for 'Star Wars.'" *BusinessWeek,* March 7, 2013. www.businessweek.com/articles/2013-03-07/how -disney-bought-lucasfilm-and-its-plans-for-star-wars.

"Let's Take a Closer Look at the New Alien in STAR WARS: EPISODE VII." *Nerdist* (blog). Accessed August 18, 2014. www.nerdist.com/2014/05/lets-take-a-closer -look-at-the-new-alien-in-star-wars-episode-vii/.

Leung, Rebecca. "I Have a Dream: College Tuition." CBS News, May 20, 2004. www.cbs news.com/news/i-have-a-dream-college-tuition/.

Levin, Samuel. "Aristotle's Theory of Metaphor." *Philosophy & Rhetoric* 15 (1982): 24–46.

Leyton Escobar, Mariana, P. A. M. Kommers, and Ardion Beldad. "Using Narratives as Tools for Channeling Participation in Online Communities." *Computers in Human Behavior* 37 (August 2014): 64–72.

Li, Cheuk Yin. "The Absence of Fan Activism in the Queer Fandom of Ho Denise Wan See (HOCC) in Hong Kong." *Transformative Works and Cultures* 10 (2012). https://doi.org/10.3983/twc.2012.0325.

"List: Huskers Land 18 Preferred Walk-Ons." *Omaha World Herald,* February 5, 2014, Big Red Today sec. http://sports.omaha.com/2014/02/05/list-huskers-land-18 -preferred-walk-ons/#.Uv5vyvbQqDO.

"Little Warrior | Mandalorian Mercs Costume Club." Accessed May 12, 2017. http://man dalorianmercs.org/who-we-are/charity/little-warrior/.

Livingstone, Sonia M., ed. *Audiences and Publics: When Cultural Engagement Matters for the Public Sphere.* Portland: Intellect, 2005.

Lopez, L. K. "Fan Activists and the Politics of Race in *The Last Airbender.*" *International Journal of Cultural Studies* 15, no. 5 (2012): 1–15.

Lopresti, Mike. "No Coach Ever Solved Lawrence Phillips." *USA Today,* August 22, 2005. http://usatoday30.usatoday.com/sports/columnist/lopresti/2005-08-22 -lopresti_x.htm.

Lord, Phil, and Christopher Miller, dirs. *The LEGO Movie.* Produced by Warner Bros., LEGO System A/S, Lin Pictures, RatPac-Dune Entertainment, Vertigo Entertainment, Village Roadshow Pictures, Warner Animation Group, and Warner Bros., 2014.

———. "Writers Built 'The LEGO Movie,' Block by Block, on Belief." *Los Angeles Times,* December 4, 2014. www.latimes.com/entertainment/envelope/la-et-mn -en-writers-lego-movie-20141204-story.html.

Lucas, Stephen E. "Coming to Terms with Movement Studies." *Central States Speech Journal* 31, no. 4 (1980): 255–66. https://doi.org/10.1080/10510978009368065.

MacDonald, Andrea. "Uncertain Utopia: Science Fiction Media Fandom & Computer Mediated Communication." In *Theorizing Fandom: Fans, Subculture, and Identity,* edited by Cheryl Harris and Alison Alexander, 131–52. Hampton Press Communication Series. Cresskill, NJ: Hampton, 1998.

Maloney, Devon. "The Marketing Tactics for Hunger Games: Catching Fire Would Make Panem's Capitol Proud." *Wired,* November 22, 2013. www.wired.com/2013 /11/catching-fire-marketing/.

Mantilla, Karla. *Gendertrolling: How Misogyny Went Viral.* Santa Barbara, CA: Praeger, 2015.

Martin, Courtney. "Fan Power: Hunger Is Not a Game, Revisited." *New York Times,* March 31, 2012, Opinionator sec. http://opinionator.blogs.nytimes.com/2012/03 /31/fan-power-hunger-is-not-a-game-revisited/.

———. "From Young Adult Book Fans to Wizards of Change." *New York Times,* March 21, 2012. http://opinionator.blogs.nytimes.com/2012/03/21/from-young -adult-book-fans-to-wizards-of-change/?scp=2&sq=the%20harry%20potter %20alliance&st=cse.

Marx, Nick, Matt Sienkiewicz, and Ron Becker, eds. *"Saturday Night Live" and American TV.* Bloomington: Indiana University Press, 2013.

Massanari, Adrienne. "#Gamergate and The Fappening: How Reddit's Algorithm, Governance, and Culture Support Toxic Technocultures." *New Media & Society* 19, no. 3 (2017): 329–46.

Massinger, Joan C. Williams and Kate Massinger. "How Women Are Harassed Out of Science." *Atlantic,* July 25, 2016. www.theatlantic.com/science/archive /2016/07/how-women-are-harassed-out-of-science/492521/.

Mathieu, David, Miguel Vicente Mariño, Maria José Brites, Inês Amaral, Niklas Chimirri, Juliane Finger, Liliana Pacheco, Bojana Romic, Minna Saariketo, and Riitta Tammi. "Methodological Challenges in the Transition towards Online Audience Research." *Participations: Journal of Audience & Reception Studies* 13, no. 1 (2016). www.participations.org/Volume%2013/Issue%201/S2/2.pdf.

"Mavs Enjoy Highlights of First D-I Campaign." omavs.com. Accessed December 12,

2013. www.omavs.com/ViewArticle.dbml?ATCLID=208641556&DB_OEM
_ID=31400.

McCaughey, Martha, ed. "The Harry Potter Alliance: Sociotechnical Contexts of
Digitally Mediated Activism." In *Cyberactivism on the Participatory Web*, 41–58.
Routledge Studies in New Media and Cyberculture 18. New York: Routledge,
Taylor and Francis, 2014.

McCready, Holly. "Don't Stop Hunger Games Fans from Fighting Hunger!" Change.org,
2012. www.change.org/p/lionsgate-don-t-stop-hunger-games-fans-from-fighting
-hunger.

McDowell, John C. *The Gospel According to Star Wars: Faith, Hope, and the Force.*
Louisville, KY: Westminster John Knox, 2007.

McGuigan, J. "The Cultural Public Sphere." *European Journal of Cultural Studies* 8,
no. 4 (November 1, 2005): 427–43. https://doi.org/10.1177/1367549405057827.

McHendry, George F., Michael K. Middleton, Danielle Endres, Samantha
Senda-Cook, and Megan O'Byrne. "Rhetorical Critic(Ism)'s Body: Affect and
Fieldwork on a Plane of Immanence." *Southern Communication Journal* 79, no.
4 (September 2014): 293–310. https://doi.org/10.1080/1041794X.2014.906643.

McIntosh, Jonathan. "A History of Subversive Remix Video before YouTube: Thirty
Political Video Mashups Made between World War II and 2005." *Transformative
Works and Cultures* 9 (2012). http://journal.transformativeworks.org/index.php
/twc/article/view/371/299.

McKinnon, Sara L, Robert Asen, Karma R Chávez, and Robert Glenn Howard, eds.
Text + Field: Innovations in Rhetorical Method. University Park: Pennsylvania
State University Press, 2016.

Medhurst, Martin. "The Academic Study of Public Address: A Tradition in Transition." In *Landmark Essays on American Public Address*, edited by Medhurst,
xi–xliii. Davis, CA: Hermagoras, 1993.

"Memorial Stadium." Huskers.com. Accessed February 14, 2014. www.huskers.
com/ViewArticle.dbml?ATCLID=208126061&DB_OEM_ID=100.

Menon, S. "A Participation Observation Analysis of the Once & Again Internet
Message Bulletin Boards." *Television & New Media* 8, no. 4 (November 1, 2007):
341–74. https://doi.org/10.1177/1527476407306621.

Mervis, Jeffrey. "NIH Program Fails to Launch Blacks in Biotech." *Science*, November 19, 2015.

———. "NSF Makes a New Bid to Boost Diversity." *Science*, March 3, 2016.

Messner, M. "Reflections on Communication and Sport: On Men and Masculini-
ties." *Communication and Sport* 1, no. 1–2 (December 30, 2012): 113–24. https://
doi.org/10.1177/2167479512467977.

Middleton, Michael K. "'SafeGround Sacramento' and Rhetorics of Substantive

Citizenship." *Western Journal of Communication* 78, no. 2 (March 2014): 119–33. https://doi.org/10.1080/10570314.2013.835064.

Middleton, Michael, Aaron Hess, Danielle Ens, and Samantha Senda-Cook. *Participatory Critical Rhetoric: Theoretical and Methodological Foundations for Studying Rhetoric in Situ,* 2015. http://search.ebscohost.com/login.aspx?direct=true&scope=site&db=nlebk&db=nlabk&AN=1134802.

Middleton, Michael K., Samantha Senda-Cook, and Danielle Endres. "Articulating Rhetorical Field Methods: Challenges and Tensions." *Western Journal of Communication* 75, no. 4 (July 2011): 386–406. https://doi.org/10.1080/10570314.2011.586969.

Mill, John Stuart. *Utilitarianism.* Edited by George Sher. 2nd ed. Indianapolis: Hackett, 2001.

Miller, Hannah. Email interview. September 19, 2017.

Mittell, Jason. "On Disliking Mad Men." *Just TV* (blog), July 29, 2010. https://justtv.wordpress.com/2010/07/29/on-disliking-mad-men/.

Molina, David, and Terry Shakespeare, dirs.. *BIONICLE: Mask of Light.* Produced by Create TV & Film, Creative Capters Entertainment, and LEGO, September 16, 2003.

Molyneaux, Heather, Susan O'Donnell, Kerri Gibson, and Janice Singer. "Exploring the Gender Divide on YouTube: An Analysis of the Creation and Reception of Vlogs." *American Communication Journal* 10, no. 2 (2008): 1–14.

Moorehead, Christina, Eti Berland, Anny Rusk, Ilana Ostrar, and Leanne Ellis. Facetime interview by the author. June 10, 2017.

Morales, Claudia. "Harry Potter Alliance Kicks off Equality FTW Fundraiser." *Geeky News,* September 12, 2013. www.geekynews.com/harry-potter-alliance-kicks-off-equality-ftw-fundraiser-18594/.

"MtvU Fandom Awards: May the Best Fans Win." MTV News. Accessed January 19, 2015. www.mtv.com/news/1849627/fandom-awards/.

Mukherjee, Roopali, and Sarah Banet-Weiser. *Commodity Activism: Cultural Resistance in Neoliberal Times.* New York: New York University Press, 2012.

Murray, Jim. "Nebraska Ought to Be Ashamed." *Los Angeles Times,* November 9, 1995. http://articles.latimes.com/1995-11-09/sports/sp-973_1_nebraska-player.

"The Mythology of 'Star Wars' with George Lucas." *BillMoyers.Com* (blog). Accessed May 13, 2017. http://billmoyers.com/content/mythology-of-star-wars-george-lucas/.

NCAA. "Graduation Success Rate Report: University of Nebraska, Lincoln." NCAA, 2013. http://fs.ncaa.org/Docs/newmedia/public/rates/index.html.

———. "2013 National College Football Attendance." NCAA, February 3, 2014. http://fs.ncaa.org/Docs/stats/football_records/Attendance/2013.pdf.

Neate, Rupert. "Lego Builds Yet Another Record Profit to Become World's Top Toymaker." *Guardian*, February 27, 2014, Business sec. www.theguardian.com/business/2014/feb/27/lego-builds-record-profit.

"Nebraska Agriculture Fact Card." Nebraska Department of Agriculture, USDA, NASS, Nebraska Field Office and N3braska Bankers Association, February 2017. www.nda.nebraska.gov/facts.pdf.

Nebraska Football 2014—Be Ready. 2014. www.youtube.com/watch?v=IXQHauJb7dk &feature=youtube_gdata_player.

"Nebraska's Five National Titles." Huskers.com. Accessed December 12, 2013. www .huskers.com/ViewArticle.dbml?ATCLID=606981&DB_OEM_ID=100.

Nerdfighter Participant AB. Online, open-ended survey, June 31, 2014.

Nerdfighter Participant AE. Online, open-ended survey, June 31, 2014.

Nerdfighter Participant AF. Online, open-ended survey, June 31, 2014.

Nerdfighter Participant AG. Online, open-ended survey, June 31, 2014.

Nerdfighter Participant AH. Online, open-ended survey, June 31, 2014.

Nerdfighter Participant AI. Online, open-ended survey, June 31, 2014.

Nerdfighter Participant AJ. Online, open-ended survey, June 31, 2014.

Nerdfighter Participant AL. Online, open-ended survey, June 31, 2014.

Nerdfighter Participant AN. Online, open-ended survey, June 31, 2014.

Nerdfighter Participant AO. Online, open-ended survey, June 31, 2014.

Nerdfighter Participant AP. Online, open-ended survey, June 31, 2014.

Nerdfighter Participant AR. Online, open-ended survey, June 31, 2014.

Nerdfighter Participant AS. Online, open-ended survey, June 21, 2014.

Nerdfighter Participant AU. Online, open-ended survey, June 31, 2014.

Nerdfighter Participant AW. Online, open-ended survey, June 31, 2014.

Nerdfighter Participant AX. Online, open-ended survey, June 31, 2014.

Nerdfighter Participant AZ. Online, open-ended survey, June 31, 2014.

Nerdfighter Participant BB. Online, open-ended survey, June 31, 2014.

Nerdfighter Participant BE. Online, open-ended survey, June 31, 2014.

Nerdfighter Participant BF. Online, open-ended survey, June 31, 2014.

Nerdfighter Participant H. Online, open-ended survey, June 31, 2014.

Nerdfighter Participant I. Online, open-ended survey, June 31, 2014.

Nerdfighter Participant L. Online, open-ended survey, June 31, 2014.

Nerdfighter Participant M. Online, open-ended survey, June 31, 2014.

Nerdfighter Participant P. Online, open-ended survey, June 31, 2014.

Nerdfighter Participant Q. Online, open-ended survey, June 31, 2014.

Nerdfighter Participant S. Online, open-ended survey, June 31, 2014.

Nerdfighter Participant U. Online, open-ended survey, June 31, 2014.

Nerdfighter Participant Z. Online, open-ended survey, June 31, 2014.

"Nerds for Obama." Accessed April 1, 2015. www.nerdsforobama.org.

"New: Arctic Oil Spill Play Set by LEGO & Shell!" Greenpeace Canada. Accessed August 24, 2014. www.greenpeace.org/canada/en/Blog/new-arctic-oil-spill-play -set-by-lego-shell/blog/50135/.

"NFL Fans Are Divided over How Players Express Themselves Politically." *NPR: Morning Edition,* September 19, 2017. www.npr.org/2017/09/19/552006632/nfl -fans-are-divided-over-how-players-express-themselves-politically.

Ng, Eve. "Telling Tastes: (Re)Producing Distinction in Popular Media Studies." *Flow: A Critical Forum on Television and Media Culture* (blog), December 17, 2010. www.flowjournal.org/2010/12/telling-tastes/.

Nicholson, Helen. "Florida: Wands and Rollercoasters at Orlando's Harry Potter Theme Park." *Daily Mail.* July 12, 2010, Online edition. www.dailymail.co.uk/ travel/article-1293774/Inside-The-Wizarding-World-Harry-Potter-Orlando.html.

"1996 Tostitos Fiesta Bowl: Nebrastka 62, Florida 24." *Husker Max* (blog), January 2, 1996. www.huskermax.com/games/1995/fiesta_recap.html.

Nørgard, Rikke Toft, and Claus Toft-Nielsen. "Gandalf on the Death Star: Levels of Seriality between Bricks, Bits, and Blockbusters." *Eludamos. Journal for Computer Game Culture* 8, no. 1 (2014): 171–98.

Northrop, John. Personal interview by the author. November 1, 2013.

obsession_inc. "Affirmational Fandom vs. Transformational Fandom." *Obsession_inc Blog* (blog), June 1, 2009. https://obsession-inc.dreamwidth.org/82589.html.

Oh, David C., and Chuyun Oh. "Vlogging White Privilege Abroad: Eat Your Kimchi's Eating and Spitting out of the Korean Other on YouTube." *Communication, Culture & Critique* 10, no. 4 (2017): 696–711.

Olson, Max. "Most to Prove in the Big 12." ESPN.com. Accessed February 1, 2014. http://espn.go.com/blog/big12/post/_/id/71210/big-12-players-coaches-with -most-to-prove.

Omi, Michael, and Howard Winant. *Racial Formation in the United States.* 3rd ed. New York: Routledge/Taylor and Francis, 2015.

O'Reilly, Lara. "Here's The Chilling Greenpeace Video That Ended Lego's $116 Million Deal with Shell." *Business Insider.* October 9, 2014. Accessed May 11, 2016. www.businessinsider.com/lego-ends-shell-deal-after-greenpeace-viral-video -2014-10.

Osborn, Michael. "Archetypal Metaphor in Rhetoric: The Light-Dark Family." In *Readings in Rhetorical Criticism,* edited by Carl Burgchardt, 3rd ed., 306–17. State College, PA: Strata, 2005.

———. "The Trajectory of My Work with Metaphor." *Southern Communication Journal* 74, no. 1 (February 2, 2009): 79–87. https://doi.org/10.1080/10417940 802559131.

Osborne, Anne C., and Danielle Sarver Coombs. "Performative Sport Fandom: An Approach to Retheorizing Sport Fans." *Sport in Society* 16, no. 5 (June 2013): 672–81. https://doi.org/10.1080/17430437.2012.753523.

Osborne, Tom. *More Than Winning: The Story of Tom Osborne.* Lincoln: University of Nebraska Press, 2009.

"Outside the Lines: Unable to Read." *Outside the Lines.* ESPN, March 17, 2002. http://sports.espn.go.com/page2/tvlistings/show103transcript.html.

Pande, Rukmini. "Squee from the Margins: Racial/Cultural/Ethnic Identity in Global Media Fandom." In *Seeing Fans: Representations of Fandom in Media and Popular Culture,* edited by Lucy Bennett and Paul Booth, 209–20. New York: Bloomsbury, 2016.

Papacharissi, Zizi. *A Private Sphere: Democracy in a Digital Age.* Malden, MA: Polity, 2010.

@PattyBones2. "Light Is about Others, Dark Is about Yourself." *Twitter* (blog), May 13, 2017. https://twitter.com/PattyBones2/status/863449115405025283.

pbegin. "LUG Statistics in the World—General LEGO Discussion." Eurobricks Forums, July 8, 2012. www.eurobricks.com/forum/index.php?showtopic=71732.

Peck, Jamie. *Constructions of Neoliberal Reason.* New York: Oxford University Press, 2010.

Penley, Constance. *Close Encounters: Film, Feminism, and Science Fiction.* Minneapolis: University of Minnesota Press, 1991.

Perren, Alisa. "Aca-Fandom and Beyond: Jonathan Gray, Matt Hills, and Alisa Perren (Part One)." *Confessions of an Aca-Fan: The Official Weblog of Henry Jenkins,* August 29, 2011. http://henryjenkins.org/2011/08/aca-fandom_and_beyond_jonathan.html.

Petroff, Alanna. "Lego Ditches Shell after Arctic Oil Protests." *CNNMoney,* October 9, 2014. http://money.cnn.com/2014/10/09/news/companies/lego-shell-greenpeace/index.html.

Pezzullo, Phaedra. "Resisting 'National Breast Cancer Awareness Month': The Rhetoric of Counterpublics and Their Cultural Performances." *Quarterly Journal of Speech* 89, no. 4 (2003): 345–65.

———. *Toxic Tourism: Rhetorics of Pollution, Travel, and Environmental Justice.* Rhetoric, Culture, and Social Critique. Tuscaloosa: University of Alabama Press, 2007.

Phillips, Forrest. "The Butcher, the Baker, the Lightsaber Maker [Symposium]." *Transformative Works and Cultures* 16 (2014). https://doi.org/10.3983/twc.2014.0498.

———. "The Star Wars Franchise, Fan Edits, and Lucasfilm." *Transformative Works and Cultures* 9 (2012). https://doi.org/10.3983/twc.2012.0385.

Phillips, Janae. "The Harry Potter Alliance." *Journal of Digital and Media Literacy* 4, no. 1–2 (2016).

Phillips, Tom. "Embracing the 'Overly Confessional': Scholar-Fandom and Approaches to Personal Research." *Flow: A Critical Forum on Television and Media Culture* (blog). Accessed May 28, 2017. www.flowjournal.org/2010/12/embracin g-the-overly-confessional/.

Pickett, David. "Part I: Historical Perspective on the LEGO Gender Gap- Sociological Images." *The Society Pages: Sociological Images* (blog), May 8, 2012. https://the societypages.org/socimages/2012/05/08/part-i-historical-perspective-on-the -lego-gender-gap/.

———. "Part IV: Historical Perspective on the LEGO Gender Gap- Sociological Images." *The Society Pages: Sociological Images* (blog), May 29, 2012. https://the societypages.org/socimages/2012/05/29/part-iv-historical-perspective-on-the -lego-gender-gap/.

Pickett, David, and Lisa Wade. "Part II: Historical Perspective on the LEGO Gender Gap- Sociological Images." *The Society Pages: Sociological Images* (blog), May 15, 2012. https://thesocietypages.org/socimages/2012/05/15/part-ii-historical -perspective-on-the-lego-gender-gap/.

———. "Part III: Historical Perspective on the LEGO Gender Gap- Sociological Images." *The Society Pages: Sociological Images* (blog), May 22, 2012. https://the societypages.org/socimages/2012/05/22/part-iii-historical-perspective-on-the -lego-gender-gap/.

Pillen, Jim. Personal interview by the author, November 1, 2013.

Plunkett, Jack W. *Plunkett's Sports Industry Almanac 2011.* Houston: Plunkett Research, 2010.

Pollock, Dale. *Skywalking: The Life and Films of George Lucas.* 1st Samuel French ed. Hollywood: S. French, 1990.

Portwood-Stacer, Laura. *Lifestyle Politics and Radical Activism.* New York: Bloomsbury, 2013.

"Preschool—LEGO Education." Accessed September 10, 2017. https://education. lego.com/en-us/preschool/intro.

Proctor, William. "'Holy Crap, More Star Wars! More Star Wars? What If They're Crap?': Disney, Lucasfilm and Star Wars Online Fandom in the 21st Century," 2013. http://participations.org/Volume%2010/Issue%201/12%20Proctor%20 10.1.pdf.

"Project for Awesome 2017." Accessed January 12, 2018. www.projectforawesome. com/.

Putnam, Robert. *Bowling Alone: The Collapse and Revival of American Community.* New York: Simon and Schuster, 2000.

Quinn, Kevin G. *Sports and Their Fans: The History, Economics and Culture of the Relationship between Spectator and Sport.* Jefferson, NC: McFarland, 2009.

Quiñones-Hinojosa, Alfredo, and Daniel A. Colón Ramos. "Racism in the Research Lab." August 4, 2016. http://kristof.blogs.nytimes.com/2016/08/04/racism-in -the-research-lab/.

Rampell, Catherine. "Football Upsets Increase Domestic Violence, Study Finds." *New York Times,* November 23, 2009, Economix sec. http://economix.blogs.ny times.com/2009/11/23/football-upsets-increase-domestic-violence/.

Ramsey, Franchesca. *Just Stop Talking about Race!!* Chescaleigh YouTube Channel, 2014. www.youtube.com/watch?v=Uo1PcovTk9o.

Ray, Angela. "The Rhetorical Ritual of Citizenship: Women's Voting as Public Performance, 1868–1875." *Quarterly Journal of Speech* 93, no. 1 (2007): 1–26.

Reid, Eric. "Opinion | Eric Reid: Why Colin Kaepernick and I Decided to Take a Knee." *New York Times,* September 25, 2017, Opinion sec. www.nytimes.com /2017/09/25/opinion/colin-kaepernick-football-protests.html.

"Retcon." TV Tropes. Accessed September 12, 2017. http://tvtropes.org/pmwiki/pm wiki.php/Main/Retcon.

Reuters. "Ex-NFL Player's Cellmate Was Strangled to Death in Cell." *Huffington Post,* April 16, 2015, sec. HuffPost Sports. http://social.huffingtonpost.com/2015 /04/17/lawrence-phillips-strangled_n_7084000.html.

Rheingold, Howard. *The Virtual Community: Homesteading on the Electronic Frontier.* Rev. ed. Cambridge: MIT Press, 2000.

Richards, I. A. *The Philosophy of Rhetoric.* New York: Oxford University Press, 1965.

Ringen, Jonathan. "How Lego Became the Apple of Toys." *Fast Company,* January 8, 2015. www.fastcompany.com/3040223/when-it-clicks-it-clicks.

Rosenberg, Alyssa. "EXCLUSIVE: As 'The Hunger Games' Opens Big, Lionsgate Tries to Shut down Anti-Hunger Advocates." *ThinkProgress,* March 23, 2012. http://thinkprogress.org/alyssa/2012/03/23/450357/exclusive-as-the-hunger -games-opens-big-lionsgate-tries-to-shut-down-anti-hunger-advocates/.

———. "How 'Harry Potter' Fans Won a Four-Year Fight against Child Slavery." *Washington Post,* January 13, 2015, Act Four sec. www.washingtonpost.com/news /act-four/wp/2015/01/13/how-harry-potter-fans-won-a-four-year-fight-against -child-slavery/.

Rowe, David. "Cultures of Complaint." *Convergence: The Journal of Research into New Media Technologies* 16, no. 3 (2010): 298–315.

Rusk, Annie. Online interview by the author. May 24, 2017.

Russo, Julie Levin, and Francesca Coppa. "Fan/Remix Video (a Remix) [Editorial]." *Transformative Works and Cultures* 9 (2012). https://doi.org/10.3983/twc .2012.0431.

Sampson, Mike. "Block Party: Talking 'The LEGO Movie' with Writer/Directors Phil Lord and Chris Miller." *ScreenCrush,* February 5, 2014. http://screencrush.com/phil-lord-chris-miller-interview/.

Sandvoss, Cornel. *Fans: The Mirror of Consumption.* Cambridge: Polity, 2005.

Scardaville, Melissa. "Accidental Activists: Fan Activism in the Soap Opera Community." *American Behavioral Scientist* 48, no. 7 (2005): 881–901.

Schmidt, Samantha. "'I'm Not a Sexist': Fired Google Engineer Stands behind Controversial Memo." *Washington Post,* August 10, 2017, Morning Mix sec. www.washingtonpost.com/news/morning-mix/wp/2017/08/10/im-not-a-sexist-fired-google-engineer-stands-behind-controversial-memo/.

Schrodt, Paul. "The 10 Biggest Blockbuster Movies of All Time, and How Much They Raked In." *Business Insider,* September 28, 2016. www.businessinsider.com/the-highest-grossing-movies-of-all-time-adjusted-for-inflation-2016–9.

Schudson, Michael. *The Good Citizen: A History of American Civic Life.* New York: Martin Kessler, 1998.

Scott, Jason. "Immersive and Interactive Adaptation and Extensions of Star Wars." In *Star Wars,* edited by Mika Elovaara, 38–47. Chicago: Intellect, 2013.

Scott, Suzanne. "Fangirls in Refrigerators: The Politics of (in)Visibility in Comic Book Culture." *Transformative Works and Cultures* 13 (2013). https://doi.org/10.3983/twc.2013.0460.

Senda-Cook, Samantha. "Rugged Practices: Embodying Authenticity in Outdoor Recreation." *Quarterly Journal of Speech* 98, no. 2 (May 2012): 129–52. https://doi.org/10.1080/00335630.2012.663500.

"Shell." Brickipedia. Accessed August 24, 2014. http://lego.wikia.com/wiki/Shell.

Sherman, Mitch. "Lawrence Phillips Continues to Cast Shadow over Nebraska, Tom Osborne." ESPN. *Big Ten Blog at ESPN.Com* (blog), April 14, 2015. http://espn.go.com/blog/bigten/post/_/id/117892.

"Show Us the Report." The Harry Potter Alliance. Accessed January 28, 2014. www.showusthereport.com.

Shropshire, Kenneth L., and Kellen Winslow. Foreword to *In Black and White: Race and Sports in America,* xi–xvi. New York: New York University Press, 1996.

Silverman, Anna. Phone interview by the author. August 15, 2014.

Silvestri, Lisa. "Context Drives Method: Studying Social Media Use in a War Zone." In *Text + Field: Innovations in Rhetorical Method,* edited by Sara L McKinnon, Robert Asen, Karma R Chávez, and Robert Glenn Howard. University Park: Pennsylvania State University Press, 2016.

Skocpol, Theda. *Diminished Democracy: From Membership to Management in American Civic Life.* Norman: University of Oklahoma Press, 2003.

Smith, Daniel R. "'Imagining Others More Complexly': Celebrity and the Ideology of Fame among YouTube's 'Nerdfighteria.'" *Celebrity Studies* 7, no. 3 (July 2, 2016): 339–53. https://doi.org/10.1080/19392397.2015.1132174.

Smith, Earl. *Race, Sport, and the American Dream.* Durham, NC: Carolina Academic Press, 2007.

Smith, Stacy, Marc Choueiti, and Katherine Pieper. "Race/Ethnicity in 600 Popular Films: Examining On Screen Portrayals and Behind the Camera Diversity." Annenberg School for Communication & Journalism, University of Southern California, 2014. https://annenberg.usc.edu/sites/default/files/MDSCI_Race_Ethnicity_in_600_Popular_Films.pdf

Snelson, Chareen. "Vlogging about School on YouTube: An Exploratory Study." *New Media & Society* 17, no. 3 (March 2015): 321–39. https://doi.org/10.1177/1461444813504271.

Snider, Mike. "Are NFL Player Protests 'massively, Massively' Hurting TV Ratings?" *USA TODAY*, September 26, 2017. www.usatoday.com/story/money/business/2017/09/26/nfl-player-protests-hurting-ratings/703619001/.

Sniderman, Zachary. "How Non-Profits Are Tapping Internet Memes & Pop Culture." *Mashable* (blog), August 30, 2011. http://mashable.com/2011/08/30/pop-culture-non-profits-memes/.

Song, Felicia Wu. *Virtual Communities: Bowling Alone, Online Together.* New York: Peter Lang, 2009.

"The Sports Market." atkearney.com. Accessed January 16, 2014. www.atkearney.com/paper/-/asset_publisher/dVxv4Hz2h8bS/content/the-sports-market/10192.

Sorokanich, Robert. "Two More Summer Lego Movies Are Coming!" Gizmodo, August 7, 2014. http://lego.gizmodo.com/two-more-summer-lego-movies-are-coming-1617579263.

Spaaij, Ramón. "Football Hooliganism in the Netherlands: Patterns of Continuity and Change." *Soccer & Society* 8, no. 2–3 (April 2007): 316–34. https://doi.org/10.1080/14660970701224566.

Star Wars. *Mark Hamill & Daisy Ridley's Epic Star Wars: Force for Change Announcement.* Star Wars YouTube Channel, 2017. www.youtube.com/watch?v=kno5kOhUQyo.

———. *Star Wars: Force for Change—Your Chance to Win an Autographed Rogue One Stormtrooper Helmet*, 2016. www.youtube.com/watch?v=907dxSVbMHA.

"Star Wars: Force for Change." Accessed August 20, 2014. http://forceforchange.starwars.com/.

"Star Wars: Force for Change | Official Site." Accessed June 5, 2017. https://forceforchange.starwars.com/.

"STAR WARS: Force for Change Raises over $4 Million, Winner Announced." *Nerdist* (blog). Accessed August 18, 2014. www.nerdist.com/2014/08/star-wars-force -for-change-raises-over-4-million-winner-announced/.

"Star Wars Legends." Wookieepedia. Accessed May 13, 2017. http://starwars.wikia. com/wiki/Star_Wars_Legends.

Star Wars Participant AB. Online, open-ended survey, May 28, 2017.

Star Wars Participant AC. Online, open-ended survey, May 28, 2017.

Star Wars Participant AD. Online, open-ended survey, May 28, 2017.

Star Wars Participant AG. Online, open-ended survey, May 28, 2017.

Star Wars Participant AP. Online, open-ended survey, May 28, 2017.

Star Wars Participant AU. Online, open-ended survey, May 28, 2017.

Star Wars Participant AZ. Online, open-ended survey, May 28, 2017.

Star Wars Participant B. Online, open-ended survey, May 28, 2017.

Star Wars Participant BB. Online, open-ended survey, May 28, 2017.

Star Wars Participant BG. Online, open-ended survey, May 28, 2017.

Star Wars Participant BH. Online, open-ended survey, May 28, 2017.

Star Wars Participant BJ. Online, open-ended survey, May 28, 2017.

Star Wars Participant BK. Online, open-ended survey, May 28, 2017.

Star Wars Participant BN. Online, open-ended survey, May 28, 2017.

Star Wars Participant BO. Online, open-ended survey, May 28, 2017.

Star Wars Participant BP. Online, open-ended survey, May 28, 2017.

Star Wars Participant BQ. Online, open-ended survey, May 28, 2017.

Star Wars Participant C. Online, open-ended survey, May 28, 2017.

Star Wars Participant E. Online, open-ended survey, May 28, 2017.

Star Wars Participant F. Online, open-ended survey, May 28, 2017.

Star Wars Participant G. Online, open-ended survey, May 28, 2017.

Star Wars Participant I. Online, open-ended survey, May 28, 2017.

Star Wars Participant J. Online, open-ended survey, May 28, 2017.

Star Wars Participant K. Online, open-ended survey, May 28, 2017.

Star Wars Participant L. Online, open-ended survey, May 28, 2017.

Star Wars Participant M. Online, open-ended survey, May 28, 2017.

Star Wars Participant O. Online, open-ended survey, May 28, 2017.

Star Wars Participant P. Online, open-ended survey, May 28, 2017.

Star Wars Participant R. Online, open-ended survey, May 28, 2017.

Star Wars Participant S. Online, open-ended survey, May 28, 2017.

Staub, Dick. *Christian Wisdom of the Jedi Masters.* San Francisco: Jossey-Bass, 2005.

Stein, Louisa. "On (Not) Hosting the Session That Killed the Term 'Acafan'—Antenna." *Antenna: Responses to Media & Culture* (blog), March 18, 2011. http://blog.commarts .wisc.edu/2011/03/18/on-not-hosting-the-session-that-killed-the-term-acafan/.

Stein, Louisa Ellen, and Kristina Busse. "SCMS 2011 Workshop: Acafandom and the Future of Fan Studies: Workshop Abstract." *Transform* (blog), March 16, 2011. http://lstein.wordpress.com/2011/03/16/scms-2011-workshop-acafandom-and -the-future-of-fan-studies/.

———, eds. *Sherlock and Transmedia Fandom: Essays on the BBC Series.* Jefferson, NC: McFarland, 2012.

SWEET Star Wars 7 Surprises! Crazier than We Thought! (Nerdist News w/ Jessica Chobot). Online video. Nerdist YouTube Channel, 2014. www.youtube.com/watch?v =LKCGkmhBOqY.

Tabb, William. *Economic Governance in the Age of Globalization.* New York: Columbia University Press, 2004.

Tabron, Judith L. "Girl on Girl Politics: Willow/Tara and New Approaches to Media Fandom." *Slayage: The Online International Journal of Buffy Studies* 4, no. 1–2 (2004). http://offline2.slayerworld.net/www.slayage.tv/PDF/tabron.pdf.

"Take the Coaches Mentoring Challenge in Iowa!" Iowa Mentoring Partnership. Accessed February 15, 2014. http://iowamentoring.org/.

Tchouaffe, Olivier. "Revisiting Fandom in Africa." *Flow: A Critical Forum on Television and Media Culture* (blog), December 17, 2010. www.flowjournal.org/2010 /12/revisiting-fandom-in-africa/.

TeamMates. "TeamMates Annual Report: 2016," 2016. https://teammates.org/wp -content/uploads/2011/01/TeamMates-2016-Annual-Report.pdf.

"TeamMates Gala." TeamMates. Accessed December 10, 2013. http://teammates.org /news-events/teammates-gala/.

"TeamMates Mentoring Program, Nebraska (NE)," May 19, 2012. http://teammates .org/news/huskers.htm.

Tegan and Sara, and The Lonely Island. *Everything Is AWESOME!!!* The LEGO Movie Soundtrack. WaterTower, 2014.

Terrill, Robert E. "Unity and Duality in Barack Obama's 'A More Perfect Union.'" *Quarterly Journal of Speech* 95, no. 4 (November 2009): 363–86. https://doi.org /10.1080/00335630903296192.

This Is Nebraska (Big Red Anthem 2). 2012. www.youtube.com/watch?v=LDRYf3vp5 Xg&feature=youtube_gdata_player.

Thomas, Lynne M, and Sigrid Ellis, eds. *Chicks Dig Comics.* Des Moines, Iowa: Mad Norwegian, 2012.

Thornton, Sarah. *Club Cultures: Music, Media, and Subcultural Capital.* 1st U.S. ed. Hanover, NH: University Press of New England, 1996.

"The Top 10 Schools in Total Academic All-America® Honorees (as of July 2013)." Capital One Academic All-America® Program by the Numbers, July 2013. http://cosida.com/Academic%20All-America/aaaselections.aspx

thruthesegates. *Morty Schapiro Interview*, 2012. www.youtube.com/watch?v=nRH 4791QSYE.

"Tom Osborne." Huskers.com. Accessed December 12, 2013. www.huskers.com /ViewArticle.dbml?ATCLID=204767407&DB_OEM_ID=100.

Tulloch, John, and Henry Jenkins. *Science Fiction Audiences: Watching "Doctor Who" and "Star Trek."* New York: Routledge, 1995.

Twenge, Jean M., W. Keith Campbell, and Elise C. Freeman. "Generational Differences in Young Adults' Life Goals, Concern for Others, and Civic Orientation, 1966–2009." *Journal of Personality and Social Psychology* 102, no. 5 (2012): 1045–62. https://doi.org/10.1037/a0027408.

"2013 NFL Football Attendance—National Football League–ESPN." ESPN.com. Accessed February 15, 2014. http://espn.go.com/nfl/attendance/_/sort/allTotal.

"University of Nebraska." Accessed December 12, 2013. http://nebraska.edu/cam puses.html.

Valinksy, Jordan. "Spoiler Alert: The Typical 'Star Wars' Fan Is a Wealthy 46-Year-Old Male Who Loves Comics—Digiday." Digiday, December 22, 2015. https://digiday .com/marketing/star-wars-demographics-male/.

Van Zoonen, Liesbet. *Entertaining the Citizen: When Politics and Popular Culture Converge.* Lanham, MD: Rowman and Littlefield, 2004.

Varela, Francisco J. *Ethical Know-How: Action, Wisdom, and Cognition.* Stanford, CA: Stanford University Press, 1999.

Vaughn, Holly. "Hunger Is NOT a Game." Harry Potter Alliance, March 1, 2012. http://thehpalliance.org/2012/03/hunger-is-not-a-game/.

Verba, Sidney, Kay Lehman Schlozman, and Henry Brady. *Voice and Equality: Civic Voluntarism in American Politics.* Cambridge: Harvard University Press, 1995.

Walker, Denny. Personal interview by the author. October 31, 2013.

Wanzo, Rebecca. "African American Acafandom and Other Strangers: New Genealogies of Fan Studies." *Transformative Works and Cultures* 20 (July 22, 2015). http://journal.transformativeworks.org/index.php/twc/article/view/699.

West, Isaac. "Analogizing Interracial and Same-Sex Marriage." *Philosophy & Rhetoric* 48, no. 4 (2015): 561–82.

"Who the &%&# Is Henry Jenkins?" Confessions of an Aca-Fan. Accessed May 24, 2017. http://henryjenkins.org/aboutmehtml.

"Who We Are." *TeamMates Mentoring* (blog), January 18, 2011. http://teammates.org /about/.

Wichelns, Herbert A. "The Literary Criticism of Oratory." In *Readings in Rhetorical Criticism*, edited by Carl Burgchardt, 3rd ed., 3–28. State College, PA: Strata, 2005.

Wiedeman, Reeves. "The Harry Potter Alliance Stages a Fast-Food Protest." *New*

Yorker, December 22, 2014. www.newyorker.com/magazine/2014/12/22 /activism.

Wilkins, Edo. *State of the Union . . . Not Good*. YouTube Channel: politicalremix, 2002. www.youtube.com/watch?v=6WtuYcn6N3A.

Wilkinson, Lili. "Nerdfighters, 'Paper Towns,' and Heterotopia." *Transformative Works and Cultures* 10 (2012). https://doi.org/10.3983/twc.2012.0374.

Wille, Joshua. "Dead Links, Vaporcuts, and Creativity in Fan Edit Replication." *Transformative Works and Cultures* 20 (2015). http://journal.transformativeworks .org/index.php/twc/article/view/663/537.

———. "Fan Edits and the Legacy of the Phantom Edit." *Transformative Works and Cultures* 17 (2014). https://doi.org/10.3983/twc.2014.0575.

Williams, Bruce, and Michael X. Delli Carpini. *After Broadcast News: Media Regimes, Democracy, and the New Information Environment*. Cambridge: Cambridge University Press, 2011.

Williams, Joan, Katherine Phillips, and Erika Hall. "Double Jeopardy? Gender Bias against Women of Color in Science." Work Life Law at UC Hastings College of the Law, 2014. www.uchastings.edu/news/articles/2015/01/double-jeopardy -report.pdf.

Williams, Rebecca. "In Focus: Ontological Security, Authorship and Resurrection: Exploring Twin Peaks' Social Media Afterlife." *Cinema Journal* 55, no. 3 (2016): 143–47.

Wootson, Cleve, Jr. "A Google Engineer Wrote That Women May Be Unsuited for Tech Jobs. Women Wrote Back." *Washington Post*, August 6, 2017, The Switch sec. www.washingtonpost.com/news/the-switch/wp/2017/08/06/a-google -engineer-wrote-that-women-may-be-genetically-unsuited-for-tech-jobs-women -wrote-back/.

Xenos, Michael, and Amy Becker. "Moments of Zen: Effects of *The Daily Show* on Information Seeking and Political Learning." *Political Communication* 26, no. 3 (2009): 317–32. https://doi.org/10.1080/10584600903053569.

Xenos, Michael, and Patricia Moy. "Direct and Differential Effects of the Internet on Political and Civic Engagement." *Journal of Communication* 57, no. 4 (2007): 704–18.

Yockey, Matt. "Aca-Fandom and Beyond: Rhianon Bury and Matt Yockey (Part Two)." *Confessions of an Aca-Fan: The Official Weblog of Henry Jenkins, September 26, 2011*. http://henryjenkins.org/2011/09/aca-fandom_and_beyond_rhianon _1.html.

———. "Wonder Woman for a Day: Affect, Agency, and Amazons." *Transformative Works and Cultures* 10 (2012). https://doi.org/10.3983/twc.2012.0318.

York, Randy. "Nebraska Fans Never Tire of Storybook Scripts Written by Walk-Ons."

Huskers.com. Accessed March 3, 2014. www.huskers.com/ViewArticle.dbml ?ATCLID=204805597&DB_OEM_ID=100.

Zaeske, Susan. "Signatures of Citizenship: The Rhetoric of Women's Anti-Slavery Petitions." *Quarterly Journal of Speech* 88, no. 2 (2002): 147–68. https://doi.org /10.1080/00335630209384368.

Zakarin, Jordan. "Lego's $116 Million Deal With Shell Oil Draws Protests, Ironic Lego Art (Photos)." TheWrap, July 1, 2014. www.thewrap.com/legos-116-million -deal-with-shell-oil-draws-protests-ironic-lego-art-photos/.

Zubernis, Lynn, and Katherine Larsen. *Fandom at the Crossroads: Celebration, Shame and Fan/Producer Relationships.* Newcastle upon Tyne, UK: Cambridge Scholars, 2012.

———. *Fandom at The Crossroads: Celebration, Shame and Fan/Producer Relationships.* Newcastle upon Tyne: Cambridge Scholars Publishing, 2012.

Zuckerman, Ethan. "New Media, New Civics? My Bellwether Lecture at the Oxford Internet Institute." Oxford, December 6, 2013. www.ethanzuckerman.com /blog/2013/12/06/new-media-new-civics-my-bellweather-lecture-at-the-oxford -internet-institute/.

Zukin, Cliff, Scott Keeter, Molly Andolina, Krista Jenkins, and Michael X. Delli Carpini. *A New Engagement?: Political Participation, Civic Life, and the Changing American Citizen.* New York: Oxford University Press, 2006.

INDEX

Brooker, Will, 138, 140–141, 145, 147–149, 155
Brown, Ramon, 64, 68–69, 76
Buffy the Vampire Slayer, 6, 15
Bugeaters, 57
business, 2, 55, 107, 113, 141, 150, 155,
196n53. *See also* Lord Business (*The LEGO Movie*)
Busse, Kristina, 9, 12–13, 36, 124
Buzzfeed, 2

Callahan, Bill, 59
campaigns
    Accio Books, 6
    celebrity charity campaigns, 135 (*see also* Omaze)
    Coaches Challenge, 16, 51–52, 55–57,
        72, 77–80, 191n126
    communication campaigns, 175
    #COP15, 28
    fan activist, 20, 174
    Force for Change, 17, 19–20, 134–137,
        150–161, 164, 175
    Grow, 170
    Harry Potter Alliance, 1, 7, 33, 170
    Hunger Is Not a Game, 7, 170–171
    media activism, 6
    mailing, 103
    Not in Harry's Name, 22, 33–35, 72
    Patronus, 16
    political campaign, 2, 21, 82, 169, 173
    #SavetheArctic #BlockShell LEGO, 17,
        19, 104–106, 123, 125, 131–133, 163,
        195n10
    TeamMates, 56
    and using fan-based civic appeals,
        174–176
    We Can Be Heroes, 175–176
causes (political), 27, 97–98, 100, 151–152,
    158–160, 168, 176
celebrity, 9, 37, 88, 135, 151, 160, 191n5,
    197n53
chapter (organization structure), 162–163,
    170

character
    fictional, 10–11, 15–16, 29, 108, 110, 117,
        121, 125, 137, 141–142, 144, 149–150
        183n96
    as moral qualities, 58, 68, 112
charity, 31–32, 69, 82, 84, 96–98, 100–101,
    103, 135–136, 147, 151, 155, 157, 159–160,
    164, 166, 168, 169, 170, 173–174, 176
Chavez, Karma, 6
children, 68, 74–76, 104–112, 118, 120, 132,
    146, 154, 157, 166, 176, 191n126, 200n22
chocolate, 6, 11, 33–34, 131, 179
Christian, 9, 101, 147
church, 9, 22–26, 28, 32, 38, 52–53, 168
citizens
    active citizen, 3
    and absent pairings, 136, 160–161
    and belonging, 39, 167–168, 180n29
    civic spaces for, 101
    definition of, 3
    entertainment media and citizens, 8
    fan-citizens, 163, 174
    and fandom, 14, 18, 20, 22–24, 35–36,
        169
    as football players, 75–76, 79
    good citizen, 3, 5, 34
    in Harry Potter, 34
    and institutions, 22, 24, 26, 28, 32, 37–
        38, 165, 167, 171
    legal-judicial citizen, 3
    and lifestyle politics, 27
    Nebraska citizens, 54, 60, 68, 72–74
    practitioners, 172
    and public issues, 7
    public subjects, 165
    relationship of citizen and state, 5
    TeamMates campaign, 51–52, 79,
        168
citizenship
    affective, 3
    definition of, 2–5
    and identity, 180n29
    legal-judicial citizenship, 3

corporations, 105, 108, 112, 118, 132, 136, 159, 169–171, 173

cosplay, 10, 139, 143, 146

CrashCourse, 93–94

creativity (LEGO ethical framework tenet), 19, 107, 113, 115–122, 124–125, 128–130, 133, 197n53

creativity, 15, 21, 37, 104–105, 143, 152–153, 164, 173, 177

critics, 4, 41, 45, 185n44

criticism. *See* rhetorical criticism

critical/cultural communication, 38

cultural engagement, 6–7

cultural power, 67

cultural studies, 7–8, 35, 102, 138

culture. *See* geek culture; internet culture; popular culture; public culture

Daily Show, The, 8

data, 41–44, 48, 50, 57, 87, 192n22

DC Entertainment, 176

DeGeorge, Paul, 21, 37

Democratic Party (U.S.), 9, 22, 26, 49, 163

demographics, 17, 83, 107, 110–111, 142, 192n22

Dewey, John, 166

DFTBA, 91

digital items, 5, 12, 19–21, 27, 40–42, 83, 101, 103, 109, 112, 123, 163, 165, 171. *See also* digital culture, internet; technology

digital culture. *See* internet culture

directors, 7, 54, 55–56, 61, 67–68, 112, 117, 121, 151–152, 170, 172–173

discourse, 2, 4, 8, 11, 13, 28, 36–37, 39–42, 51, 53, 59–60, 79, 112, 123, 171, 180n29, 183n6, 185n44, 192n22, 197n53

discussions

discussion of public issues, 23–24, 172

discussion boards and forums, 9, 82, 84, 96, 104, 109, 139, 140

Nerdfighter discussions, 91, 93–94, 98, 100, 103

Star Wars discussions, 144, 156, 160–161

Disney, 19, 107, 134–137, 141, 150–151, 157–160, 175

diversity, 17, 87–88, 113, 142–143, 147, 173

Doctor Who, 10–11, 21, 82, 95, 97, 174, 192n27

domestic violence, 61–62, 66, 97

dominant interpretations, 37, 147

donations

Harry Potter Alliance donations, 1

Hunger Games fan donations, 170

Justice League fan donations, 176

LEGO fans donations, 129, 133

Nerdfighter donations, 19, 103

Star Wars fans donations, 19, 136, 151, 153, 160, 166, 168, 175

down-to-earth (Husker ethical framework), 18, 57, 60–62, 79, 164

Dumbledore's Army, 1

DUPLO, 107, 110

EcoGeek, 81

education, 8, 17, 55, 58, 66, 81, 94, 104, 112–114, 146, 158, 167, 191n126

Emmet (*The LEGO Movie*), 119, 121, 125, 128

empathy (Nerdfighter ethical framework tenet), 91–96, 101

Empire, The (Star Wars), 134, 148–150, 153–154

entertainment, 8, 29, 53, 71, 100, 123, 157, 176

enthusiasm, 1, 2, 8, 12–13, 21, 85–86, 91, 93, 96–97, 101

environment, 39, 105, 128, 131, 162, 167

environmental communication, 123

equality, 1, 15, 28, 37–38, 114, 147

Equality Now, 15

ethics, 9, 22, 29, 30–31, 51, 131, 144, 146, 184n36

ethical framework

agreement on, 35–36

definition of, 18, 29–33

Harry Potter, 34–35, 38, 170

Husker, 18, 51–52, 54, 57–69, 73, 78–80, 164, 191n126

Index

Patronuses, The, 163
Pelini, Bo, 59, 73–74
performance, 1, 4–5, 20, 66, 77, 81, 102, 105, 129, 136
personalized politics, 27–28, 49
petition, 27, 33–34, 105–106, 129–130, 132–133, 170
Pew Research Center, 52
Phillips, Lawrence, 61–62
Pillen, Jim, 60, 63, 75, 79
place, 1, 6, 14, 17, 30, 36, 43, 48, 52, 55, 57, 75, 90, 92, 95, 111, 114–115, 138, 144, 156, 176, 196n24
play, 8, 11, 15, 19, 27, 32, 37, 48, 52–53, 55, 57, 59, 61, 64–65, 89, 104, 106–108, 111, 115, 117, 118, 128–129, 132, 139, 141, 174, 188n20, 191n126
PodCon, 43
podcast, 11, 43, 141, 201n61
policies, 2, 6–7, 25–26, 124, 163, 170–172, 185n38
politics. *See* lifestyle politics
political communication, 5, 8, 22–24
political community. *See* community: political
polysemy, 185n51
popular culture, 8–9, 16, 18–20, 22–23, 28, 35–39, 49, 67, 69, 71, 86, 88, 161, 164–166, 171, 174–175, 183n6, 185n51
poster, 5, 73, 77, 90–91
Pottermore, 29
power, 2, 4–5, 12, 20, 34, 38–39, 41, 49, 52–53, 57, 65, 67–69, 73, 80, 95, 99, 101, 103, 108–109, 122, 130, 133, 144, 153, 157, 160, 162–163, 166–168, 171, 173, 175, 184n15, 185n44, 190n91, 199n10
practitioners, 20, 172–176
preferred pairings, 31, 49, 163
preferred readings/interpretations, 147, 185n51
preferred uses, 28–29
presidents, U.S., 5, 40, 68, 162. *See* also 2016 U.S. presidential election

press release, 40, 72, 76, 115, 139
privilege, 27, 30, 59, 68, 114–115, 122, 140, 167
process, 4, 8, 18, 22, 30–31, 44–45, 49, 60–61, 70, 73, 91, 103, 106, 116, 136, 145, 165, 176–177, 203n8
production, 6, 15, 67, 126, 131, 156, 165, 181n51
program, 29–30, 54, 58–60, 112–113, 116, 170
Project for Awesome, 16, 19, 81–85, 96–103, 160, 163–165, 168–169
protest, 2, 11, 14, 27–28, 42, 53, 123
public culture, 5, 8, 16, 18, 19–20, 23–24, 54, 82, 84, 101–102, 123, 133, 136, 152, 160–161, 164–167, 172, 175
public engagement, 1, 3–5, 7, 14, 30–31, 53, 120, 133, 162, 172, 174, 176. *See also* civic engagement
public exhibition, 105, 109, 110, 120–122
public issues, 2, 7, 18, 20, 24, 71–72, 98, 100–102, 136, 156–160, 164, 166, 168, 172, 175
public life, 3, 165
public modalities, 31
public relations, 132, 151
public schools, 51, 55
public sphere, 171
public subjectivity, 25–26, 165 (*see also* subjectivity)
public outreach (LEGO ethical framework tenet), 107, 115, 120–122, 128–130, 133
public values, 2, 39, 103, 166–167

queer, 15, 46

race, 4, 11, 114, 118, 140, 142, 154, 184–185n38
racialized boundaries, 114–115
racism, 27, 53, 59, 67, 87–88, 113, 140, 144, 167–168
rape, 66, 101
Ray, Angela, 4, 94

Index